The Education of the Hero in Arthurian Romance

The Education of the Hero
in
Arthurian Romance

❧

by Madeleine Pelner Cosman

THE UNIVERSITY OF NORTH CAROLINA PRESS · CHAPEL HILL

To
B C M D and the CORRELATIVE IMAGINATION
and to
MARIN and CLIFFORD
who, in their enfances, *love medieval things*

৵৹ Acknowledgments

Of all obligations, gratitude is the pleasantest to acknowl-
edge; my obligations to people and to institutions are four-fold:
intellectual, financial, practical, and affectionate.

First, three scholars from Columbia University have seen this
book in some form more than once. Professor W. T. H. Jackson's
influence and critical approach will be reflected in the better parts
of these chapters. Professor Lawton P. G. Peckham commented
upon the Old French materials in the manuscript, and Professor
Howard Schless made welcome editorial suggestions. Two friends,
while not directly concerned with the production of this book, indirectly inspired its contents. Professor Helaine Newstead, of
Hunter College of the City University of New York, was the first
guide for my Arthurian passions during a year of memorable
tutorials; and Professor W. Cabell Greet long ago initiated an
academic progress by transforming an eager Barnard premedical
student into a medievalist.

Second, for generous fellowships, I am grateful to the Faculty
of Philosophy of Columbia University, to the Hunter College

Graduate Program, and to New York State. For publication of this book, City College of the City University of New York awarded a substantial grant from its Research Foundation funds.

Third, several ladies graciously aided: Mrs. Ruth Donnelly typed the penultimate draft of this essay; Mrs. Charlotte Fine typed the final version. Mrs. Viola Watts of New York, and later, Mrs. Eileen Tanner of London gave special assistance and friendship.

These three categories of gratitude plus the last I offer to Dr. and Mrs. Louis Pelner, who have always helped—without my request and without their question—in at least these four ways.

The final thanks are the dedication.

Table of Contents

✑ List of Abbreviations

ADA	*Anzeiger für deutsches Altertum*
ALMA	*Arthurian Literature in the Middle Ages,* ed. R. S. Loomis (Oxford, 1959)
BBSIA	*Bulletin Bibliographique de la Société Internationale Arthurienne*
BEITRÄGE	*Beiträge zur Geschichte der deutschen Sprache und Literatur*
CFMA	*Classiques français du moyen-âge*
DVLG	*Deutsche Vierteljahrsschrift für Literaturwissenschaft und Geistesgeschichte*
GR	*Germanic Review*
JEGP	*Journal of English and Germanic Philology*
MGH	*Monumenta Germaniae Historica*
MLN	*Modern Language Notes*
MLR	*Modern Language Review*
MPh	*Modern Philology*
PL	Migne, *Patrologiae cursus completus. Series latina*

PMLA	*Publications of the Modern Language Association of America*
RP	*Romance Philology*
RR	*Romanic Review*
SP	*Studies in Philology*
ZCP	*Zeitschrift für celtische Philologie*
ZDA	*Zeitschrift für deutsches Altertum*
ZDP	*Zeitschrift für deutsche Philologie*
ZFSL	*Zeitschrift für französische Sprache und Literatur*
ZRPH	*Zeitschrift für romanische Philologie*

𝒆𝓇𝓸 Introduction

Accounts of the births and childhoods of religious and mythical figures at once prefigure and explain their later powers; so the medieval romancer justifies his hero's extraordinary prowess by defining his early, extraordinary promise. Almost every important Arthurian hero is first a prodigious youth. Presented either as wonderfully precocious or as exceptionally naïve, nevertheless each hero for whom there is an *enfance* is portrayed as remarkable. These youthful portraits and childhood adventures directly and significantly affect the romances which contain them.

This prefacing of a hero's adult adventures with his childhood exploits—his *enfance*—is a very prevalent romance phenomenon. W. P. Ker has written about the "empty patterns" which captivate poets' minds; for the romance writers the *enfance* appears to be one of these patterns. These *enfances* encompass the period between the birth of the hero and the ceremony of his knighting. Rarely have they been studied as literary entities;[1] their significance as artistic

1. One of the only studies dedicated specifically to *enfances* is Professor Helaine Newstead's exhaustive and enlightening "The 'Enfances' of Tristan and English Tradition," *Studies in Medieval Literature in Honor of Albert Croll Baugh*, ed. MacEdward Leach (Philadelphia, 1961), pp. 169-85.

representations or as romance patterns transformed by individual writers has not been examined.

The origins of recurrent motifs within the *enfances*, however, have long interested scholars of legend and folklore.[2] Many of these motifs—such as the hero's incestuous, secret, or tragic birth, his upbringing with a foster parent, his temporary exile and eventual return to his patrimony, his namelessness or belated discovery of his name, his mission to avenge iniquity or insult to his father, and his quest for advice—may originate in Celtic or classical tradition. But one repeated *enfance* motif stands apart from these traditional themes and becomes most significant in the better romances; that motif is the education of the hero. Little bound by traditional proscription, the theme of the hero's learning is very susceptible to emendation for the artist's purpose. The period of the Arthurian knight's *enfance* and specifically the education within the *enfance* is the subject of this study.

Tristan, Perceval, and Lancelot are the major Arthurian heroes, each of whose educations appear in more than one significant medieval romance.[3] Restricting consideration to these knights' educations makes possible a detailed examination of characteristics specific to each yet common to all. This analysis permits the tracing of possible literary influences existing between certain of the texts and reveals literary progressions in the utilizations of this romance theme. The important texts in which the *enfances* educations appear are preserved in Old French and Middle High German, with some other romance versions in Middle English, Icelandic, Italian,

2. The theories and bibliographies for the traditional elements of Arthurian *enfances* appear in the notes to each chapter.

3. Knights such as Gawain and King Arthur himself are not considered. Although their *enfances* appear in more than one version, none of these is a recognized major romance. Versions of Gawain's childhood exploits may be found in: "Les Enfances Gauvain: fragments d'un poème perdu," ed. P. Meyer, *Romania*, XXXIX (1910), 1-32; "De Ortu Walwanii," ed. J. D. Bruce, *Hesperia* (Göttingen, Baltimore, 1913); Wace's *Brut*, ed. I. Arnold (Paris, 1938-1940), II, 518 f.; and *Perlesvaus*, ed. W. A. Nitze (Chicago, 1932-1937), I, 307 f., II, 327 f. Arthur's *enfances* are enumerated by E. S. Ownbey, *Merlin and Arthur: A Study of Merlin's Character and Function in Romances Dealing with the Early Life of Arthur* (Nashville, 1933). Other knights for whom there is but one extant education text, such as Ruodlieb, also are not examined in this essay. A modern edition and translation of *Ruodlieb* is by E. H. Zeydel (Chapel Hill, 1959), especially pp. 73-77.

and Welsh. Most date from the late twelfth and early thirteenth centuries, while a few are fourteenth-century works.

In the analyses of these *enfances*, each knight's education is discussed in terms of its components and its development within the complete romance. A consideration of the hero's curriculum, the type and nature of his tutor(s), and the characterization of the hero as a student is followed by an examination of the effects of this characterization, this tutoring, and this learning upon the later portrait of the knight as warrior and lover. The traditional elements of each *enfance* and education are summarized. Possible literary influences upon each text are discussed, and possible effects of that work upon other romances are suggested.

The simpler versions of the knightly education consist of a list of subjects that the youthful hero is taught. The more complex texts present not only the curriculum but the immediate effects of study, the display of new learning in action, and the formation and cultivation in childhood of those abilities which later distinguish the hero's manhood. Whereas the tutor, in the more primitive versions, simply is designated the master, and whereas his influence ceases at the close of the educational period, in the more sophisticated romances the tutor becomes an important character whose qualities of spirit, methods of teaching, and prolonged influence as mentor and companion are carefully delineated. In the less refined texts the characterization of the hero as a youth and the elements of his learning have no bearing upon the rest of the romance. But, the accounts of the hero's education in the more refined works introduce significant romance themes which are later developed and allow the exposition of pedagogical and social interests of both the author and his age.

Tristan's education is the subject of the first chapter. The romances discussed suggest that music and manners make the man. The poems of Thomas of Britain and Gottfried von Strassburg, and to a lesser degree Eilhart von Oberg's *Tristrant*, the English *Sir Tristrem*, the French *Prose Tristan*, and Malory's "Book of Sir Tristram of Lyones," demonstrate the development of the learned knight whose artistic and intellectual exploits not only parallel his chivalric adventures but supersede them. Perceval's education, considered in the second chapter, is not the portrait of precocity but rather the progress of a brave man only slowly wise. The educations of the *Dümmling* hero in Chrétien de Troyes' and Wolfram von Eschenbach's poems determine the characterizations and structures of the complete romances. Consideration of these two works is augmented by reference to five other Perceval versions, *Peredur*, *Sir Perceval*, *Carduino*, *Bliocadran's Prologue*, and the *lai* of *Tyolet*. Lancelot's tutelage is examined in the third chapter. Represented only in Ulrich von Zatzikhoven's *Lanzelet* and in the *Prose Lancelot*, the hero's childhood learning first displays his ultimate concerns with the altar, the bower, and the sword.

The final chapter turns from literary criticism to literary history in order to consider the prevalence and the provenance of the educations of romance heroes. Representative minor Arthurian romances, as well as medieval romances whose heroes are not Arthurian, are examined for their expression of the theme of the hero's education. Consideration of such romances as *Galeran*, *Wigalois*, *Wigamur*, and *Sone de Nausai*, while indicating the frequency with which this motif occurs in medieval romance, also demonstrates the commonplace qualities and the rudimentary forms of this theme. The several versions of the exploits of the "Seven Sages" hero and the multiple texts of the adventures of Alexander not only further indicate the frequency of the theme but also exhibit its susceptibility to artistic development.

The provenance of this prevalent medieval romance theme is sought in both "fictional" and "theoretical" works of classical, Celtic, and medieval literature. Epics of earlier and later antiquity, from Homer to Statius; classical treatises upon statecraft, from Plato to Plutarch; Irish saga versions of exploits of Cuchulainn, Finn, and Lug, as well as Old Irish instruction books for princes (the *tecosca*); medieval French and German epics, and more importantly, medieval *miroirs de princes*, from John of Salisbury to William Perrault; all of these are examined for the possible origins of the theme of the Arthurian romance hero's education. Both the philosophical concept of an educated hero as well as the narrative details of the acquisition of learning are considered in these works. From this background a combination of topical and traditional material is proposed as the provenance of the Arthurian *enfance.*

Medieval romancers ascribe an education to their heroes almost as routinely as they do a battle or a love affair. Great writers freely embellish this theme of the knight's education for their special artistic purposes. In their depictions of youthful learning these writers define their knights' chivalry and determine their heroes' love. Since the educations emphasize important romance themes, it is profitable to examine the contemporary influences upon them, the literary interrelationships among them, and the artistic uses of the *enfance* pattern which includes them. Appreciation of the formation, the development, and the utilization of the *enfance* and the education of the Arthurian hero provides fresh insights into the medieval romancer's style, intention, and art.

traditional material is proposed as the possessor of the Arthurian

The Education of the Hero in Arthurian Romance

Chapter I

The Education of Tristan

✑ Music and Manners
Make the Man

De la fu li contes estrez
Qui tesmoingne l'estoire a voire:
Por ce fet ele mialz a croire.
Par les livres que nos avons
Les fez des ancïens savons
Et del siegle qui fu jadis.
Ce nos ont nostre livre apris
Qu'an Grece ot de chevalerie
Le premier los et de clergie.
Puis vint chevalerie a Rome
Et de la clergie la some,
Qui or est an France venue.

—*Cligès*

$\mathcal{T}$ristan is not an Arthurian knight. But he is one of the most significant knights of Arthurian romance. In no major version does Tristan owe direct allegiance to King Arthur or his court, and in few versions is Arthur mentioned at all. However, for the literary genre characterized by knights and ladies in quest of adventure and love—romance—the tale of Tristan proved vigorous and compelling. In some versions Tristan's exploits are as typically Arthurian as are most tales of Lancelot and Gawain. But in others, the Arthurian milieu is but bare framework for the artistic emendation and transformation of traditional themes by great artists of the Middle Ages; in these, the transformation of the romance pattern in the *enfance* of Tristan is particularly interesting to examine.

Tristan's *enfance* in all its versions is primarily a program of education which is presented dramatically. The education is important both in the characterization of the hero and in its contribution to the special qualities of those romances in which it is prominent. In all the fragmentary Tristan versions in which the appropriate part is extant, there is an *enfance* text. Nothing of the *enfance* is preserved in Béroul's poem, the Oxford and Berne fragments, *Le Chèvrefeuil*, or the *Tavola Ritonda*; therefore these works are not referred to in this study. Among the earliest statements of Tristan's education is in the late twelfth-century *Tristrant* of Eilhart von Oberg. Though perhaps contemporaneous with Eilhart, Thomas of Britain presents an education with a different emphasis and development of incident. These undergo astonishing transmutations in the work of Thomas' follower, Gottfried von Strassburg. In later texts, too, *Sir Tristrem*, the *Prose Tristan*, and Malory's "Book of Sir Tristram of Lyones," although the education has less significance for the hero and for the romances, the *enfance* of Isold's lover is well worth considering.

Gertrude Schoepperle established that Eilhart's *Tristrant*[1]

1. Franz Lichtenstein (ed.), *Eilhart von Oberge* ("Quellen und Forschungen zur Sprach und Culturgeschichte der Germanischen Volker," Vol. XIX [Strassburg, London, 1887]).

represents the closest extant version of the lost French *estoire* from which most other Tristan versions are descended.[2] Examination of Tristan's youth and education in this Middle High German poem is therefore important for its probable representation of the earliest form of the hero's youthful exploits, and for the elements of that statement of Tristan's education which were so radically altered and developed by Thomas and Gottfried. When compared to these two works, Eilhart's is the most straightforward and psychologically the most simple. Yet it is the longest and most various. The description of education is the most detailed not only of all Tristan texts but of the *enfances* of every other Arthurian hero, with the single exception of the *Prose Lancelot*'s. Early critics recognized the unusual fullness of Eilhart's *enfance*: A. Schultz, in *Das höfische Leben*,[3] cites it as an example of the "historical" education of a German knight, and Bédier indicates its "principaux traits différentiels" are "si vraiment singuliers qu'il paraît inutile de les discuter."[4]

Tristrant's education in Eilhart has an aura of refined courtliness, of *hoveliche dinge* that is indeed striking in this least courtly of the Tristan romances. Three periods constitute the total education: care by a woman, instruction by the tutor Kurneval, and tutelage by a polished courtier of King Mark, Tînas von Lîtan. Tristrant spends his first years with a nurse,

> einer ammen die sîn plag,
> und zôch daz wol biz an den tag
> daz ez mochte gerîten.
>
> (123-25)

After her care, Kurneval tutors the youth in five subjects. The first courtly concerns are "harfin unde setin klingen." After

2. *Tristan and Isolt: A Study of the Sources of the Romance* (2 vols.; 2nd ed.; New York, 1960), I, 7-8; Frederick Whitehead, "The Early Tristan Poems," in *Arthurian Literature in the Middle Ages* [hereafter referred to as *ALMA*], ed. R. S. Loomis (Oxford, 1959), pp. 134-38. Earlier valuable discussions of sources are Lichtenstein, *op. cit.*, pp. xlvii f., and E. Muret, "Eilhart d'Oberg et sa source française," *Romania*, XVI (1887).

3. *Das höfische Leben zur Zeit der Minnesinger* (2 vols.; Leipzig, 1889), I, 171.

4. Joseph Bédier (ed.), *Le Roman de Tristan par Thomas* (2 vols.; Paris, 1902), I, 31.

musical instruction comes intellectual training—reading, writing,
languages, and law; and third, coaching in physical feats of agility
and chivalric expertise—putting the stone, jumping, wrestling,
riding, and wielding the lance and spear. Fourth is training in
hunting. Courteous behavior and deportment constitute the fifth
area of learning. Later at King Mark's court, Tristrant refines
these achievements. In this final period of instruction, he is taught
by Tînas von Lîtan's example all he needs to know of knighthood;
courtesy, largesse, and delicacy of spirit are perfected.

> he bat daz ingesinde
> daz sie im gût wêrin
> und in vor allen swêren
> wolden hehûten
> daz wolde he mit gûten
> vordînen um sie alle.
> (334-39)

Eilhart's emphasis is upon the instruction of his hero in all
arts of courtly life:

> he lêrte im manchir hovesheit
> und lêdete im di unkûscheit.
> Waz sal der rede mêre?

He is taught to achieve worthiness and honor by cultivating both
body and mind. Line for line, less detail is devoted to Tristrant's
intellectual development than to his preparation for the exercise of
bohurts and the straits of battle. But "êre," "lobe," "sîn
getrûwe," "tugend," and "guter zuchte" are Eilhart's descriptions of his hero's achievements and the goals of his education. As
Schultz puts it, "Es ist hier dem Erzieher also nicht bloss die
musicalische und militärische Ausbildung seines Zöglings anver-
traut, sondern derselbe überwacht auch dessen moralische Entwicklung und leitet ihn an zu guten Manieren, wie sie einem wohler-
zogenen jungen Manne anstehen."[5] For Eilhart's young hero,
manners are the expression of morality.

This education of Tristrant seems to be one of the few aspects of

5. *Op. cit.*, 1, 171.

Eilhart's poem not prescribed by traditional origins, although most other incidents and many characterizations have Celtic backgrounds. Miss Schoepperle's comparison of Tristrant's youthful accomplishments in strength and skill to the exercises of Old Irish heroes reveals that some of Tristrant's feats are comparable only to those of minstrels and jongleurs in other texts, "whereas, in Irish they are still appropriate to heroes."[6] A feature Professor Helaine Newstead considers part of Celtic tradition is Tristrant's ability in hunting.[7] While Miss Schoepperle recognizes that harping for Tristrant, as for an Old Irish hero, is an almost necessary accomplishment, she yet maintains that Tristrant excels in the pursuits cultivated by the knights of the time.[8] Her conclusion about the hero's education is much the same as for his conception and birth: "Whether these accounts are modifications of Celtic tradition or the invention of the French redactors, it is impossible to definitely decide."[9]

It seems likely, then, that Tristrant's education in Eilhart is a reflection of contemporary example. The correspondences between Tristrant's tuition and those of other twelfth-century romance heroes are too specific to be accidental,[10] yet too consistent with

6. *Op. cit.*, II, 288.

7. Helaine Newstead, "The 'Enfances' of Tristan and English Tradition," in *Studies in Medieval Literature in Honor of Professor Albert Croll Baugh*, ed. MacEdward Leach (Philadelphia, 1961), p. 177; see also Rachel Bromwich, "Some Remarks on the Celtic Sources of 'Tristan,' " *Transactions of the Honorable Society of Cymmrodorion* (1953), pp. 32, 45.

8. *Op. cit.*, II, 281-82.

9. *Ibid.*, II, 281.

10. Among such heroes are Apollonius, in *Historia Apolonii regis Tyri*, ed. A. Riese (Leipzig, 1893); Florentine, in Killis Campbell (ed.), *The Seven Sages of Rome* (New York, 1907), as well as in *Dolopathos* of Johannis de Alta Silva, ed. A. Hilka (Heidelberg, 1913); and Alexander, in the various versions of the *Roman d'Alexandre*, particularly those of Alberic de Pisançon, the decasyllabic version, and Pfaffe Lamprecht, Milan S. La Du (ed.), *The Medieval French Roman d'Alexandre* (Text of the Arsenal and Venice Versions, "Elliott Monographs," No. 36 [Princeton, 1937]), and other texts in the same series, ed. E. C. Armstrong and others. For a version of the education of Alexander from the *Secretum Secretorum*, see Gower's *Confessio Amantis*, ed. G. C. Macauley (Oxford, 1899-1902), Books VII and VIII. The implications of the "royal" background of such educated heroes and the possible relationships to the learned hero of romance will be discussed in chap. iv, below.

chronicle evidence to be specifically literary.[11] Eilhart's stress
upon courtliness in the *enfance* text suggests that the sources of
detail in the educational program were the very courts where this
romance and others like it were heard.

Although the derivation of the hero's education is probably not
traditional, there are, however, aspects of it which are specific to
many versions of the Tristan story.[12] Other Tristan romances
maintain Eilhart's references to the hero's unparalleled assiduity
in study and superiority in mental and physical prowess to any
other youth.[13] The first two phases of education, with the nurse
and Kurneval, also appear in Gottfried's poem; but here, as in
Thomas, there is no third tutor at court. In Eilhart, Tristrant's
learning requires the polish of court example, but in Thomas and
more so in Gottfried, Tristan's youthful cultivation is so remarkable that he tutors the courtiers. The triumvirate of tutors in
Eilhart—the woman, the "governor," and the courtier—represents
a recurring theme in the *enfances* of other heroes, and the three
instructors of Perceval and Lancelot will be considered in the next
chapters. Tristan's training in hunting and languages remain con-
stants of his education. Most interestingly, music and specifically
harping—the first skill Eilhart's hero is taught, here mentioned
without elaboration—is the study which supersedes all others in the
Tristan narratives. In Thomas and Gottfried, music is not merely
one of several arts but a major concern of the whole romance. Not
present in the other versions, however, is the fullness of Eilhart's
curriculum in physical activity: in Thomas, none is mentioned; in
Gottfried and those later, it is given brief notice without the
particulars listed in Eilhart.

What these romances possess which Eilhart's version does not

11. Schultz, *op. cit.*, I, 170-72. The specific "topicality" of the education
of heroes will be suggested in chap. iv, below.

12. It is not to be implied that Thomas or Gottfried used or knew Eilhart's
version or his immediate source. The sequence of *enfance* considerations in
this chapter is not necessarily controlled by chronology, but rather, indicates a
progression from simpler to more complex *enfance* versions.

13. Romance examples of the ideal of nurturing a noble young man to un-
equalled excellence are so frequent that it is surely a panegyrical *topos*,
probably originating in praise of rulers. Curtius discusses such *topoi* in
European Literature in the Latin Middle Ages, trans. W. Trask (New York,
1953), pp. 176-82.

is the interpretation of detail and the use of incident for specific purposes. The education of the hero has little or no importance for the rest of Eilhart's *Tristrant*. Tristrant's youthful learning and refinement do not have noteworthy repercussions later in the romance. The books, arts, and talents of his youth do not essentially refine Tristrant's manhood. Tutelage does not prepare for his way of loving Isolde, nor for his betraying Mark. In Eilhart, Tristrant's tragic passion is not born young.

For Thomas of Britain's *Tristan*[14] and for Gottfried von Strassburg, who claims Thomas as his source, the hero's education in the *enfance* bears a crucial relationship to the later parts of the narratives. It is unfortunate that considerations of the *enfance* in Thomas must partake as much of the methods of typological archeology as those of literary criticism. No original octosyllabic *vers* of this *enfance* survives. The whole romance can be reconstructed only from fragmentary remains, and that whole judged as a fusion of its fragments and reconstructed components. What Brother Robert, in his Norwegian translation and redaction, retained of his original can be ascertained only by informed speculation based on comparison of Thomas' extant words with Brother Robert's corresponding passages.[15] However, recognizing Robert's methods of handling Thomas' text and believing, with Chaucer, that we can and must "maken virtue of necessitee," permits examination of Tristan's *enfance* in Thomas' poem.

What is, in Eilhart's version, a statement of the hero's youthful activities pursued with gusto is in Thomas an account of sedentary pursuits peerlessly performed; what is a detailed curriculum for the cultivation of mind and body in the first is a general outline for the stimulation of youthful intellect in the second; what is in Eilhart a series of actions without emphasized results is in Thomas

14. Eugene Kölbing (ed.), *Tristrams Saga ok Isondar*, Vol. I of *Die nordische und die englische version der Tristan-sage* (Heilbronn, 1878).

15. See Bartina H. Wind's Introduction to her *Les Fragments du Tristan de Thomas*, (Leiden, 1950); Kölbing, *op. cit.*, I, xviii f.; F. Piquet, *L'Originalité de Gottfried de Strasbourg* ("Travaux et Mémoires des Facultés de l'Université de Lille," N.S. No. 5 [Lille, 1905]); Philip Mitchell, *ALMA*, p. 465; W. T. H. Jackson, *ALMA*, p. 146. Robert's apparent interest in action rather than characterization made him supplant monologue and dialogue with straight narration, and exclude details which retard action.

an intimation of the effects and ramifications of nurture. Thomas' text of the education the faithful seneschal Roald gives to his foster son and lord is brief and vague. Tristan learns "book knowledge," the seven chief arts, languages, and the seven types of music.[16] There is but one phase to his education; there is no distinction between types of instruction, degrees of readiness or progression, or times of tutelage. No tutors are specified. Roald "made him learn"—which can mean (in a direct causal grammatical construction) "taught him," or (in a construction of cause at one remove) "had someone teach him." Tristan learns nothing of the physical arts of chivalry. He has no training in hunting, no physical recreation nor expertise in sports, no training in laws and customs of other lands. He is not said to know how to write. Thomas' Tristan is not taught to display moral worth by good manners.

Many details of Tristan's education, though not stated as a curriculum, are, however, revealed in action. Within the *enfance*, although there is no mention of his instruction in hunting, there is mention of Roald's gift of hunting gear (xvii) and of Tristan's display of virtuosity in the ceremonies of venery (xxi). Tristan's particular instruction and talent in playing the harp is not stated, but the value of that fine harping to King Mark on sleepless nights (xxii) and the impression Tristan's musicianship makes on the king's court (xxii) are portrayed dramatically. No tutor is mentioned in the education, but Tristan's master Gorneval, whose name is not revealed until much later in the tale (xciii), remains on board the Norwegian merchant ship, is initially abducted with Tristan, set adrift, and forced to return alone to Roald with tidings of foreboding and gloom (xviii).

Details of the hero's instruction which are both specific to the

16. Since music is one of the Quadrivium, one wonders about the meaning of "seven types of music." Medieval classifications such as the familiar Boethian *musica mundana, musica humana, musica instrumentis constituta* usually are constituted by two, three, or four "types" (it is so in such writers as Cassiodorus, Isidore of Seville, John of Salisbury, Johannes de Grocheo, Hermannus Contractus) but not seven. Thomas' use of the number either is meant to unite some two classifications of three and four categories, or it is a structural parallel to "seven arts" and a statement of emphasis upon this musical study.

text of the education and revealed in action, both within the *enfance* and later, pertain to languages and music. Tristan's knowledge of diverse languages allows him to bargain with the foreign merchants for the seven falcons; this bargaining becomes his undoing (xviii). Abandoned in England, one of the youth's primary fears—even taking precedence over dread of fierce lions—is the possibility he might not know the language of the land's inhabitants (xx)! Later, King Mark's barons, expecting to rid themselves forever of Tristan, suggest him as being the best suited for the expedition to win Isolt because of his skill in the Irish tongue (xxxiii). More numerous and more significant than these references to languages are the details of Tristan's musicianship. Tristan announces himself to the English court by his long, elaborate horn fanfare when coming to Tintagel with the "present" of the hunt (xxii); once at court, after recognizing the melody played by a harper, he takes up the instrument to display his own extraordinary skill (xxii); he specifically pleases King Mark with music (xxii). Later, Isolt, betrayed by one man's music, is then rescued by another's: she is lost to Mark by Gandin's rote and won back by Tristan's harp (1). A second Isolt, White Hands of Brittany, also is won by his music (lxix).

Consideration of the *enfance* points up Thomas' interest in his hero's intellectual attainments. Eilhart's Tristrant is cunning but the poet does not stress that education makes him so. Thomas' hero is even more clever, and his learning in the *enfance* subtly changes the nature of his later adventures. Tristan's education, particularly his musical prowess, is significant for the course of the poem. This *enfance* portrait of Thomas' hero adumbrates the later characterization of the tragic lover and learned knight.

Tristan's youthful training as a musician becomes most important when he asumes his "Tantris" disguise in Ireland (xxx). His harping strikes the attention of the Irishmen to the injured minstrel-knight adrift in his rudderless boat. Tantris' musicianship and display of artistic accomplishments cause word of him to come to young princess Isolt who consequently asks to become his pupil to learn to harp, to write, and to compose verses. And once the killer of Morholt is healed of his poisoned wound, he instructs

Isolt in harping and all manner of other stringed instruments, in writing, and in knowledge of all crafts, so that her fame for learning and courtly graces waxes wide. Once again, now as a man in Ireland, just as before when a youth in England, music is Tristan's herald. It is his means by which he saves his life, and it is his introduction to Isolt. Moreover, it is a significant part of his instruction of the young woman who must later understand his language of fatal passion. Tristan and Isolt are brought together by music and learning.

Whether Thomas further developed these two themes of music and learning, whether he emphasized an equality of refinement for the lovers, or whether he intimated that culture affects the ways of loving—these are queries that Robert's version of Thomas does not answer. Since Brother Robert's *Tristrams Saga ok Isondar* is not an exact translation, the suspicion can be raised that Thomas described the education of his hero in more detail and developed the theme more fully in ways which the Norwegian redactor excluded.[17] Gottfried's elaboration of the theme of the knight of

17. Bédier arrives at his conjectural restoration of the *enfance* of Tristan by similar reasoning. His reconstitution of the education text reads: ''La femme de Foitenant éleva donc Tristan comme eut fait une mère. Mais quand il eut accompli sa septième année, son père le maréchal le reprit aux femmes et le confia à un sage maître. Celui le mit aux lettres, et Tristan s'y appliqua d'un tel zèle qu'il en eut bientôt plus que tout autre enfant. Il apprit les sept arts et devint habile à parler divers langages. Puis il apprit les sept branches de la musique, en sort qu'il n'y eut pas de musicien plus renommé que lui. Il apprit encore à chevaucher en portant l'écu et la lance, à éperonner adroitement les deux flancs du destrier, à le faire sauter hardiment, volter, galoper, le frein abandonné, à presser des genoux. Il apprit à bien s'escrimer, à lutter vaillamment, à courir et à sauter, à lancer l'épieu; à berser et à chasser, si bien qu'il devint la plus habile des veneurs. Il apprit les diverses manières de jeux qui se jouent dans les hautes cours. Il observa et connut les lois et coutumes de la terre'' (*Op. cit.*, I, 28-29). While refuting other parts of the restoration text, Miss Schoepperle takes no issue with this education construction (*op. cit.*, I, 1-10; 66-120; II, Appendix II, 518-23). Professor Newstead suggests that the *enfance*, as it now exists in Thomas, was determined by the author's ''instinct for the dramatic which governed his selection of narrative material. Instead of merely listing Tristan's accomplishments, he presents them as a series of vividly dramatic scenes'' (*op. cit.*, p. 181). However, the combination of Thomas' usual method of describing causes and effects, Robert's usual method of excluding ''motivation,'' and Gottfried's specific statement of including education details ''from my source,'' makes it more probable that the vague summary of Tristan's education is Brother Robert's and not that of Thomas, his source.

learning, music, and love may have been more directly derived from Thomas, his claimed source, than the extant romances indicate.

Thomas' text, as we have it, suggests collateral considerations. One of Thomas' contributions to the Tristan tradition consists in his adaptation of story and ideal to twelfth-century literary standards. This is manifest in his portrayal of the love between Tristan and Isolt. Consideration of the *enfance* of the hero and its relationship to the whole romance suggests that another concept, just as important as the description of love and contributing to that portrait, is the presentation of the lover as learned. Although there is some literary example for the learned hero,[18] the education and *enfance* of Tristan appear to reflect contemporary interests. The many indications that Thomas' poem particularly mirrors the temper of the court at Anjou[19] make it possible that not only general ideas but specific figures of the court of King Henry II and Queen Eleanor affected Thomas' concept of his hero and his hero's youthful exploits. While it is not necessary to attribute to history what may be poetic invention, contemporary examples for comparison between life and literature exist. Pierre Jonin's *Les personnages féminins dans les romans français de Tristan* testifies to the

18. Apollonius of Tyre is an example. See Professor Newstead, *op. cit.*, pp. 176 f. Alexander of Macedon best exemplifies the historical king transfigured to twelfth-century gentleman of prowess. Significant studies are Paul Meyer, *Alexandre le Grand dans la littérature française du moyen-âge* (Paris, 1886), 2 vols.; George Cary, *The Medieval Alexander* (Cambridge, 1956); and K. Sneyders de Vogel, "L'Education d'Alexandre le Grand," *Neophilologus*, XXVIII (1942-1943), 161-71.

19. The theory of relationship between Thomas and Henry II or his successors has long been championed by R. S. Loomis: twice in 1922, "Tristram and the House of Anjou," *MLR*, XVII, 24-30, and in *Burlington Magazine*, XLI, 54-64; earlier, in *Illustrations of Romance on Tiles from Chertsey Abbey* ("University of Illinois Studies in Language and Literature," Vol. II, No. 2 [Urbana, 1916]); and later, in his and Laura Hibbard Loomis' *Arthurian Legends in Medieval Art* (New York, 1938). So too agrees Rita Lejeune, "Rôle littéraire d'Aliénor d'Aquitaine et de sa famille," *Cultura Neolatina*, XIV (1954), 5-57; A. T. Hatto, "Tristan's Angevin Escutcheon," Appendix III of his *Gottfried von Strassburg's Tristan* (Baltimore, 1960); and Amy Kelly, *Eleanor of Aquitaine and the Four Kings* (Cambridge, Mass., 1952), p. 87. Cf. Margaret M. Pelan, *L'Influence du Brut de Wace sur les romanciers français de son temps* (Paris, 1931), chap. ii. See also Friedrich Heer, *The Medieval World*, trans. Janet Sondheimer (Cleveland, 1962), pp. 123-57.

validity of studying contemporary influences upon Thomas' poem.[20] Recognition that Celtic literature and the classics are not the only sources of idea and incident in courtly romance permits suggestion that the origin of certain details in Thomas may be found in records of the courtly milieu.

In one of the chronicles of Anjou, the *Historia Gaufredi Ducis Normannorum et Comitis Andegavorum* of Jean de Marmoutier,[21] there is a startling resemblance between the childhood exploits and characterization of Count Geoffrey the Handsome and Thomas' Tristan. In both texts a brilliant youth is versed in both the arts of chivalry and learning. He crosses the Channel from France to England and there astounds the king, the knights, and the assembled court with his erudition and learned speech. He is profoundly interested in and moved by music and song. In common with the king, he delights in hunting and its ceremonies. He is befriended by the monarch, retained, treated as, and even called, a son. He is dubbed knight by this king of England, who is the guardian of this knight's future beloved. The Anjou lion escutcheon is represented in his arms and dress; at his investiture he receives "marvelous" arms. His clothing is given detailed description. A ceremonial bath is significant for the course of his life. He "loses his companions while hunting" and is put on the right path by a man (men) who does not know him, who yet recognizes that he is a superior, and who reveals facts he seeks.

Since Geoffrey the Handsome was the father of King Henry II, details such as these might have been included by Thomas in his characterization of Tristan as a compliment to Henry and his

20. *Les personnages féminins dans les romans français de Tristan au XIIe siècle. Étude des influences contemporaines* ("Publications des Annales de la Faculté des Lettres d'Aix-en-Provence," N.S., No. 22 [Gap, 1958]), particularly pp. 2-55, 249-335, and 373-450.

21. The best edition of Jean's *Historia* is published in Louis Halphen and Réné Poupardin (eds.), *Chroniques des comtes d'Anjou et des seigneurs d'Amboise* (Paris, 1913), pp. 176-231. An older edition important for comparison and for supplementary material is Paul Marchegay and André Salmon (eds.), *Chroniques des comtes d'Anjou receuilliés et publiées pour la Société de l'histoire de France* (Paris, 1856-1871), with a valuable introduction by Émile Mabille. Louis Halphen's *Le comté d'Anjou au XIe siècle* (Paris, 1906), contains a useful critique of method and content of this chronicle, as does Kate Norgate's *England Under the Angevin Kings* (2 vols.; London, New York, 1887), I, 258-62.

queen. Interestingly enough, the major evidence adduced for Thomas' having written at the Anjou court has been the lion device on Tristan's arms;[22] the relationship between Thomas' poem and the Angevin chronicle account may buttress this attribution. Thomas' designation of Mark as king not merely of Cornwall but of all England—a change from tradition which thus far has been explained only tentatively[23]—might be an implied reference to the historical king of England, Henry I. Thomas' panegyric passages on London and England would then be entirely consistent.[24]

There are several difficulties in this interpretation. First, any one of the details listed exists alone elsewhere and could be considered a stock motif or incident in folklore or romance.[25] However, it is their remarkable congruence in both texts that is here impressive. Second, some of the details appear in conjunction in other stories, such as in versions of Apollonius of Tyre.[26] But these similarities are general in outline and do not invalidate the conten-

22. References are listed in note 19, above.

23. Professor Newstead explains Mark's kingship this way: ''The complimentary references to England and London, as well as the description of the hunting ritual and the extension of Mark's kingdom to the whole land, could have been introduced to please an Anglo-Norman audience by the same *conteur* who developed the story of the *enfances* from tradition current in the east of England'' (*op. cit.*, p. 182). Cf. her ''King Mark of Cornwall,'' *RP*, XI (1958), 240-53.

24. Bédier discusses these *encomia*, *op. cit.*, I, 397 f., as does Wind, *op. cit.*, p. 163 f. The possible Geoffrey-Tristan relationship gives added meaning to the very three changes from tradition which Whitehead recognizes: Thomas' ''residence in England presumably led to the encomium of London; his court connections may have led him to attribute to Tristan the royal arms; for less clear reasons he rejected all connection with Arthur and made Mark king not only of Cornwall but of all England'' (*ALMA*, p. 141).

25. Gertrude Schoepperle says, ''It is usual in primitive stories for the hero to be brought up in obscurity, to display extraordinary powers in his youth, and then, coming to a brilliant assembly, to surpass the greatest in the land'' (*op. cit.*, II, 208). Cf. J. G. von Hahn, *Sagwissenshaftliche Studien* (Jena, 1876), pp. 341 f.

26. *Historia Apolonii regis Tyri*, ed. Riese. Similarities between Tristan's early life and Apollonius' have been noted frequently: S. Singer, *Apollonius von Tyrus, Untersuchungen über das Fortleben des antiken Romans in spätern Zeiten* (Halle, 1895); A. B. Smyth's Introduction to *Shakespeare's Pericles and Apollonius of Tyre* (Philadelphia, 1898); Elimar Klebs, *Die Erzählung von Apollonius aus Tyrus* (Berlin, 1899); C. Voretzsch, *Epische Studien* (Halle, 1900) I, 144-46; J. Bédier, *op. cit.*, I, 94, n. 1; Laura Hibbard, *Medieval Romance in England* (New York, 1924), pp. 164-73; and most recently and most completely by Professor Newstead, ''The 'Enfances' of Tristan and English Tradition,'' pp. 176 f.

tion that the essential details in Thomas have their source else-where. Third, material of chronicles was frequently modeled on popular romance material, either written or oral.[27] And therefore the chronicle account of Geoffrey the Handsome could have been, in turn, effected by unknown Tristan versions. Finally, since the dates for neither Thomas' nor Jean's works are established exactly —though both are thought to have been written between 1160 and 1180—precedence cannot be positive. Thomas, however, could have heard or seen a version of this chronicle before or after its com-pletion, or he could have heard from Geoffrey's friends the very anecdotes out of which the *Historia* is largely made.

Although certainty is impossible, the suggested relationship offers a more consistent and more complete justification for certain elements in Thomas' poem than otherwise has been proposed. If the concept has validity, it affords an explanation for Mark's king-ship over England, a firmer connection between Thomas of Britain and the Angevin court, and a topical significance to certain details of description and incident in *Tristan.*

The more one reads in the chronicles of Anjou, the more one is struck by the progressively assiduous intellectualism of the Angevin rulers as represented by their "biographers." The prevailing philosophy apparently was *Quia rex illiteratus est quasi asinus coronatus.*[28] The accounts of the education and cultivation of Folque the Good, for example, and records of the educations of his sons Gui and Drogon read like *miroirs de princes.*[29] But not until

27. A convenient summary of evidence for this may be found in Reto Roberto Bezzola's *Les Origines et la formation de la littérature courtoise en occident, 500-1200* (Paris, 1944-1960), II, Seconde Partie, 326 f. Of the chronicles of the Angevin court in particular he says, "l'historien de la maison d'Anjou, conscient de la culture littéraire demi-savante, demi-populaire, demi-ecclésiastique, demi-profane aussi de ses seigneurs, fait entrer les différents éléments qui la composent..." (p. 343).

28. The devout and erudite Folque the Good is reported to have written to Louis IV: "Regi Francorum comes Andegavorum. Noveritis, domine, quia rex illiteratus est asinus coronatus" (Halphen and Poupardin, *op. cit.,* p. 140). This familiar saying has been attributed in its Latin and vernacular forms to many princes and many writers. John of Salisbury has the Roman Conrad III state it; Hennig Brinkmann attributes it to various princely spokesmen in *Entstehungsgeschichte des Minnesangs* (Halle, 1926), p. 19. The chronicler Jean de Marmoutier himself recognizes the idea as proverbial (Halphen and Poupardin, *op. cit.,* pp. 140 f.).

29. Halphen and Poupardin, *op. cit.,* pp. 34 f., 140 f.

Jean de Marmoutier's history of Henry II's father, Geoffrey the Handsome, is there description of such artistic unity of action and learning: of a knight's passion for languages, devotion to hunting, concern with music, delight in artful ceremony, and studiousness so pervasive that a learned tutor accompanies him to battles.[30] Thomas' Tristan is just such a knight.[31]

If Thomas wrote his *Tristan* for Henry and Eleanor with the hero's *enfance* as an implied panegyric on his patron's father, he was not the only poet of the Angevin court to compliment the king by praising the count. Étienne de Rouen commemorates the cultured Count Geoffrey in a poem dedicated to Henry II and appended to Jean de Marmoutier's *Historia*:

> Sola solus patriae, speculum lux atque sophiae,
> Artibus imbutus septenis, sensus acutus,
> Precluis orator, logicae nec segnis amator,
> Rethoricus flores edoctus sive colores. . . .[32]
>
> (32-35)

This poem, though characterized by the eulogistic language of antiquity, has as its subject the intellectual concern of Anjou—that same interest in a noble knight's learning which is displayed in the chronicle of Jean de Marmoutier and in the romance of Thomas of Britain.

Thomas' poem, then, represents an approach to the hero quite at variance with Eilhart's. In his youth, Eilhart's hero studies but he is not learned. Thomas introduces a new emphasis in Tristan's characterization in the *enfance*. He emphasizes the display of Tristan's learning and gives significance to gentlemanly scholarship and, most particularly, to music. Unlike Eilhart's work in

30. *Ibid.*, pp. 37 f., 218 f.

31. The significance of historical personages for the character and development of the *chanson de geste* has long been recognized. (Bédier's theory on the William cycle amply demonstrates this point.) The role of an Angevin count in French epic is suggested by Ferdinand Lot, ''Geoffroi Grisegonelle dans l'épopée,'' *Romania*, XIX (1890), 377-93. I propose that just as the martial exploits of certain noble knights affected the *chanson de geste* so did the intellectual interests and cultivation of other noble men affect the romance.

32. Marchegay and Salmon, *op. cit.*, pp. 311-15, and in R. Howlett's edition of the Norman monk's works in *Chronicles of the Reigns of Stephen, Henry II, and Richard I* (London, 1886), II, 772.

which the *enfance* qualities have no effect upon later incidents and characterizations, in Thomas ramifications of Tristan's education are displayed later in the romance. The incomplete state of Thomas' work invites speculative considerations, and those parts of the poem which have survived the vagaries of time only in translation stimulate a quest for contemporary influence upon the author's conception of his hero. Thomas' *Tristan* can be mined not only for evidence of "courtliness"[33] but for possible relationship to one specific courtier and that courtier's characteristics. Out of Thomas' romance, Tristan emerges the learned knight.

The *enfance* in Thomas' *Tristan*, for all its interest, is more significant as a literary Janus. One face reflects the past and the other prefigures the work of Gottfried von Strassburg,[34] who took Thomas' poem as a model. With his "cristillinen wortelin," Gottfried makes Thomas' grotto into a shrine; he transmutes the love affair into a mystic union; from the educated knight, he derives the perfect artist.

The education and *enfance* of Gottfried's *Tristan* portray the knight as tutored and tempered to apprehend music, love, and life as art. Far more learned than Tristan is in Thomas' poem, Gottfried's hero is an erudite musician with the qualities of composer and performer. His education is more particular and more significant for his spirit and destiny than in any other version. Important themes stated in the education text are developed later in the romance. Aspects of the hero's characterization and those of subsidiary personages such as Kurneval are first introduced in the *enfance* and developed later. In considering this *enfance*, it is

33. "Nineteenth century scholars agreed in regarding the poems of Eilhart and Béroul as essentially a single version (*version commune* or *version des jongleurs*) and in contrasting it with that of Thomas and his derivatives (*version courtoise*)" (Whitehead, *ALMA*, pp. 136-37). This dichotomy has been endlessly reiterated. Jonin's study, however, documents his important demur: "Cette même épithète de courtoise, nous renonçerons à appliquer à Thomas malgré la tradition, précisément parce que nous ne croyons pas trouver en lui les éléments suffisants pour la justifier" (*op. cit.*, p. 454).

34. Wolfgang Golther (ed.), *Tristan und Isolde von Gottfried von Strassburg* (Berlin, Stuttgart, 1888), and Friedrich Ranke (ed.), *Gottfried von Strassburg, Tristan und Isold* (Berlin, 1963). Though older, yet still easily accessible, Golther's edition has been preferred. All quotations are from this edition. (Golther's line numbers are generally two lines behind Ranke's, e.g. Golther's line 2050 appears in Ranke as 2052.)

therefore necessary to range throughout the poem to follow the meaning and development of the childhood exploits. This is in contrast to the more self-contained *enfances* in Eilhart and in Thomas. Gottfried's consummately courtly romance emends and transcends the basic tenets of the genre; the education of the hero introduces and exemplifies many of these distinctive changes. Within the *enfance* the poet dramatizes the characteristics of education, the character of the educator, and the uses of education. He expresses the educated romancer's view of contemporary love, lovers, and love stories. His *Tristan* is an exposition of a new type of knighthood in which love cannot ennoble the chivalric lover until he, by art, ennobles it.

Professor W. T. H. Jackson's "Tristan the Artist in Gottfried's Poem"[35] makes consideration of Tristan as an educated knight more derivative than original; but there is yet much to examine in Gottfried's portrait of his hero's education and the uses to which the poet puts the *enfance* for his expression of a love unbound by traditional chivalry and uncircumscribed by worldly codes.

Whereas Eilhart lists Tristan's various subjects for study, and whereas Thomas gives a generalized outline of education, Gottfried indicates both the educational endeavors and the immediate changes these force upon his hero. Tristan's tutelage has two separate periods. The first embraces his years from baptism until age seven. Floraete, his foster mother, cares for him so carefully and affectionately that she would have him always walk on velvet (2050). The next seven years bring the tutor, the travel abroad, and the studies which harden yet refine, free yet imprison, liberate the imagination yet control the heart. Kurneval is the tutor with whom Tristan is sent abroad to study. Of his five areas of instruction, books and languages take precedence; they are the first studies and the most important. Tristan devotes himself to books "vor aller slahte lêre" (2065); this study "und ir getwanc/was sîner sorgen anevanc" (2083-84). While mastering books and languages, he learns to play many kinds of stringed instruments and practices these diligently.

35. *PMLA*, LXXVII (1962), 364-72.

so vertete er sîner stunde vil
an iegelîchem seitespil:
dâ kêrte er spâte unde fruo
sîn emzekeit sô sêre zuo
biz er es wunder kunde.
                    (2093-97)

Third are physical skills. He learns the chivalric art of riding with shield and lance and the recreational sports of fencing, wrestling, running, leaping, and javelin-throwing. Tracking and hunting are the fourth study. Finally, he excels at all courtly pastimes —"aller hande hovespil"—and has many at his command (2119-20). At fourteen years of age, he returns home for travel through his own lands and among his own people.

The constituents of this learning are not markedly different from those in Eilhart and Thomas. With the addition of physical training, Gottfried's text maintains the elements present in Thomas. The relationship to Eilhart is much closer,[36] but there are differences in the order and the emphasis of the studies. Gottfried includes nothing of manners as morality's expression. He gives less space and fewer particulars than Eilhart does to training of body. Instead of music's being the first study, as it is in Eilhart, Gottfried makes it succeed books and languages. Yet, the musical education is given some detail, and its prominence in the whole *enfance* is Gottfried's most noteworthy difference in subject emphasis. Gottfried's Tristan needs no king's courtier to refine his youthful instruction as he does in Eilhart, and he therefore has no subsequent training. Instead of a third period of instruction, Tristan's arrival at Mark's court is made a brilliant performance of expertise.

The striking quality of Gottfried's description is its statement on the effects of learning. While Eilhart and, to a lesser degree, Thomas stress subject matter, Gottfried describes the difficulties

36. The scholarly consensus is that Gottfried probably did not know Eilhart's poem. Johannes Gombert, *Eilhard von Oberg und Gottfried von Strassburg* ("Beiträge zur Tristanforschung" [Rotterdam, 1927]); F. Piquet, "Le Problème Eilhart-Gottfried," *Revue Germanique*, XX (1929), 109-54; and H. Stolte, *Eilhard und Gottfried, Studien über Motivreim und Aufbaustil* (Halle, 1941).

and glories of disciplined study and the antithetical dualities (love
and hate, pleasure and pain) which characterize the transition
from carefree innocence to responsible, sensitive manhood.

> daz was sîn êrstiu kêre
> ûz sîner frîheite:
> dô trat er in daz geleite
> betwungenlîcher sorgen,
> die ime dô vor verborgen
> und vor behalten wâren.
> in den ûfblüenden jâren,
> dô al sîn wunne solte enstân,
> dô er mit fröuden solte gân,
> in sînes lebenes begin
> dô was sîn beste leben hin:
> do er mit fröuden blüen began
> do viel der sorgen rîfe in an
> der maneger jugent schaden tuot,
> und darte im sîner fröuden bluot.
> in sîner ersten frîheit
> wart al sîn frîheit hin geleit.
>
> (2066-82)

The pain of learning is its most immediate effect. Gottfried
portrays this suffering in learning as necessary and inescapable.
For him and for his hero, unfettered joyousness is incomplete.
The yoke of knowledge allows increase of both the heights and
depths of emotional range. Young Tristan suffers to learn but
learns, also, to suffer well.

Tristan's education in the *enfance* inculcates the attributes of
grace and thoughtful self-criticism. These characterize his display
of learning in action. Grace and thought unite in each of the
youth's endeavors. This unity astounds his beholders and leads
to the hero's childhood tribulations and successes.

First, his display of accomplished elegance causes his abduction.
Not only courtly demeanor, chessmanship, and language skill stimulate the merchants to kidnap the youth—these are the motivations in Thomas—but the small talk of fashion, the exotic (well-
pronounced!) vocabulary in chess, and the subtle songs sung, the

chansons,   refloits, and *estampies* (2281-93), confirm Tristan's worth.[37]

A second example of learning displayed in action is his calculation of effects and his graceful execution of the ceremony of the hunt once he is abandoned in Cornwall. The four rituals of hunting the hart—the excoriation, fourchie, quarry, and present—appear in Thomas.[38] In Gottfried, however, Tristan carefully presents each of these foreign terms with due recognition of their fascination to the Cornish courtiers; they seize each word, repeat it, and marvel at his learning (2925 f.). This young master of artful effects begins to excoriate the hart by first preparing himself for the task by rolling his sleeves and by smoothing his hair above his ears (2841 f.) ; when nearing the animal's large intestines he calls for serving men to do this less ceremonial part of disembowelment. Finally, when time comes to make the present of the hunt to the king, Tristan (not merely given a horn to blow, as he is in Thomas), specifically chooses a small high-pitched instrument, "ein kleine hellez hornelin" (3202), splendidly leads the courtiers to follow his measure (3208 f.), fills Tintagel Castle with his music (3220 f.), and plays a complex solo fanfare in foreign style (3246). This hunt, like the performance aboard ship before abduction, is a work of planned artistry.

A third revelation of training in action within the *enfance* occurs at King Mark's court. This long scene (3378-3754), in which the singular education of the young musician is admired by Mark and the courtiers and in which Tristan receives the epithet *niuwe spielmann,* displays the major concept of the *enfance,* the importance of music. Essentials of this court scene are present in Thomas: music heralds the hero, his music produces admiration, and music binds the friendship with King Mark; but the significance of music to Gottfried's poem appears in the proliferation of detail, as well as in the comments of the poet. One can say of

37. Surely the dirge Tristan utters when aware of his betrayal (2330 f.) is sung as a formal *klagelied*!

38. Discussions of these hunt scenes and of Tristan as master-hunter include François Remigereau, "Tristan 'Maître de Vénerie' dans la tradition anglaise et le roman de Tristan," *Romania,* LVIII (1932), 218-37, and H. L. Savage, "Sir Gawain 'Fer Ouer þe French Flod,' " *JEGP,* XLVII (1948), 48 f.

Tristan, as W. P. Ker said of *Beowulf*,[39] that the "traditional essentials" of romance are placed at the outer edges and the "irrelevancies" at the center. Here, Tristan's music, like Beowulf's dragon, is central to the tale. Two noteworthy elements of Tristan's musicianship at court are the effects of his music upon others and the artistic temperament of Tristan as musician.

Horns of the hunt, followed by strains of the harp, captivate King Mark's court. First the hunting horn thrills Mark and "does him and others good to hear it" (3454-56) just as, in the earlier chase, the huntsmen, for sheer joy, can scarcely wait to follow his measure (3208-16). So haunting are the first flourishes of Tristan's harping that Tintagel's household is drawn from all points of the castle at a run (3571). And so enthralling is the playing of the music, that the listeners doubt their senses.

> daz maneger dâ stuont unde saz,
> der sîn selbes namen vergaz :
> da begunden herze und ôren
> tumben unde tôren
> und ûz ir rehte wanken ;
> dâ wurden gedanken
> in maneger wîse vür brâht.
>
> (3589-95)

Tristan's second *lai* is sung (in Breton, Welsh, Latin, and French) as well as harped.[40] The courtiers now must weigh two wonders, instrumental and vocal perfection (3631). They question his training in instruments (3654) ; they test his linguistic skill (3688 f.) ; and their hearts yearn for his accomplishments.

> "â Tristan, waere ich also duo !
> Tristan, dû maht gerne leben :
> Tristan, dir ist der wunsch gegeben
> aller der fuoge, die kein man

39. W. P. Ker in *The Dark Ages* (Edinburgh, 1904) maintains that the radical defect of *Beowulf* is a disproportion that "puts the irrelevancies [the dragon] in the center and the serious things on the outer edges" (pp. 252-53).

40. The possible significance of the conjunction between words and music in the Breton *lai* is considered by Ferdinand Wolf's still not superseded *Über die Lais, Sequenzen und Leiche* (Berlin, 1841). Cf. T. Gérould, *La musique au moyen-âge* (Paris, 1932).

ze dirre werlde gehaben kan.''
ouch macheten sî hier under
mit rede michel wunder!
''hôrâ!'' sprach dirre, ''hôrâ!'' sprach der
''elliu diu werlt diu hoere her:
ein vierzehnjaerec kint
kan al die liste, die nu sint!''

(3708-18)

King Mark offers the final compliment, which is the invitation to
companionship and the schedule of their future activities: hunting
by day, harping and singing by night (3725-29). The extraordinary power and success of Tristan's music encourages others
to emulate him, to become utterly engrossed by it, to envy him, to
love him; his listeners thus yearn both with him and for him.

The young musician is a performer with an artist's temperament. Gottfried portrays him responding to good music played
well by another, striving for perfection in his own, and recognizing
the musician's need for performing ''with the whole heart.'' After
his arrival at Mark's court, Tristan intently listens to a fine Welsh
harper and becomes so involved with the music he cannot keep from
speaking even were he threatened by death.

waer' ez im an den lîp geboten
ern möhte ez niht verswigen hân.
sîn muot begunde im ûf gân.
sîn herze daz wart muotes vol.

(3516-19)

When offered that harp himself, he does not immediately set to
playing but first ''warms up'' by striking a few preludes and disparate phrases (3551-53). He adjusts pegs and strings to his
satisfaction (3556-59). He concludes his *lais* only when they are
''to his pleasure'' (3644-45). While playing, he executes his office
as *niuwe spielmann* with all his concentration on it: ''sin niuwez
ambet huob er an mit flîzeclîchem ruoche'' (3562-63). (Just as in
later harpings in Ireland, mind and emotion determine the results
of art; first, he plays with his heart not in his music [7528-40];
then, he plays with all his heart and desire to make fine music

[7670-76] ; and still later, he harps better than ever before because, now, not playing as a lifeless man, he dedicates all his spirit to performance [7824-36].)

Versatility is also a feature of Tristan's musicianship, and modesty the sign of his manner. The harp is but one of seven instruments he knows.

> "mich lêrten Parmenîen
> videln und symphonîen;
> harphen unde rotten
> daz lêrten mich Gâlotten,
> zwêne meister Gâloise.
> mich lêrten Britûnoise,
> die wâren ûz der stat von Lût,
> rehte lîren unde sambiût."
> "sambiût, waz ist daz, lieber man?"
> "daz beste seitspiel, daz ich kan."
>   (3673-82)

Before Tristan's music is heard at all he twice demurs when asked whether he can play (3534-43; 7809-12); his astonishing recital concluded, he diffidently says "I have studied sporadically for seven years, but would gladly play better" (3668-72).

These three *enfance* scenes, the abduction, the hunt, and the young musician at court, demonstrate Gottfried's emphasis upon music's significance to Tristan in his youth.[41] These descriptions of

41. There seems never to have been a study of music in the curriculum of the medieval youth; paucity of evidence makes this understandable, for it is mostly in the romances that reference to youthful musical training is found. However, the subject is given passing notice in studies on medieval university life, including: Nan Cooke Carpenter, *Music in the Medieval and Renaissance Universities* (Norman, 1952); Simon Sommerville Laurie, *The Rise and Early Constitution of Universities, with a Survey of Medieval Education* (New York, 1903); Hastings Rashdall, *The Universities of Europe in the Middle Ages* (3 vols.; Oxford, 1895), especially Vol. I on Paris; Vol. II, Pt. I on other universities in France and in Germany; and Vol. II, Pt. II on English universities; and L. J. Paetow, *The Arts Course at Medieval Universities, with Special Reference to Grammar and Rhetoric* (Urbana, 1910). An example of Music's plight (in education) in medieval allegory is found in Henri d'Andeli's *La bataille des septs arts*, trans. L. J. Paetow, *The Battle of the Seven Arts* (Berkeley, 1914). The literary tradition of the musician, particularly the harper, as *vates* or clever maneuverer is long and complex: elements are discernible in such diverse sources as Orpheus legend, Bede's Caedmon, King Alfred's harper disguise, Geoffrey of Monmouth's *Historia Regum Britanniae*

his musical training and performance—so detailed and so unusual for Arthurian romance—constitute the large center of the hero's *enfance*. At the outer edges, virtually as prologue and epilogue, are the common romance narrative themes, the story of the hero's parents and the reunion and revelation of identity before the king. Gottfried's outstanding preoccupation with music and artistic perfection in his portrait of the young hero surely is not accidental.

The musical perfection Tristan displays in his youth, consisting of thoughtful criticism of his performance and grace of technique, is cultivated throughout the later life of Gottfried's hero. As in Thomas, music saves Tristan's life among the hostile Irish (7494 f.); music is his introduction to Isold and constitutes most of his instruction of the young princess (7696 f.); it rescues Isold from Gandin's ruse with the rote (13279 f.); it is part of his wooing of Isold of the White Hands (19200 f.). But, Gottfried goes beyond Thomas in his elaboration of detail; his emphases on emotional and intellectual effects of youthful training distinguish Gottfried's poem. In addition, music is twice Tristan's Galleotto.

Princess Isold is taught music and *moraliteit*[42] by Tantris until she masters "the pick of his attainments" (7966 f.), so that like her lover Tristan she finds solace, understanding, and mystical perfection in love through music. Troubled by "l'ameir" on board ship after their *Minnetrank*, Isold assuages her passionate discomfort by speaking to Tristan of his tutelage (11950-53); sorrowful because of Mark's suspicions, she distracts herself with the harp and lyre (14955-56). In the *Minnegrotte* she and Tristan fulfil their love in filling their equally tempered spirits with music (17204 f.). The second time Tristan loves an Isold he is drawn to her and she to him by music. He keeps company with Isold of the White Hands by singing, harping, and composing, partly for her diversion but mostly for his own comfort, while resolving his conflict between loyalties to two Isolds. For her Breton courtiers

---

(IX, 1). An interesting study of such figures in German texts is George W. Schoolfield, *The Figure of the Musician in German Literature* (Chapel Hill, 1956).

42. W. T. H. Jackson defines *moraliteit* as: "not 'morality' but the total 'mores' of a man, his character viewed as an abstraction. . . . It links the higher spirits and pleases both the human and the divine" (*op. cit.*, p. 370).

he composes "schanzûne, rundate und höveschiu liedellîn," always
with the same ambivalent refrain:

Îsôt ma drûe, Îsôt m'amie
en vûs ma mort, en vûs ma vie!
(19217-18)

That refrain langorously sung compels this young Isold of the
White Hands to love—"daz locte ir herze allez dar" (19415-16).

Evidence of the predominance of music throughout Gottfried's
poem is the number of types of music mentioned.[43] The specific
references to varieties of instruments include: the harp (*harphen*)
(3508, 3675, 8065, 13101 f.); lyre (*liren*) (3680, 8068); rote
(*rotten*) (3675, 13101 f.); sambuca (*sambiût*) (3680); symphonium
(*symphonien*) (3674); and viol (*videln*) (3674, 8062). Among the
examples of song are: folate (8078); "songs from Sans and St.
Denis" (*fremdiu notelîn von Sanze und San Denîse*)[44] (8063-66);
little courtly airs (*höveschiu liedelîn*) (19215); lais (*leich*) (8063);
pastourelle (*pasturêle*) (8076); refloit (2295, 8078); retrouange
(*rotruwange*) (8077); rondel (*rundate*) (8077, 19215); chanson
(*schanzûne*) (2292, 8078, 19214); and estampie (*stampenîe*) (2295,
8062).

But Tristan's musical training is not the only part of his
enfance with special significance for the rest of the poem. Several
other aspects of the *enfance* which bear examination are striking
in their novelty in an exposition of a hero's youth and in their
contribution to the special character of Gottfried's romance. The
pain of learning, the significance of restraint, the training in guile,
all are parts of the total effect of the hero's education. The role of
the tutor has some specific importance in Gottfried's work different
from the master's role in other Tristan versions. The concept

43. Descriptions of many of the instruments and song types cited may be
found in Bernhard Bergemann, *Das höfische Leben nach Gottfried von Strassburg* (Halle, 1876), chap. vi; Schultz, *op. cit.*, pp. 521 f.; F. Fétis, *Histoire
générale de la musique* (Paris, 1869-1876), V; J. Ruhlmann, *Die Geschichte
der Bogeninstrumente* (Braunschw., 1882); Gustave Reese, *Music in the
Middle Ages* (New York, 1940).

44. Professor Jackson convincingly associates these not with the saints but
with the places named after them: the schools which made St. Denis and the
ecclesiastical province of Sens famous music centers (*op. cit.*, p. 368 and p.
368, n. 14).

of preparation before action as well as the presence of humor and satire within the *enfance* are also novel features.

That learning is painful Gottfried makes plain by imagery and direct statement. Tristan, sent abroad to study, finds that at the very unfolding of his life, his best life is over (2075 f.); when just beginning to bloom with delight, the frost of care withers the blossoms of his joy (2072 f.). With Tristan's first true freedom his whole independence is cut short (2081-82). The antitheses in these lines, the paired antinomies of freedom and imprisonment, commencement and conclusion, delight and pain have their parallels in Gottfried's portrait of the pain of love. The pain of education during the *enfance* prefigures the later pain of love. The antithetical dualities of passionate devotion—first, to cultivating the senses in learning, and, then, to using them in love—punctuate the romance. From the oxymorons of the Prologue, through the joy and pain in the love of Riwalin and Blanscheflur (839 f.); their love and death in their conception of Tristan their son (1436); the success and misfortune (*leides unde linge*) paired in him (5074); Isold's recognition of her lover as death and life, joy and sorrow, and these same qualities joined in the *Minnetrank* (11710 f.); Tristan's realization that his life's death is his best life, Isold (18438-41), his life and death, his living death (18471-72); to the sweet and good pain of Tristan's love for Isold of the White Hands who, as his pleasure and disease, soothes yet hurts him (18991 f.): this unity of opposites in emotion is Gottfried's theme. The pain of education, like the tragic love, can be interpreted as an extension of the preoccupation of the *Minnesänger*, like many troubadours before them, with the antitheses of passion. The lyric poets' vocabulary of intellectualized love is pressed into the service of romance narrative; it serves strikingly well in Tristan's education.

Tristan's studied restraint and talent for invention also appear in the *enfance*. The discipline of education and the exercise of intellect limit the youth's uncensored expression. Gottfried repeatedly remarks upon young Tristan's thought before action and his weighing of possibilities before decision. Abandoned in Cornwall and forlorn, now fearful and full of tears, now in perfect control of his feelings, Tristan tells a carefully contrived lie to the pilgrims (2693 f.).

> Tristan der was vil wol bedâht
> und sinnesam von sînen tagen.
> (2690-91)

His speech and demeanor are under fine restraint (2737 f.). Shortly after, upon meeting King Mark's hunters, he slowly and subtly fabricates his story (3090-91);

> sîn rede diu enwas kinden
> nicht gelîch noch sus noch sô!
> (3092-93)

In much the same manner, his true feelings and true purposes are portrayed as under restraint during his arrivals in Ireland. Bearing the stench and pain of his poisoned wound, Tristan contrives to harp and sing beyond his strength and beyond his artist's heart for his music in order to win favor (7670-76). When sent by Mark to woo Isold he analyzes his danger and bluntly remarks:

> den muoz ich liegen disen tac
> swaz ich in geliegen mac!
> (8709-10)

Tristan's lies, ruses, and disguises are present in all versions of his legend. The hero disguised is a recurring motif of popular tradition,[45] but what Gottfried makes distinctive is Tristan's thought behind each decision for disguise and his delight in the cleverness of deception. This is evident in the poet's frequent attribution to Tristan of a "need for a good story" and in Gottfried's own comments upon his hero's talent for invention.

Tristan's ability gets him out of trouble but also gets him into it. Those who admire him consider his talent ingenuity, those who hate him (such as King Mark's envious barons) consider it sorcery. ("Er waere ein zouberaere" [8335]; "ez waere ûz zouber geschehen" [8340]; "der parâtiere, wie kan er/gesehendiu ougen blenden" [8350-51]; "durch dise rîche linge/zouberlîcher dinge"

45. See Gertrude Schoepperle, *op. cit.*, "Tristan's Disguises," I, 239 f.

[10799-800].) It is interesting that the single subject for Tristan's disguises—in the *enfance* and beyond it—to which he returns, which he artfully varies, and which is uniformly successful, is the merchant. For Tristan, the role of merchant or merchant's son is both the disguise of anonymity and the guise of respectability. The hero is made to use this at three critical moments in the romance: first, within the *enfance*, in his meeting with Mark's huntsmen (3095 f.) and during the subsequent explanation of his plight to the King and courtiers (3597 f.); later, in his role of Tantris (7564 f.) in which, having previously been a minstrel, he becomes a merchant when gain goes to his head! (7573-76); and finally, in his justification to Isold for having killed the dragon which ravaged Ireland (9521 f.). "Künde in fremeden landen/diu rîchet den koufman" (9540-41). In no other version is Tristan disguised as a merchant at all these junctures. In Thomas, Tristan appears as a Flemish merchant in the dragon episode, but not at King Mark's nor in Ireland as Tantris.[46] The likely explanation for Gottfried's repetition of this single topic for his hero's inventive talent, in this romance dedicated to "edelez herzen," is his admiration of Strassburgian culture.[47] "Koufman" and "edelez herzen" are united in Gottfried's epithets for the men of trade and in statements by his characters; for example, King Mark's admiring courtiers say of young Tristan:

> wie kunde ein werbender man
> sîn kint sô schône erzogen hân
> ez enmüese ûz edelem herzen gân?
> (4090-92)

Gottfried's emphasis in the education of his hero upon the pain of learning, upon the restraint in action enforced by learning, and

46. Near the conclusion of Thomas' poem, Caerdin, disguised as a merchant, comes to Isolt to beg her help for Tristan, who is dying in Brittany; but Gottfried's incomplete poem breaks off before that point.

47. As A. T. Hatto states it, Gottfried was probably a "member of the urban patriciate, a class of men who, by the beginning of the thirteenth century, were growing in wealth and self-assurance and were soon to play a part in literature" (*op. cit.*, p. 10). On the merchant's position in medieval London's cultural life, a fascinating study is Sylvia Thrupp's *The Merchant Class of Medieval London* (Ann Arbor, 1962).

upon the uses of guile create a *puer senex*[48] and contribute to the unusual nature of Tristan as youth and as learned knight.

The role of the tutor in Gottfried's poem is also of considerable interest for the *enfance* and for its relationship to the rest of the poem. Kurneval, "einem wîsen man" (2059), with whom young Tristan goes abroad to study, is described this way:

> daz knappe nie von hövescheit
> und von edeles herzen art
> baz noch schôner geedelt wart;
> und was der Kurvenal genant.
> er hete manege tugende erkant,
> als er dem wol ze lêre zam,
> der ouch von siner lêre nam
> vil manegiu tugentlîchiu dinc.
> (2260-67)

This cultured squire is Tristan's faithful companion in happiness and in adversity, accompanying him from accomplishment to adventure and from land to land. In the *enfance* he is abducted with Tristan (2254 f.), set adrift (2338 f.), and he arrives home with dire tidings to Rual (2371 f.). In this abduction scene Gottfried shifts his focus away from the well-bred youth, who is the object of the treachery, to the tutor kidnapped along with him. Not merely the merchant's perfidy but Kurneval's own noisy misery causes him to be put to sea alone. Stimulated by Tristan's lament at their plight, Kurneval weeps with him from the very depths of his heart (2333); such is his lamentation that the merchant crew grows sullen and angry because of him (2337). Therefore, given an oar, a bread-loaf, and a skiff, he is left to drift—and to pray:

> Ouwê got wie gewirbe ich?
> i'ne wart alsus besorget nie.
> nu bin ich âne liute hie
> und kan ouch selbe niht gevarn.
> got hêrre, dû solt mich bewarn

48. This panegyrical *topos* for the ideal noble life, which strikes the balance between the opposites of youth and age, is discussed in Curtius' *European Literature*, pp. 98-101.

> und mîn geverte hinnen sîn!
> ich wil ûf die genâde dîn
> des ich nie began, beginnen:
> wis mîn geleite hinnen!
>
> (2358-66)

Later in the poem, after Tristan returns to his fatherland and avenges himself upon Morgan, he makes courtly Kurneval his knight (5745) who then accompanies him back again to Cornwall (5855). Still later, Kurneval goes with "Tantris" on the first Irish voyage (7337) and returns there with Tristan on the second (8757)—where he examines the burnt remains of Tristan's horse and the dragon and so believes his student and master dead (9640). Finally, Kurneval carries Tristan's harp into banishment (16658). While maintaining residence at court (16777), Kurneval returns to the *Minnegrotte* once every twenty days (16805) and ultimately acts as King Mark's ambassador to Tristan and Isold to announce the king's desire for their return (17686).

In no other Tristan text is Kurneval so ubiquitous or so fully portrayed. In Eilhart he is "eine knapin der hiz Kurvenal" (129) who teaches Tristrant his broad curriculum of *hovelichen dingen* and suggests the uses of travel abroad (185). In Thomas, Gorneval does not appear until Tristan's abduction (xviii). *Sir Tristrem* presents no tutor but the knight's foster father "Rohand þe trewe" (xxvii). The French *Prose Tristan* portrays Curneval, despite his checkered past, as Merlin's choice of tutor to the motherless babe;[49] and Malory sends Tristan with Gouvernail to France to learn languages, "nurture," and deeds of arms,[50] after which point the teacher is referred to merely as Tristan's "man."

Gottfried, on the other hand, distinctly emphasizes the character of his hero's tutor and again and again refers favorably to the teaching profession.[51] King Mark allots the fullness of praise for

49. E. Löseth (ed.), *Le roman en prose de Tristan, le roman de Palamède, et la compilation de Rusticien de Pise. Analyse critique d'après les manuscrits de Paris* (Paris, 1891), p. 16, sec. 20.

50. Eugène Vinaver (ed.), *The Works of Sir Thomas Malory* (3 vols.; Oxford, 1947), I, 375.

51. Possible influence upon the romancers' interest in the role of the tutor and in methods of teaching, coming from sources classical (including Plato

Tristan's musical accomplishments to the tutor's honor: "der dich
dâ hât gelêret/der sî vor gote geêret" (3647-48)! Just as he does
for Kurneval, Gottfried describes the talents and culture of another
tutor, the priest who instructs both Queen and Princess Isold.

> wan er ouch selbe kunde
> list' unde kunst genuoge,
> mit handen manege fuoge
> an iegelîchem seitespil
> und kunde ouch fremeder sprâche vil.
> an fuoge unde an hövescheit
> het er gewendet unde geleit
> sîne tage und sîne sinne.
>
> (7704-11)

Gottfried intimates, for both instructors, that the more learned the
tutor, the more learned the student can be "in turn" (2266). This
is virtually a *translatio studii.* Learning passes from Kurneval to
Tristan, and later, from Tristan to Isold.

Tristan himself is a superb tutor. Gottfried tells more of
Tristan's pedagogic method than his mere assiduity—as it appears
in Thomas. Tristan's approach to his tutor's task partakes of the
Abbeye de Thélème's philosophy: *Fais ce que voudras.* The student may choose the best the master knows, and, in voluntary
learning, achieve mastery.

> Sît gie diu junge künigin
> alle zît ze sîner lêre:
> an die sô leite er sêre
> sînen flîz und sîne stunde;
> daz beste daz er kunde
> sô schuollist, sô hantspil,
> daz ich niht sunder zalen wil:
> daz leite er ir besunder vür
> daz si nâch ir selber kür
> ze lêre dar ûz naeme,
> swes sô si gezaeme.
>
> (7966-76)

---

and Seneca) and medieval (including *miroirs de princes*) will be considered
in chap. iv.

Slowly, during the course of six months (8034), Tristan introduces subjects which Isold studies to perfect.[52] Tristan's tuition of *moraliteit*[53] polishes her manners and her mind; this study, not bound by lines of subject, pervades all aspects of behavior before God and the world (8015). Tristan's instruction in this causes her to achieve serenity as well as charm:

> hie von sô wart si wol gesite
> schôn' unde reine gemuot
> ir gebaerde süeze unde guot
> (8028-30)

It would seem that the achievement of *moraliteit* is *consonantia* of the intellect.

The learned hero makes of Isold the learned heroine.[54] He does not need to teach her the rudiments of her studies (as Tristan in Thomas teaches Isolt "from scratch," "þviat hun vill furst nema"

52. Isold's curriculum is noticed briefly in H. Jacobius' "Die Erziehung des Edelfräuleins in alten Frankreich nach Dichtungen des XII, XIII, und XIV Jahrhunderts," in *ZRPh*, XVI (Halle, 1908). An interesting comparison to Isold's student life is Vincent of Beauvais' *De Eruditione Filiorum Nobilium*, ed. Arpad Steiner (Cambridge, Mass., 1938). Young analyzes the education of Virginia in Chaucer's "Physician's Tale" in *Speculum*, XVI, 340. Of interest is A. A. Hentsch's *De la littérature didactique du moyen-âge s'adressant spécialement aux femmes* (Paris, 1903).

53. The correspondence between *moraliteit* in Gottfried and *moralitas* in Boethius' *De Musica* has been demonstrated by Professor Jackson, *op. cit.*, p. 370.

54. There are few other learned heroines in medieval literature. We know little about Guinevere's education and literary tastes and even less about Perceval's ladies'. Several learned women appear in Geoffrey of Monmouth's *Historia Regum Britanniae*, such as Hélène, mother of Constantine, learned in all arts, especially music. Two romance ladies of high cultivation are associated with the Prince of Tyre: Apollonius' learned princess wife, and their daughter Thaïs, whose learning is so great she overcomes—by wisdom— those who would sell her into prostitution and instead becomes a tutor of music and science to young ladies of station (*Historia Apolonii regis Tyri*). The literary history of Isold leads one to postulate that, in the romances of the twelfth century, her heritage of magic and the arts of healing is replaced by more mundane, though still in their way extraordinary, pursuits of learning. Miss Schoepperle discusses Isolt as healer, *op. cit.*, I, 194-203, and II, 375-90, as does Muriel Hughes in *Women Healers in Medieval Life and Literature* (New York, 1943). The Celtic background of this tradition is discussed in James Carney's *Studies in Irish Literature and History* (Dublin, 1955), pp. 189-242, while the "healer" as a "type" is the concern of Oscar Kühn in "Medizinisches aus der altfranzösischen Dichtung," in *Abhandlungen zur Geschichte der Medizin* (Breslau, 1904).

[xxx]), but rather he imparts the methods and flourishes of refinement. Just as Tristan was, during his education in the *enfance*,
Isold is taught to perform with thought and grace (8041-8135).
Again like her master, her accomplishments, artfully displayed,
beget envy and desire (8089 f.). Gottfried's specific portrayal of
Isold as student has significance for his portrait of her as queen.
She has learned the uses of beauty, and she is not guileless. Most
importantly, the tutor and the tutored, the lover and beloved, are
made equal in appreciation of artistic endeavor and demand
artistic perfection of others as well as of themselves. They are
prepared for an emotional experience to be an aesthetic one. For
Tristan and Isold, learning and love involve a *translatio*; symbolically and literally this *translatio* is a passing of the harp.

For Gottfried, the prerequisite to perfect love is preparation.
Professor Jackson says, ''Both Tristan and Isold required to be
trained before they were capable of the highest form of love.
Tristan was trained in books and music until he was intellectually
and spiritually capable. This training he subsequently imparted
to Isold.''[55] Gottfried makes specific his proposition that preparation is needed for worthy love. Reiterating the Biblical image of
reaping the fruit sown, Gottfried exhorts:

> tuo uns daz leit iht sêre wê,
> sô bedenken ez ê,
> saejen bezzer unde baz
> unde snîden ouch daz.
> wir, die zer werlde haben muot,
> swie sô er si boes' oder guot,
> wie tuon wir unseren tagen
> die wir vertrîben unde verjagen
> in dem namen dar minne
> und vinden niht der inne
> niwan die selben arebeit
> die wir haben an si geleit
> misselinge und ungeschiht!
>
> (12257-69)

55. *Op. cit.*, p. 372.

den vindet man ie lützel nuo:
als vorwerke wir dar zuo.
(12281-82)

Preparation for love, preparation before all action is one of Gottfried's constant themes. This motif first appears in the *enfance*
and is later varied. Gottfried makes many references in the *enfance*
to the uses of education, stesses studied invention as the component
of Tristan's ability which leads to success, and makes gnomic statements upon foresight and preparation (7909-14). The need for education before creative action may be the significance of the unusual
statement in the *Einleitung*: To the world of those able to endure
sorrow as well as bliss, let my life be given, says Gottfried, to be
damned or saved with it:

ich bin mit ir biz her beliben
und hân mit ir die tage vertriben,
die mir ûf nâhe gêndem leben
lêr' unde geleite solten geben.
(67-70)

If the education of the hero and the exploits of his youth may
be viewed as preparation—with recognition of Gottfried's purposeful design of a knight of learning—what then is the nature of the
life Tristan is prepared for? Is the Tristan of this consummate
courtly romance a romance knight? Is his sedulous preparation
necessary or proper for an Arthurian hero? These questions raise
the issue of the poet's creative intention. Wolfgang Mohr's pro-
vocative study suggests that Tristan is a *spielmann*.[56] This concept,
with the relegation of the hero to a social position as court entertainer, seems less than completely credible. Although Gottfried
himself calls Tristan *niuwe spielmann* in the arrival scene at
Tintagel, the poet uses that epithet as a temporary description of
young Tristan *as he plays*, not of his true position at court. Tristan
can act the *spielmann*, but he is of a nature far greater. Professor
Jackson has demonstrated that the preparation of the hero as

56. "*Tristan und Isold* as Künstlerroman," *Euphorion*, LIII (1959), 153-
74. Mohr also finds other talents of an entertainer in Tristan: "wir sehen da
für einen Moment der Künstler als Mimus—und zwar hinter den kulissen," (p.
159) as well as the roles of Prometheus, Loki, and Pygmalion! (p. 161).

artist serves his role as lover.[57] The combination of the interpretations of Tristan as *spielmann* and Tristan as artist reveals a third possibility. The life Tristan is prepared for may be that of a minnesinger.

Not much is known of the lives of the minnesingers[58] save that until Walther von der Vogelweide they were not professional poets but were usually educated, cultured gentlemen practicing the art when leisure and inspiration permitted. They were, in effect, learned knights. The characteristics of their songs can all be found in Gottfried's poem.[59] In vocabulary, poetic structure of lines, imagery (such as the free falcon, the limed bird analogies), allegorization (such as the personification of Love, the Dawn, the Moon), allegorical *topoi* (such as the *paysage idéal*), statements of psychological introspection, interest in the antitheses of love, and preoccupation with the *spannung* of desirability and accessibility—for all of these, Gottfried's *Tristan* offers multiple examples. In addition to the stylistic devices of *Minnesang* which characterize *Tristan*, much of the action and two of the main scenes of the poem may owe their inspiration to lyric love poetry: the *Minnegrotte* scene and the literary *excursus*.

In the romantic exploits of Tristan, Gottfried makes dramatic the narrative *topoi* of *Minnesang*. Introspection, for example, is not merely stated but dramatically portrayed. *Spannung* is not only described but endured. However, the man who is singer and poet does not suffer alone, as so often in *Minnelieder*, but has as his beloved one trained to worthiness of his mannered praise. Yet, Gottfried intimates that even equal capacities for the sacredness of

57. *Op. cit.*, pp. 368 f., 370.
58. Most studies of the minnesingers are concerned with the poems produced, not with the composers themselves. But reviews of the ''evidence'' and speculation about their lives can be found in Brinkmann, *op. cit.*; J. Schwietering's *Die deutsche Dichtung des Mittelalters* (Potsdam, 1941); and in Lachmann's introduction to his *Des Minnesangs Frühling* (new ed.; Stuttgart, 1959). More references are listed in note 61.
59. With varying degrees of inclusiveness, scholars have recognized stylistic similarities between *Minnesang* and Gottfried's poem; Bechstein in the commentary to his now outdated edition of *Tristan,* originally published, 1889, and in a 5th edition (Leipzig, 1930), was one of the first to do so; A. T. Hatto in the Introduction to his *Tristan* translation, (Baltimore, 1960), is one of the most recent.

Minne are insufficient. Even in the *Minnegrotte*, where the influence of *Minne* of the court,[60] handmaid to the ideal *Minne*, is obviated, the unity of bodies and spirits which is the true Ideal[61] is achieved but cannot be perpetuated. The *Minnegrotte*, then, may be interpreted as an embodiment of the *spannung* of *Minnesang*.[62] The recognition of the futility of *Minne* is tripartite (virtually representing the tripartite construction of classic *Minnelieder*): the approach to *Minne*, then its limited power to endure (the two *Stollen* of the *Aufgesang*), followed by the ultimate rejection of it and return to the world (the *Abgesang*).

Gottfried's literary *excursus*, in particular praise of lyric poetry and its practitioners, is the other section of the poem testifying to his special interest in that art. The *excursus* is remarkable as much for its position in the romance as for its content. The

60. In "The Role of Brangaene in Gottfried's *Tristan*," *GR*, XXVIII (1953), 290-96, W. T. H. Jackson maintains that Brangaene symbolically represents the spirit of Minne, Frau Minne. "As long as the lovers remain under her influence and act according to her advice their love remains a furtive affair . . ." (p. 292). A comparison is J. Schwietering's "Isolde ist insigel der minne" (*Die deutsche Dichtung des Mittelalters*, p. 190). Another possible interpretation of Brangaene and the type of love she represents is: *Minne*-as-practiced-at-Court, but not the celebrated ideal.

61. The critical studies defining *Minne* are nearly as numerous and controversial as are the medieval works in which that word appears. It is clear that *Minne* is more than and other than Heinrich von Morungen's "Minne, diu der werlde ir froide meret" (*Mirst geschen als einem kindeline*). One of the most recent and comprehensive studies of *Minne* as word and ideal (as well as its distinction from *Liebe*) is H. Kolb's *Der Begriff der Minne und das Entstehen der höfische Lyrik* (Tübingen, 1958). Earlier works, though also concerned primarily with lyric poetry, are: P. Schmid, "Die Entwicklung der Begriff 'Minne' und 'Liebe' im deutschen Minnesang bis Walther," *ZDP*, LXVI (1941); A Moret, "Qu'est-ce que la Minne? Contribution à l'étude de la terminologie et de la moralité courtoise," *Études Germaniques*, IV (1949), and sections of Margaret Richey's *Essays on the Medieval German Love Lyric* (Oxford, 1943). Consideration of convention and psychology in Gottfried's representation of *Minne* is found in E. Nickel's monograph, *Studien zum Liebesproblem bei Gottfried von Strassburg* in *Königsberger deutsche Forschungen*, I (Gräfe, 1927).

62. Other interpretations may be found in J. Schwietering, *Die Tristan Gottfrieds von Strassburg und die Bernhardische Mystik* (Berlin, 1943); R. Ranke, *Die Allegorie der Minnegrotte in Gottfrieds Tristan* ("Schriften der Königsberger Gelehrten Gesellschaft, geisteswissenschaftliche klasse," Vol. I, No. 2 [Königsberg, 1925]); and G. Weber, "Liebesideologie und Weltbildhaltung der Tristandichtung im Rahmen der Hochmittelalterlichen Geistesgeschichte" in his *Gottfrieds von Strassburg Tristan und die Krise des Hochmittelalterlichen Weltbildes um 1200* (Stuttgart, 1953), Vol. I.

culmination of Tristan's preparation and practice for knighthood is not the anticipated *swertleite*, with its emphasis upon physical and chivalric attributes, but rather is this initiation into the world of (*Hohenstaufen*) artistry and this introduction to the great composers in the double art of poetry and music.

Whether educated to be a minnesinger or not, Gottfried's Tristan is singular among medieval knights. Many of his actions and statements in the *enfance* and later violate the basic components of courtly romance. Indeed, some of the knight's adventures are inversions of chivalric conduct, which hardly can be fortuitous. Examples of these inversions with their humor and irony represent a last aspect in which material in the *enfance* helps illuminate the poet's intent.[63]

Kurneval's weeping misery aboard the abduction ship, followed by his fears, when set adrift, because of his untried seamanship—"nu bin ich âne liute hie/und kan ouch selbe niht gevarn" (2360-61)—is one example of Gottfried's interjection of an unexpected light flourish in a scene of serious import. When Tristan is ultimately abandoned in Cornwall, the homeless boy can do nothing but cry—this, the usual response of children when crossed!

> Nu wie gewarp dô Tristan?
> Tristan der ellende? jâ
> dâ saz er unde weinde aldâ;
> wan kint enkunnen anders niht
> wan weinen, alse in iht geschiht.
> (2480-84)

The young hero's dread of wild animals, his damning of the sparrowhawks, falcons, merlins—"*die* hânt mich mînen vater benomen" (2595)—make this unbelievably learned and restrained *puer senex* momentarily a boy.[64] This scene, coming after the assiduous edu-

---

63. The few studies on medieval irony and its techniques take no notice of humor or irony in Gottfried. A. Hübner, for example, *Die Mittelhochdeutsche Ironie* (Leipzig, 1930) devotes his emphasis to litotes in lyric poetry, and P. Lehmann's subject is particularly medieval Latin lyric poetry, *Die Parodie im Mittelalter* (Leipzig, 1922). A doctoral dissertation on medieval irony, especially in Chrétien de Troyes, is being written at Columbia University by Mr. Peter Haidu.

64. In addition to the *puer senex*, another panegyrical *topos* from late

cation and before the display of valor in learning, is the first in
which the poet portrays his serious young hero humorously.

Aspects of the *enfance* hunt scene are also characterized by
humor. With King Mark's huntsmen gathered round expectantly,
the well-nurtured youth rolls his cloak, smoothes his hair, pats
down his sleeves, tucks up his robe, goes up to the hart to teach
proper excoriation, takes hold of it, tries to lay it on its back, and
then fails to budge it because of its too great weight for his youthful figure. And he must call for help (2841 f.)! Then, the courtiers three times repeat the exotic hunting term ''enbesten'' (2813,
2818, 2820) and jump upon his statement of ''furkîe'' (2925), and
after this, ''curîe'' (2959) :

> ''curîe? dê benîe!''
> sprâchen s' alle, ''waz ist daz?
> wir vernaemen sarrazênesch baz.
> was ist curîe, lieber man?
> swîc unde sage uns niht hie van.''
>   (2960-64)

This, after Tristan has carefully given grammatical roots and
derivations for each term which he presents with such calculation!
The very contrast between the lively excitement of the elder
courtiers and the calm control of the boy is doubtlessly intentional
and humorous in effect.

Much in the way that the courtiers repeat the foreign terms of
venery, Rual, joyous at the news his search for Tristan is near an
end, entreats the pilgrims to repeat the name of the place where last
they saw him, ''Tintagel,'' over and over and over (3829). And
when Rual, Tristan, and Mark are finally reunited and Tristan's
readiness for the knight's accolade discussed, the impetus for
knighthood young Tristan feels is not ordinary. It is based on his
reading (4415-37)!

---

antiquity may be appropriate to the youthful Tristan; *ludicra-seria* in
description of the hero, which is so frequent in eulogy of rulers and in hagio-
grapha, may here have its place in romance. The tradition is considered in
''Jest and Ernest in Medieval Literature,'' Excursus IV of Curtius' *European
Literature*, pp. 417 f.

> wan ritterschaft, alsô man seit,
> die muoz ie von der kintheit
> nemen ir anegenge
> oder sî wirt selten strenge.
> daz ich mîn unversuochte jugent
> ûf werdekeit unde ûf tugent
> sô rehte selten geüebet hân
> daz ist vil sêre missetân
> und hân es an mich selben haz.
> (4415-23)

These *enfance* examples set the tone of the poem. They are grace notes and cadenzas, sounded in complimentary major modes, interspersed within the stately minor modes of the whole. Much of this mockery may be interpreted as deliberate parody.[65] Indeed, it appears that much of the poem which is not concerned with the exposition of Tristan and Isold's sacred love and the preparation for it is characterized by humorous incident. Illustrations of this are numerous. To consider some of these briefly, there is the sophistry of Tristan's sharing himself equally, as if cut in two—his wealth to one father, Rual; his person to another father, Mark—just as neatly as one divides an egg (5685 f.). Then, the fight against Morold in which the poet asks, when the hero's strength fails: "Got unde reht, wâ sint si nuo?" (6984); and when Tristan is triumphant, there is the mock-heroic concern that all three pieces of the hacked-apart knight be laid together so that none gets lost on the way home to Ireland (7147 f.). These ironic comments upon Tristan's battle with Morold, his first enemy, are paralleled by Gottfried's comedy in the battle with the Beast of Anferginan, Tristan's first dragon. Spear resolutely lowered, Tristan meets the fiery serpent head-on with such shock his horse dies under him (8985 f.); but the dragon carefully attacks the dead horse, consuming it as far as the saddle. An army by itself, that beast takes

65. Petrus W. Tax in *Wort, Sinnbild, Zahl in Tristanroman* (Berlin, 1961), and W. T. H. Jackson, in "Tristan the Artist," have suggested the satiric intent of several scenes. Cf. Jkvr. M. J. Härtsen's *Der Zweispalt in Gottfrieds "Tristan" und die Einheit der Ritterlich-Höfischen Kultur* (Amsterdam, 1938).

smoke and steam to battle along with its other equipment of fire
and teeth. The knight must therefore take cover.

> dâ mite treip er in umbe
> manege ängeslîche krumbe
> von boumen ze buschen:
> dâ muose er sich vertuschen
> und fristen, swie er mohte,
> wan ime der kampf niht tohte.
>   (9029-34)

That dragon's grisly death cry greatly *startles* Tristan—"Tristan
harte sêre erschrac" (9059). And when the cowardly seneschal
arrives to claim the prey and the princess, Gottfried's hyperbole
reaches hilarity (9077-9267).

Other examples of humor are the delightfully disparaging
descriptions of the barons who accompany Tristan to Ireland.
They, among all the mercenaries, are the only ones who come
grudgingly, "âne golt" (8594); while proclaiming their bravery,
they entreat a speedy retreat to the luxuries of home (8633-62);
they quibble noisily and pettily among themselves (9680-82).
Particularly in the scenes most basic to the Tristan story, there are
humorous touches: the Bath, the Ordeal, the Tryst beneath the
Tree, the Trap within the Garden. Helping Tristan bathe, Isold
scans him up and down studying his arms and most particularly
his legs, which so openly told what he had tried so hard to keep
secret (10001-7)! At the time of ordeal, not pity nor sense of injustice but rather Isold's figure and flimsy garment attract comment (15655-71). (To this may be compared Gottfried's initial
description of the queen's French clothes in which her girdle hangs
"dâ der borte ligen sol" [10912], her mantle clings between her
knees "als iuwer iegelîcher wil" [10920], and is so tight that "dâ
man diz unde daz dâ sach—ich meine vederen unde tach" [10951-
52].) For Melot and Mark, the attempt to spy on the expected
tryst is fraught with exertion; they can climb the tree only with
much effort (14614); and when Mark gains the proof of infidelity,
his evidence is Tristan and Isold peacefully locked in embrace
"after some exertion or another"—"ine weiz, nâch waz unmuoze"
(18218).

These examples of humor, irony, and parody in the *enfance* and later in the poem are surely intentional. There are many more. Interestingly enough, in number and quality they have not been recognized before. They lend credence to calls for reinterpreting Gottfried's poem—poetry with which noble hearts can laugh.

What does Gottfried mock and how does he do it? As these are exemplified in the romance literature of his day, Gottfried laughs at traditional chivalry and traditional *Minne*. His parody consists in isolating one action or part of an action, together with its expected decorations, from its traditional Arthurian milieu and inserting into it a character or action from another. By deliberate inversion, or inflation, or introduction of realistic detail into a stock romance context, Gottfried achieves his parodistic smile. His is a playful blasphemy against serious romance canons and a usage of its patterns for purposes other than those for which they were developed. In mockery, as in his elaboration of the concept of the learned knight, Gottfried denies the very characteristics of the genre and achieves greatness in that denial. For the serious poet seeking beyond what Hugo Kuhn calls ''unterhaltungsliteratur,''[66] courtly romance may be the vehicle but not the consummate expression of an exposition of mystical love. Gottfried's deviations from the characteristic romance patterns signal the excellence of his achievement.

After Gottfried's *Tristan*, all treatments of the tale seem anticlimactic. The later *Sir Tristrem*, the *Prose Tristan*, and Malory's ''Book of Sir Tristram of Lyones,'' the other three texts in which there is an *enfance* of the hero, were not in any way influenced by the German poem. These *enfances*, while adding little to the understanding of the works in which they appear and nothing to the concept of Tristan as learned knight and lover, yet indicate some of the changes in courtly romance when written some time after its moments of excellence.

In the early fourteenth-century English *Sir Tristrem*,[67] a tradition other than Gottfried's is reflected in the intentions and ideals

66. *Dichtung und Welt im Mittelalter* (Stuttgart, 1959).

67. Eugene Kölbing (ed.), *Sir Tristrem*, Vol. II of *Die nordische und die englische version der Tristan-sage* (Heilbronn, 1882). Another edition is G. P. McNeill's, for the Scottish Text Society, Vol. VIII (1885-1886).

of a rhymer-redactor who quotes one "Tomas" as his source.[68]
Only two out of the 304 staccatto, compressed, ingenuously vigorous
rhymed stanzas are devoted to the education of Tristrem by Rohand
"trewe so stan." The youth has no tutor but this, his foster father.
During the educational course of fifteen years, Tristrem studies
books, instrumental and vocal music, contemporary and old law,
and, particularly, hunting[69]—but, as in Thomas of Britain, no
physical or chivalric pursuits. He is unsurpassed in all "craftes"[70]
studied. Although Rohand is Tristrem's tutor, Kurneval is not
absent from the story. After the wound Mohand inflicts on
Tristrem begins to fester, so that "No man no miȝt for stink/Come
þer Tristrem ware," only Gouernayl, called Tristrem's "man,"
remains with him and then accompanies him to Ireland. Later in
the rhyme, Gouernayl joins and then flees from the fight with Sir
Canados (cclxxxvi).

The only significance of the education in this text is its presence.
The author, who omitted so much incident and characterization
usual to the Tristan story, yet included the educational curriculum
which most other versions possess. In this humorous tale, in which
morality and devotion are direct functions of money,[71] and in

68. The "Tomas" five times referred to in this poem has not been definitely
identified, though as a whole, the influence of Thomas of Britain's version
seems to be reflected. The rhymer's source is thought to be either Thomas of
Erceldoun (according to two editors of the work, Sir Walter Scott and G. P.
McNeill) or Thomas of Kendale (according to Kölbing).

69. Tristan's expertise in hunting and his epithet as "founder" of the
art are discussed by Remigereau, *op. cit.* That ascription appears in Malory
(Vinaver, *op. cit.*, 682.26-683.4) and, earlier, in medieval hunting treatises.
Vinaver cites the *Book of St. Albans* and *The Noble Art of Venerie or Hunting*
as examples of this "notion peculiar to the English versions of the Tristan
romance" (*op. cit.*, III, 1497). Cf. Chrétien's *Cligès* in which the hero is
described as surpassing the epitome of the hunter in his own art: Cligès knows
more about the bow, about birds and hounds than does King Mark's nephew
(v. 2761-92).

70. The word "craftes" appears similarly in the education text in Eilhart
("daz er zu den creftin tochte," v. 187) and in Gottfried ("daz tete er
wol nach siner kraft," v. 2114). Is this coincidence? The medieval German
and English usages of the word were similar and this is an entirely predictable
context for it. Or is there some possible connection among the three versions
at this point?

71. Seven times money is specified in the poem: (1) in a game of checkers
with the merchant-mariners who later abduct him, Tristrem gambles and wins
100 pounds; (2) he offers 10 shillings and *pens* to the Pilgrims to bring him
to court; (3) Rohand meets them later and gives them 10 shillings "and

which animals partake of the fated passion,[72] there is no artistic relationship between the *enfance* of the hero and his later adventures.

The French *Prose* version[73] of Tristan's *enfance* presents an interesting problem. There is neither specific nor general description of Tristan's education, yet this French text is accepted as the source for Malory's story of Tristan's youth.

The French *Prose enfance* of Tristan begins in a forest where Merlin discovers Helyabel, wife of King Meliadus, near death in childbirth. We know only that Gurvenal is chosen as Tristan's tutor by the enchanter Merlin; that Gurvenal has a past history of fratricide but is yet fit to educate the newborn prince; that King Meliadus accepts his son's tutor; and that Gurvenal shows lifelong faith to his charge. The tutor's function consists not in instructing nor advising but in recognizing Tristan's destiny—revealed in letters engraved on a marble block beside the ''Fontaine brahaigne ainsi nommée parce que l'eau en rendait les femmes steriles!''[74]

Malory's treatment of the hero's *enfance*,[75] both in narrative details and in philosophy of exposition, makes it most unlikely that the French *Prose Tristan* was the source for the *enfance*, even

more''; (4) back home to slay Morgan, Tristan gives Rohand payment; (5) Tantris gets gold and silver for teaching Ysonde; (6) Ysonde bribes the churls with gifts to bring Brengwain back; (7) the ''gleeman'' (Gandin) gives Tristan 100 pounds and *pens* for playing the harp.

72. After Brengwain gives the love philter to Tristrem and Ysonde, Hodain the dog licks the cup—therefore ''Þai loved wiþ al her miȝt/And Hodain dede also.'' Hodain and Peticriu accompany the lovers to their home in the forest. And when Ganhardin goes to Cornwall to see how beautiful Ysonde is, he greets her and Brengwain and ''stroked þe hounde Peticriu.'' (This stroking of the dog, which appears but humorous detail here, has specific justification in Thomas of Britain. There it is to reveal Tristan's ring [Isolt's pledge of faith, and their recognition token], worn by Kaherdin, to Isolt).

73. E. Löseth, *op. cit.* Commentary on sources and style is found on p. xvi f. Cf. H. Oscar Sommer's analyses in his edition of *Le Morte Darthur: The Original Edition of William Caxton* . . . (3 vols.; London, 1889-1891), pp. 279-90.

74. One manuscript, the M.S.B.N. fr. 103, has somewhat more detail than the others: Tristan knew ''tant des eschez et des tables que nul ni l'en peust mater, et de l'escremie plus que nul. Et chevauchoit si bien que nul plus'' (f. 30ᵛ, col. 2). Vinaver, *op. cit.*, III, 1445.

75. Eugène Vinaver's edition of the Winchester MS, ''The Book of Sir Tristram de Lyones'' is in Vol. I of *The Works of Sir Thomas Malory*, pp. 375 f. For the education of the hero the differences between the Winchester and Caxton versions are minimal; Sir Thomas Malory, *Le Morte d'Arthur*, ed. William Caxton (2 vols.; London, New York, 1956), I, 241.

though every other part of Tristan's biography in Malory is thought to be derived from the *Prose*.[76] Malory's Tristram is sent to France by his father, King Meliodas, with Gouvernail (a "gentleman well learned and taught") "to learn the language, and nurture, and deeds of arms." Tristram returns home after more than seven years to study harping and musical instruments— "and so learned to be a harper passing all other." Hunting and hawking are his next pursuits in which he not only excels but creates ceremonies and the very vocabulary for them.

He began good measures of blowyng of beasts of venery, and beasts of chase, and all manner of vermin, and all these terms we have yet of hawking and hunting. And therefore the book of venery, of hawking and hunting, is called the book of Sir Tristram, wherefore, as meseemeth, all gentleman that bear old arms ought of right to honour Sir Tristram for the goodly terms that gentlemen have and use, and shall to the day of doom. . . .[77]

Elements familiar to Tristan's *enfance* in the medieval poems are present in Malory's text: the presence of the named tutor who is instructor as well as companion, the travel abroad, and the studies of language, deeds of arms, music, and hunting. Similar also are the seven-year periods of instruction, described by Gottfried and intimated by Eilhart. In Malory one difference in the curriculum is that hunting replaces music as the hero's special

76. Vinaver, *op. cit.*, III, 1437-38. "'The content of Malory's immediate source is found in four MSS of the Prose Romance. . . . His immediate source was probably a single work which followed alternately each of the three versions." (M.S.B.N. fr. 334; M.S.B.N. fr. 103; M.S.B.N. fr. 99 [with which MS Chantilly 316 is almost identical]). Vinaver takes note of the disparity between the *enfances* in the *Prose* and in Malory but considers the education text the invention of Malory (*op. cit.*, III, 1445, n. 375.12-29). He has discussed the over-all relationship between the *Prose* and Malory in two studies: *Le Roman de Tristan et Iseut dans l'oeuvre de Thomas Malory* (Paris, 1925), especially pp. 35-40, 91-129, 156-70; and *Études sur le Tristan en prose: Les sources, les manuscrits, bibliographie critique* (Paris, 1925). A review of Vinaver's *Le Roman* is L. E. Winfrey's, in *MP*, XXVI (1928-1929), 231-33. The recent comprehensive critique of Malory's use of sources is R. M. Lumiansky's fascinating *Malory's Originality: A Critical Study of Le Morte Darthur* (Baltimore, 1964). See also the unpublished Ph.D. dissertation of Thomas C. Rumble, "The *Tristan* Legend and its Place in Malory's Morte Darthur" (Tulane University, 1955).

77. There are only minor divergencies in phraseology between Caxton's text and that of the Winchester MS, and minor omissions of words. The only other difference in the two texts is the age until which Tristan resides in Cornwall: nineteen years old in Caxton, eighteen years old in the Winchester.

skill. Whether Malory formed his education for Tristram from a lost version of the *Prose*, or from a medieval poetic version, or from a prose Tristan story in another language,[78] or from example in his own English milieu, it is not possible to determine.

But in Malory, as in the French *Prose* and the metrical English stories, the education of the hero sows no seeds for a second reaping; it has therefore no aftermath. The two English romances and the prose exemplify the biographical approach to romance in the decadence of the courtly genre. Such *seriatim* narratives, in which a story begins with its hero's birth and concludes with his death, are guided by few dramatic principles, or none at all. The education of the hero merely spans the time between infancy and knighthood.

Consideration of the education of the hero in these major and minor versions of his story reveals aspects of poetic methods, standards, and achievements. The use of material introduced in the *enfance* is characteristic of the more complex and poetically accomplished versions. In these, study of the education within the *enfance* suggests possible influences from contemporary example. Consideration of the education theme also illuminates individual writers' alterations of traditional elements for specific artistic purposes. The lack of such development and elaboration defines the artistically imperfect works. Thus, while the education Eilhart affords Tristan is abundant in detail, it is ultimately a list of activities with no clear significance for the rest of the romance. In the late English and French works, the education of the hero is either neglected, absent, or unelaborated. The brief outline of the hero's education in the English *Sir Tristrem* indicates only that its redactor recognized the importance of the hero's tutelage in the sources he employed. The French *Prose* gives no educational detail but, rather, presents an *enfance* characterized by magic, incest,

78. Thomas Rumble recognizes that both a Spanish and an Italian prose romance offer parallels closer to Malory's text than do the French prose versions (Lumiansky, *op. cit.*, pp. 118-83). This appears to be true particularly for the *enfance* of the hero. The Spanish text is edited, with a very useful introduction, by C. T. Northup, *El Cuento de Tristan de Leonis* (Chicago, 1928); the Italian, by Luigi di Benedetto, *La Leggenda di Tristano* ("Scrittori D'Italia," Vol. 189 [Bari, 1942]). Definitive relationships between these texts and Malory's have not yet been established.

and wildly indiscriminate use of stock romance incident. In Malory, the hero's education is detailed but contributes no themes developed in his later adventures.

In Thomas, and much more so in Gottfried, the intellectual hero and musician emerges. In both texts, the education of the child fathers the qualities of the man as knight and hero. The content and characteristics of the *enfances* in these two works permit reappraisal of the whole poems in their light. In Thomas and Gottfried there appears the concept of the learned knight, the ideal of the romance hero trained in both letters and arms. Thomas' version particularly lends credence to the supposition that contemporary noblemen known to the romancers, or feudal leaders whose exploits were recorded in family chronicles available to romance writers, inspired details in the texts which otherwise cannot be accounted for. Gottfried's poem, the greatest Tristan story, displays the splendid adaptation of the *enfance* to a new design for chivalry, for the chivalric lover, and for courtly romance.

In Thomas and Gottfried, Tristan is portrayed as studious, introspective, and cultivated. More than any other romance figure, Tristan signifies the culmination of the battle between *miles* and *clericus*. For Tristan the man of learning, and for Tristan the artist knight, learning is the better part of valor.

Chapter II

The Education of *Perceval*

A Brave Man Slowly Wise

Do not heap up many words.
—Matthew 6:7

Omnia in mensura et numero et
pondere disposuisti.
—Wisdom of Solomon 11:21

$\mathcal{N}$o Kurneval educates Perceval. Young Perceval, the antithesis of Tristan the learned knight, is a rustic *Dümmling*. Guileless and ingenuous, he knows nothing of knowledge or restraint. His arrival at court, rather than exciting marvel at his culture and refinement, stimulates laughter at his ignorance and simplicity. Raised in virtual isolation because of his mother's desire to shield him from knighthood, Perceval's forest values and lack of formal education cause clumsy, humorous ineptitude in all courtly pursuits. But although he has no tutor, no travel, and no intellectual nor musical studies, Perceval is portrayed as passing through periods of deliberate instruction. In some versions, his education consists of Instruction and Advice[1] from his mother and from the nobleman Gornemant de Gohort; in others, merely his mother's Advice before their parting sends Perceval from rusticity to the court. When employed artfully, the education of the hero is significant for the hero's characterization and for the structure of the romances. Indeed, Perceval's adventures in chivalry and in love and his quest for the Holy Grail directly depend on this youthful education.

Most criticism of Perceval romances has been devoted either to a search for their traditional sources and analogues[2] or to exegesis—

1. For convenience in distinguishing these specific components of the hero's education, these terms will be capitalized throughout this chapter.

2. The parallels between the Perceval story and the Irish tradition have long been recognized. A selective list of works dealing particularly with the *enfances* includes: A. T. Nutt, *Studies on the Legends of the Holy Grail* (London, 1888); E. Brugger, ''Ein Beiträg zur Arthurischen Namenforschung. Alain de Gomeret,'' in *Aus romanischen Sprachen und Literaturen, Festgabe für H. Morf* (Halle, 1905); J. L. Weston, *The Legend of Sir Perceval* (London, 1906); Mary R. Williams, *Essai sur la composition du roman gallois de Peredur* (Paris, 1909); C. Strucks, *Der junge Parzival in Wolframs von Eschenbach Parzival, Crestiens von Troyes Conte del Gral, englischen Syr Percyvelle und italienischen Carduino* (Borna, Leipzig, 1910); R. H. Griffith, *Sir Perceval of Galles: A Study of the Sources of the Legend* (Chicago, 1911), especially pp. 14-77; W. A. Nitze, *Perceval and the Holy Grail* (Berkeley, 1949), pp. 312 f.; W. A. Nitze, ''The Sister's Son and the Conte del Graal,'' *MP*, IX (1912), 291 f.; R. B. Pace, '' 'Sir Perceval' and the 'Boyish Exploits' of Finn,'' *PMLA*, XXXII (1917), 598-604; A. C. L. Brown,

religious and philosophical—of their Grail mysteries.³ Analysis of
the romances from the standpoint of the hero's education permits a
slightly different perspective: it attempts to define not out of what
nor why the works were written, but rather how this single
romance feature, the *enfance*, expresses the poets' artistic methods
and intentions. Chronologically, Chrétien's *Perceval, le Conte
del Graal*⁴ (*ca.* 1191), presents the earliest statement of Perceval's

"The Grail and the English Sir Perceval," *MP*, XVI (1919), 553 f., XVII
(1920), 361 f.; F. C. J. Los, *Das Keltentum in Wolframs Parzival* (Amsterdam, 1927), especially pp. 84-102; E. Brugger, "Bliocadran, the Father of
Perceval," *Medieval Studies in Honor of Gertrude Schoepperle Loomis* (New
York, 1927), pp. 147 f.; H. Newstead, "Perceval's Father and Welsh Tradition," *RR*, XXXVI (1945), 1 f.; M. F. Richey, *MLR*, XLVII (1952), 350-61;
one of the most comprehensive studies is R. S. Loomis, *Arthurian Tradition
and Chrétien de Troyes* (New York, 1949), pp. 335-62.
   3. Those studies consulted which consider the *enfances* of Perceval include:
M. A. Rachbauer, *Wolfram von Eschenbach, A Study of the Relation of the
Content of Books III, VI, and IX of the Parzival* (Washington, 1934);
G. Weber, *Der Gottesbegriff des Parzival* (Frankfurt, 1935); and his *Parzival,
Ringen und Vollendung* (Oberursel, 1948); Hermann J. Weigand, "Die
epischen Zeitverhältnisse in den Graldichtungen Chrestiens und Wolframs,"
PMLA, LIII (1938), 917-50; B. Mergell, in *ADA*, LVIII (1939), 121-25; J.
Schwietering, *Parzivals Schuld, Zur Religiosität Wolframs in ihrer Beziehung
zur Mystik* (Frankfurt am Main, 1946); Hermann Schneider, *Parzival-Studien*
("Sitzungsberichte der Bayerischen Akademie der Wissenschaften, Philos.-
Hist. Klasse, 1944-6," IV [München, 1947]); U. T. Holmes, *A New Inter-
pretation of Chrétien's Conte del Graal* ("University of North Carolina
Studies in Romance Languages and Literature," VIII [Chapel Hill, 1948]);
P. Wapnewski, *Wolframs 'Parzival': Studien zur Religiosität und Form*
(Heidelburg, 1955); Sister A. Klenke, *Liturgy and Allegory in Chrétien's
Perceval* (Chapel Hill, 1951); U. T. Holmes and A. Klenke, *Chrétien, Troyes
and the Grail* (Chapel Hill, 1959); H. Adolf, *Visio Pacis: Holy City and
Holy Grail: An Attempt at an Inner History of the Grail Legend* (State
College, Pa., 1960); Susan B. Snyder, "The Paradox of Despair: Studies in
the Despair Theme in Medieval and Renaissance Literature" (unpublished
Ph.D. dissertation, Columbia University, 1963), pp. 112-47.
   4. Alfons Hilka (ed.), *Der Percevalroman von Christian von Troyes* (Halle,
1932). The editions of the other Perceval texts to be considered in this chapter
are: G. Jones and T. Jones (trans.), *Peredur* in *The Mabinogion* (London,
New York, 1957), pp. 183-228; *Sir Perceval* in J. Campion and F. Holthausen
(eds.), *Sir Perceval of Gales* (Heidelburg, 1913); Pio Rajna (ed.), *Carduino*,
in *Poemetti Cavallereschi* (Bologna, 1873); "Bliocadran's Prologue," in
Hilka, *Der Percevalroman* pp. 430-54 and 489-90; G. Paris (ed.), *Tyolet*, in
Romania, VIII (1879), 40-50; and *Parzival*, in K. Lachmann (ed.), *Wolfram
von Eschenbach* (6th ed.; Berlin, 1926). The *enfances* of Perceval in the *Prose
Lancelot* and the *Prose Tristan* are not pertinent to this chapter; a convenient
description of them based upon examination of MSS and editions is A. Hilka,
"Die Jungendgeschichte Percevals im *Prosa-Lancelot* und im *Prosa-Tristan*,"
ZRPh, LII (1932), 513 f. Printed editions of the two romances are referred to
in the notes to chaps. i and iii.

education, and it is one of the two most sophisticated. Though later
in time, the Welsh *Peredur*, the English *Sir Perceval*, the Italian
Carduino, the French "Bliocadran's Prologue," and the Breton *lai*
of *Tyolet* preserve elements of an earlier tradition from which
Chrétien himself must have drawn. Since the value of the hero's
education in these texts lies not in literary statement but in
preservation of traditional vestiges, they will be discussed only
within the analysis of Chrétien's poem. No reference will be made
to three Perceval romances, also later works: the Icelandic *Perceval*, which has the briefest mention of youthful instruction, or the
Didot Perceval and *Perlesvaus*, which have no education of the hero
whatsoever. Besides Chrétien's, the other romance in which Perceval's learning is documented and developed is Wolfram von
Eschenbach's *Parzival*. Basing conception and characterization in
part upon Chrétien, in part upon other tradition, and in greatest
part upon personal interests and skills, Wolfram transforms the
education themes and their expressions to their greatest beauty.

Chrétien describes the two periods of Perceval's education in
the *enfance* with exuberant humor. Each of these periods, the one,
in the forest with his mother as tutor, the other, with Gornemant de
Gohort at his castle, has two phases: one of specific Instruction and
one of Advice before parting. From his mother, Perceval gets
religious Instruction, and from Gornemant, chivalric. Upon parting from each tutor, the Advice Perceval receives specifically affects his subsequent exploits. The special qualities of the two
periods of education, their reflection in Perceval's attempts to put
precept into action, and his characteristics as student, inform the
Dümmling hero's progress from blunders through follies to
spiritual crises. Chrétien's careful structures of each educational
episode in the *enfance*, their parallels, and their interesting congruence to a time of tutelage later in the romance are noteworthy.
To one viewing the whole of the poem from the *enfance*, even with
the inevitable parallax of such consideration, *Perceval* appears to
be an elaborate structure of preparations and culminations, an
educational progress of a knight not yet made moral.

Perceval's mother teaches him that devils are the most terrible
beings, that angels are the most beautiful, except for God who is

even more beautiful (114-16; 141-45). She also reveals that some angels terrorize and murder those whom they meet (396 f.). The youth knows to cross himself, to bow down "to honor and adore" God, to recite a creed and prayers, and to commend people to the Lord (151 f.). These rudiments of religious Instruction are revealed not in a scene of mother instructing son in answer to his childish questions, as in every other version, but rather, in soliloquy and in action. Mistaking knights for devils, the youth who is innocent of all chivalry hears the crashing and clanging of armor and says to himself: "My mother told me that devils are most terrible and to cross myself. . . . But I'll scorn her teaching and strike them with my 'javeloz' " (113-25). Seeing the glitter of their burnished armor and their regal demeanor, Perceval's humorous arrogance turns into adoration. "Ma mere . . . me dist qui li ange estoient/ Les plus beles choses qui soient,/Fors Deu," at which he bows down in the path of the oncoming horses to honor the knights by prayer. The handsomest knight denies that he is God, in answer to Perceval's question, "Estes vos Deus?," names and explains the uses of each piece of his equipment, again in answer to comically repeated questions, and reveals that King Arthur "makes knights."

Perceval, coming home to his mother, reproving her for lying about angels' beauty when knights' glory is superior, prepares to leave the Welsh forest for Arthur's court. He receives four dicta of Advice: (1) Aid a lady or maiden, for in this all honor lies; yield honor to ladies, serve them, avoid displeasing or offending them, take from them no more than a kiss, "por moi," but do take the token of a ring or a purse (533-56); (2) Inquire the names of men whose company you keep (557-62); (3) Speak with "pro-domes" and take their advice (563-66); and (4) Enter churches and minsters to pray to God to give you honor and a good end (567-72). To Perceval's questions "Que est iglise?", "Et mostiers quoi?" his mother replies with descriptions of the houses of worship.

In every other version of Perceval's education, including Wolfram's, there is a specific Instruction scene. Only the short *lai* of *Tyolet* is without such a scene, though it too has implications of Instruction. In *Sir Perceval*, the fifteen-year-old youth learns only about God. Told to pray to Him, Perceval asks: "Whatkyns a godd may þat be?" (242). His mother's reply, that God is the great God of Heaven who made the world within seven days, sends him to the forest to "meet with that man" (250). Carduino, upon finding hunters' spears, learns that God sent those "darts" to him (IX,5–X,8). From afar, seeing knights for the first time, *Peredur*'s hero asks, "What are those yonder?" "Angels," replies his mother (184). Devils are the subject of Perceval's Intruction in the "Bliocadran's Prologue"; if beings "covered with iron" are met in the forest, the youth is to say his "credo" and speedily return home (751-67). In each of these texts, the hero next meets with knights whom he mistakes for divine beings and whom he questions about their armor.

The elementary dialogue of question and answer in these Instruction incidents represents a far simpler literary device than Chrétien's dramatic revelation of Perceval's religious training. These five versions essentially have two sequential question-and-answer scenes, one with the mother, one with the knights accidentally met; on the other hand, Chrétien achieves an artistic blend of monologue with question and answer. It is within Perceval's soliloquy that his mother's simple Instruction is revealed; Chrétien thereby increases the emphasis and heightens the humor of the encounter with the knights. Questions to the mother about religion, however, are not absent but only postponed. Chrétien later introduces a series of Perceval's questions about churches following the mother's Advice. This postponement, in addition to the detailed questioning of the knights, puts the emphasis in the *Waldleben* not only upon the hero's ignorance but upon his single most striking youthful trait—one with important implications later in the romance—his tendency to ask questions.

The episodes of the mother's Advice in the five later works also are indicative of less narrative sophistication than Chrétien's. The English Sir Perceval is told to (1) "be of mesure," (2) be generous, "fond to be fre," and (3) take off his hood to a knight (who can be identified because fur lines the hoods of knights) and "haylse hym in hy" (389-416). Carduino is to (1) serve King Arthur as he would his mother, (2) obey the king, and (3) avenge his father's death (XXVII-XXIX). Peredur is enjoined to (1) recite a *pater noster* to a church, (2) take food if he needs it even when it is not offered, (3) go to a woman's cry if he hears it, (4) take a jewel if he sees it and give it to another, and (5) make love to a fair lady even though she is unwilling (184-85). The hero in *Tyolet* is to (1) go to King Arthur's court, and (2) keep company only with those of noble birth (269-74). The "Bliocadran's Prologue" breaks off before the point of Advice. The injunctions-before-parting in these texts have features in common with one another and, since literary history makes interdependence unlikely, they probably derive from a common source or series of sources.[5] They preserve elements which in Chrétien have no place, yet they have enough features similar to Chrétien's to make it likely that these poems represent aspects of the written or oral tradition from which Chrétien formed his four dicta.[6] It is also possible, though not likely, that Chrétien's poem was known to these writers.[7]

Just as there is a dramatic relationship between Chrétien's Instruction of the hero and his first adventure, whereas the other texts present two simple scenes, so there is a relationship between the Advice and Perceval's later exploits in Chrétien which the other texts lack. In Chrétien, the mother's Advice causes three episodes of blunder: the adventure in the tent, the arrival at King Arthur's court, and the approach to the second period of education, the meeting with Gornemant de Gohort. The five later Perceval stories present some connection between the Advice and the tent incident, little correspondence between the Advice and court scene, and no correlation whatever between the Advice and meeting with Gornemant.[8] Rather than analyzing each of these relationships between Advice and action in the cruder romances, a

5. Weston, *op. cit.*, pp. 92-93; Strucks, *op. cit.*, pp. 74 f.; Griffith, *op. cit.*, pp. 32 f.; Loomis, *op. cit.*, pp. 335-55.

6. Weston, *op. cit.*, p. 93; Strucks, *op. cit.*, pp. 29 f.; Griffith, *op. cit.*, pp. 29-40.

7. The arguments for Chrétien's provenance, only a few of which today can be considered valid, are best found in W. Golther, *Chrestiens conte del graal in seinem verhältniss zum walschen Peredur und zum englischen Perceval* (Munich, 1890), pp. 174-217, and in his *Parzival und der Gral* (Munich, 1908); also, in W. W. Newell, *The Legend of the Holy Grail and the Perceval of Chrestien of Troyes* (Cambridge, Mass., 1902).

8. Cf. Griffith, *op. cit.*, pp. 37-38; 40-47.

single example and the features they all share may be noted. To
the English Sir Perceval, the philosophical enjoinder to *moderatio*,
"Be of mesure," means simply: measure things in half! He
consequently takes only one half of the food stolen from the lady
in the tent (here a "hall") and halves the oats he eats with the
bony mare he rides (436 f.). All of the five romances are written by
what may be called the omniscient-humorist-technique. Humor
directly depends upon the writer's overt ridicule of his hero. The
audience is told what Perceval does wrong and just how ignorant
he is for having done so. Blatant and coarse, the humor of the
hero's actions is all in the foreground, with little reference to
things past or to future characteristics. No subtlety and no variety
inform the nature of the hero; the writers of his exploits call him
and make him "Idiot," "Simpleton," "Foolish Youth," "Ridiculous Bumpkin," and "Fool of the Field." His foolish adventures
do not advance his fortunes, as they do in Chrétien and Wolfram;
his attempts to obey represent no progression but merely repetition.
Aside from the traditional incidents, the single factor common to
these romances and to Chrétien's is Perceval's literal interpretation and application of his instruction.

Chrétien, however, never once calls his hero "fool"; indeed, he
characterizes him fully—though not so subtly nor sympathetically
as does Wolfram. Chrétien gives special qualities to the tutelage
which, in turn, affect the hero's adherence to it. The *Dümmling*
character is created by the conjunction of methods of education
and Perceval's qualities in applying his lessons.[9] Chrétien artfully
turns the first period of education, the mother's Instruction and
Advice, to purposes of characterization and structure.

The mother's suggestions to her son are specific and disjunct.
The four Advice precepts, separated only by her affectionate epithet "Biaus filz," cryptically encompass what a lifetime of courtesy
might achieve: proper behavior toward women, other men, one's
elders, and God. In all her teaching the mother stresses appearances and externals. The differences between angels and God, or

9. In one of the few studies devoted to Chrétien's characterizations, H.
Königer, *Die Darstellung der Personen bei Crestien von Troyes* (München,
1936), essentially ignores the importance of this education as a contribution to
the portrait of the hero.

between devils and angels, are a matter only of beauty. Perceval is taught to recognize but not to understand. Although she speaks plainly, Perceval's mother's words yet are more symbolic than he can appreciate. Her explanations of what Perceval can expect in the world beyond the forest (for example, "King Arthur will make you a knight; he must do so" [512 f.]) mean much more in their associations and ramifications than ingenuous Perceval can apprehend.[10] All-knowing to her son, and permitting him no other formal education than her own, the mother makes it inevitable that Perceval will be incapable of judgment which modifies or counters hers.

Perceval leaves the Welsh forest with uncritical obedience to his mother's teachings, with Advice for which he has no preparation, and with no discretion. In each of the adventures which follow his first educational period, those at the tent, the court, and Gornemant's castle, the hero makes three errors: mistaken identifications, mistaken applications, and mistaken expectations of functions. Thinking the many-colored, jeweled tent a church, Perceval says a *pater noster* to it with the hope of gaining food; then he enters to find the elegant Lady whom he roughly kisses, from whom he takes a finger ring, whose lover's food he eats; leaving her in tearful distress, he commends her to God (635 f.). His next adventure, at King Arthur's court, has him entering the grand hall mounted on his hunter, impertinently demanding knighthood in the arms of the Red Knight, following the seneschal Kay's sarcastic command:

10. Perceval's religious education by his mother has excited some controversy. Omer Jodogne, in "Le Sens chrétien du jeune Perceval dans le *Conte du Graal*," in *Lettres Romanes de Louvain*, XIV (1960), 111-21, and Paul Imbs, in an unpublished paper presented to the Strassburg Colloqium, on "le sens religieux dans le Conte du Graal," quoted by Jodogne, insist that Chrétien portrays young Perceval as devout, faithful, and the possessor of an elaborate Christian indoctrination. These conclusions are based upon Perceval's mention of a "credo" and his repetition of such formulaic expressions as "By my faith," and "By my soul." (M. Jodogne also maintains that Perceval knew about communion, possibly from a chaplain on his mother's manor, and that the youth wished to take his mother to a convent to end her years! Unfortunately, Chrétien says nothing about such matters in the poem.) A happy corrective to these untenable views is Mario Roques' review of Jodogne's article (in *Romania*, LXXXI [1960], 271-73) in which he repeats his earlier conclusion (in *le Graal de Chrétien et la demoiselle au Graal* [Paris, 1955]) that Perceval is a romance of education.

"Alez li tolir or androit/Les armes, car eles sont voz" (1004-5), killing the knight for the armor, and learning from the Squire Yonet some few essentials of arming and horsemanship (873-78). The third episode consequent upon his mother's education brings him to the castle of his second tutor, Gornemant de Gohort. Here, riding clumsily, asking for a night's harborage, indicating, in answer to his host's queries, his complete ignorance of chivalric activities, he gains from Gornemant the spur, sword, and accolade of knighthood and promises faith to his tutor's Instruction and Advice (1031 f.).

Each of these incidents is constructed similarly. Chrétien's hero makes his three errors, every one of which is either prefaced or followed by the words or implication: "Thus my mother told me." To Perceval things are what they seem. His mistaken identifications of the tent for a church, of Kay's malicious jest for King Arthur's promise of arms, and of Gornemant's bestowal of knighthood for mere hospitality are misinterpretations of surface impressions. His mistaken applications of past learning to behavior with the Lady of the Tent, to his demands for the Red Knight's armor (and his ignominious achievement of it), and to use of his war horse for riding up hill and down dale as well as use of his brilliant armor for putting on and putting off—these are literal adherences to incomplete conceptions. His mistaken expectations of functions derive from Perceval's confusion of metaphor and symbol with concrete realities. He believes that praying is for food when hungry, that knighthood is merely for the asking, and that a knight's advice is for literal obedience. As Chrétien presents them, not one of his hero's silly early exploits is without basis in his education. In contradistinction to all other versions, except Wolfram's, each blunder of Chrétien's Perceval is a misguided attempt to act just as he had been taught.

Chrétien's characterization of the naïve hero depends for its excellent humor upon the incongruity inherent in good advice well followed by the wrong person in the wrong place. Many of Perceval's actions would not appear folly if they took place in the forest. But Perceval's rustic standards which are sufficient for the forest are absurd for the court. Ignorance of knighthood does not hinder life in the Welsh woods where Arthur's men had not yet come. But while the youth's "javeloz" serves well for killing bucks and hinds, it leaves something to be desired for chivalrous battling against knights. His clumsy ways of love-making suffice for the bitter lips of his mother's serving maids (725) but not for the more refined Lady of the Tent. His ubiquitous words, "ç'a m'anseigna ma mere," are proper for speaking with servants on his mother's manor (who also are beholden to her instructions) but not for conversation with Arthur's courtiers or with Gornemant. The ingenuous arrogance of the child ("What I see, I want") is sufficient for Perceval's leaving the forest and beginning a quest but not for achieving more than the externals of knighthood nor for returning to that forest of innocence. So also, the child's penchant for questioning the unknown suffices for the simple problems of appearances in the forest but not, when superficially censored, for the high mysteries of the Grail. Chrétien's hero, then, suffers not from natural witlessness but from circumstantial ignorance. In this first period of education Chrétien emphasizes his hero's rusticity as the cause of his follies; even his clothing, considered so ludicrous by the courtiers, is not fool's dress, as it is in Wolfram's and other versions, but merely Welsh. It seems that from the folklore motif of the *Dümmling*,[11] combined with some suggestion from Celtic tradition,[12] Chrétien fashioned the rustic *Dümmling*—the Waleis who appears foolish (to the courtly) because he is rustic.

11. One of the most complete studies of this subject is M. Ramondt's "Zur Jugendgeschichte des Parzival," in *Neophilologus*, IX (1923), 15-22. Important material is contained in A. Aarne, *Types of the Folktale*, trans. Stith Thompson ("Folklore Fellows Communications," No. 74 [2nd ed.; Helsinki, 1961]), especially motif numbers 460-62, 465, 1204, 1691, 1693, 1696; J. Bolte and G. Polivka, *Anmerkungen zu den Kinder- und Hausmärchen der Brüder Grimm* (Leipzig, 1913), especially I, 299 f.; G. Ehrismann, "Märchen im höfischen Epos," *PBB*, XXX (1905), 14 f.; J. de Vries, *Betrachtungen zum Märchen* (Helsinki, 1954); and H. Sparnaay, *Verschmelzung legendarischer und weltlicher Motive in der Poesie des Mittelalters* (Gröningen, 1922). Considerations of other *Dümmling* heroes include, A. Mennung, *Der Bel Inconnu des Renaut de Beaujeu in seinem Verhältnis zum Lybeaus Descilus, Carduino und Wigalois* (Halle, 1890); W. H. Schofield, *Studies on the Libeaus Desconus* (Boston, 1895); E. Brugger, "Bliocadran, the Father of Perceval," pp. 166-70; A. Dickson, *Valentin and Orson: A Study in Late Medieval Romance* (New York, 1929), pp. 128 f.; and W. Hertz, in his translation of *Parzival von Wolfram von Eschenbach* (7th ed.; Berlin, 1927), pp. 443 f.

12. Loomis, *op. cit.*, pp. 339 f.; T. P. Cross, *Motif-Index of Early Irish*

Perceval's ineptitude reaches its highest point at Gornemant's castle. His first period of education brings him only so far as to cover his Welsh brogues with shining spurs and his canvas suit with vermilion armor. The rustic *Dümmling* by circumstance, but the potential knight by nature, needs more teaching to make the image of the knight reflect his essential chivalry. Chrétien thus gives his hero a second education period during which he receives the garments more conventionally worn beneath knightly mail than those his mother gave him and the Instruction and Advice which ought to better prepare him for his coming adventures.

Recognizing Perceval's marvelous ignorance of chivalry, Gornemant teaches such things as "Qu'au besoing mestier li eüssent" (1577). His Instruction consists in lessons in arms, in how to hold a lance, spur and check a horse, display a pennon, hold a shield, and wield a sword (1433 f.). Delighting in Perceval's aptitude for these skills—Perceval "comança a porter/si a droit la lance et l'escu/Con s'il eüst toz jorz vescu/An tornoiemanz et an guerres" (1474-78)—Gornemant invites him to remain at the castle. Upon Perceval's refusal to stay more than a single night because of his hope to return to his mother, Gornemant gives four counsels of Advice before parting. These are: (1) When you are winning in combat with a knight, have mercy and do not willingly kill him (1639 f.); (2) Beware of talking too much and of gossiping; no one talks too much without being rude; it is said: "Qui trop parole, pechié fet"; hence I forbid too much talking (1648 f.); (3) If a man or woman is in distress, and if you have the power to help, then advise, "conseilliez," as well as you can (1657 f.); (4) Enter minsters to pray to God to have mercy on your soul and to keep you a good Christian in this life (1667-70).

This second education period is surprisingly absent in every other Perceval text—with the exception of Wolfram's. There is no chivalric Instruction or Advice from Gornemant in *Sir Perceval*, *Carduino*, or *Tyolet*. *Sir Perceval* has a visit to a maternal uncle before the hero's adventure at Lufamor's castle (parallel to

Literature ("Indiana University Publications, Folklore Series," No. 7 [Bloomington, 1952]). Cf. A. T. Nutt, "The Aryan Expulsion-and-Return Formula," *Folk-Lore Record*, IV (1881), 1-44.

Chrétien's "Belrepaire" incident) which may conceivably have some distant though not very significant relationship to the Gornemant scene,[13] but there is no teaching and no learning in this episode. *Peredur* preserves a visit to an unnamed, lame uncle who is first met while he watches youths fishing. From him, Peredur receives a single piece of Advice, after a demonstration of conduct in sword-play: "Even though you see what is strange to thee, ask not after it, unless there be such courtesy that thou be told of it. Not upon thee will thy fault be, but upon me, for I am thy teacher" (191). This maimed Fisherman is clearly a doublet of the maimed Fisher King whom Peredur meets but a few lines later,[14] and this Advice undoubtedly was created by a confusion among the hero's "uncle" characters and their literary functions.[15] This Advice given the nephew bears no particular relationship to Peredur's later adventures except in that the hero does not ask the Grail question. The attribution of fault for behavior, however, is a fascinating example of garbling, misinterpretation, fission of character, and fusion of characteristics. Probably working with material similar to Wolfram's, the Welsh writer retains the majestic yet humble offer to take on another's guilt—which appears in the German as Trevrizent's "Give me your sin"—but here gives it to the hero's wrong uncle. In some manner, either from Wolfram, from a source based upon his poem, or from the material from which Wolfram himself drew, an injunction against questions and a relationship between that injunction and its consequence to some later exchange of fault were known to the writer of *Peredur*.[16] Other than this visit to an uncle's castle, there is no other vestige of an education in the Welsh text, nor in any other Perceval version.

Chrétien's second period of Perceval's tutelage apparently is his own invention. Although there is a vague hint of such an incident in Irish literature,[17] there is no known source for Gornemant's education of the hero. This whole episode appears to be a

13. Griffith, *op. cit.*, pp. 41-77.
14. Williams, *op. cit.*, pp. 109-12; Loomis, *op. cit.*, p. 361.
15. Williams, *op. cit.*, pp. 109 f., 117; Loomis, *op. cit.*, p. 361.
16. Cf. Williams, *op. cit.*, pp. 81-95.
17. Loomis, *op. cit.*, pp. 361 f.

eflection of social interest in the arts of chivalry, a literary expres-

reflection of social interest in the arts of chivalry, a literary expression of a major concern of the courtly audience for which *Perceval* was written.[18] The necessities of Chrétien's narrative must have stimulated the creation of this incident. First, the portrait of an honored knight, accustomed to riding a hunter bareback in Welsh brogues and carrying a willow switch for crop, mounted upon a charger which cost "one hundred marks" (1443), would be inconsistent with Chrétien's rationalism in the description of familiar things.[19] Second, for the sake of the characterization of a hero rustic not by nature but only by appearance, the incident allows revelation of Perceval's inherent chivalric capabilities; Chrétien says: "Ne li peut estre riens grevainne/La ou nature et cuers se painne" (1483-84). Third, this second education period serves the purpose of a structural parallel to the first period of education and is an intimation of the later one with the Hermit. Examination reveals that, just as for the first period, qualities of the education and qualities of the attempts to follow it define the hero's progress.

Gornemant's Instruction directly affects Perceval's method of fighting during his first adventure at Belrepaire castle where he twice relieves the besieged lady who ultimately becomes his bride. Chrétien makes the correlation between Instruction and action plain by permitting all of the hero's martial triumphs but one to be consistent with his chivalric learning; however, during Perceval's fight with Anguingeron, Chrétien makes his hero face a problem for which Gornemant had given no training. Perceval therefore stops short, dismounts, and positions himself for familiar methods and expected results:

18. Weston, *op. cit.*, pp. 86, 88. Cf. W. Kellermann, *Aufbaustil und Weltbild Chrestiens von Troyes im Percevalroman*, Beihefte zur *ZPR*, LXXXVIII (1936). The similarity between the education in chivalric arts given Perceval by Gornemant and that given Lanzelet by Johfrit in Ulrich von Zatzikhoven's poem has been noted many times; first by G. Paris, "Etudes sur les romans de la table ronde: Lancelot du Lac," *Romania*, X (1881), 473; and also by Philipot, *Romania*, XXVI (1897), 290 f.; A. C. L. Brown, *MP*, XVII (1919) 369, n. 4; and Loomis, *op. cit.*, p. 361. This point will be discussed in chap. iii.
19. Chrétien's fidelity to reality in the description of courtly customs is striking. Interesting discussions of this realism are contained in W. Kellermann, *op. cit.*, and in J. Frappier, *Chrétien de Troyes, l'homme et l'oeuvre* (Paris, 1957). Cf. Dorothy Everett, "A Characterization of the English Medieval Romances," in her posthumous collection, *Essays on Medieval English Literature*, ed. Patricia Kean (Oxford, 1955).

Et li vaslez a pié desçant
Qu'il nel set a cheval requerre;
Del cheval est venuz a terre,
Puis tret l'espee, si li passe. . . .

(2224 f.)

Just as in the first period of education, it is the tutor's Advice
rather than the Instruction which has the greater repercussions for
the hero's later actions. Here again, three incidents bear the mark
of the youthful learning: the encounters at Belrepaire, at the Grail
Castle, and with the Proud Knight of the Glade.

The newly made knight coming to Belrepaire sits so silently
beside his hostess Blanchefleur because of the charge which "li
prodon," Gornemant, had laid upon him against speaking (1855 f.)
that the courtiers ask one another, "Is he mute? They look like a
good pair but will never get anywhere if he makes no first move"
(1862 f.). Fighting his lady's enemy, Anguingeron, Perceval van-
quishes him but will grant no mercy until he remembers that
Gornemant had taught him never to slay willingly a knight after
overcoming him (2236 f.). And when the knights of Belrepaire,
less knowledgeable in the ways of honor than Perceval, ask why
he sent Anguingeron as captive to King Arthur instead of bringing him or his head back to them, Perceval passes on Gornemant's
Advice:

Trop eüst an moi po de bien,
Des que je au desore an fui
Se n'eüsse merci de lui.

(2348 f.)

At the Grail Castle, seeing the marvel of the bleeding lance, Perceval, ever mindful of Gornemant's warning "de trop parler se gar-
dast" (3207-9), and fearful of being considered rude for asking
(3211), holds his peace. Seeing the Damsels carrying the Grail,
he does not dare ask about it because he kept in his heart the words
of the wise nobleman (3244 f.). Still he does not speak when the
Grail passes again, restraining himself because "le prodome se
tenoit/Qui doucement le chastia/De trop parler," and he treasured
this and remembered it (3290 f.). At each successive passing of

the Grail he asks no questions, though he would have liked to know
the answers (3303). Instead, he postpones his queries until the
morning (3307) but it is then too late. Finally, in the third incident in which action is specifically dependent upon Advice, Perceval overcomes the once Proud Knight. His plea for mercy is
granted because the hero never forgets "Le prodome, qui li pria/
Que ja chevalier n'oceïst/Puis que merci li requeïst" (3933 f.).

These adventures are, of course, traditional in origin,[20] and
were possibly connected with Perceval before Chrétien refined
them. However the distinctive characteristic of these—the com-
plexities of the Grail visit notwithstanding—is Chrétien's specific
reference to and emphasis upon Perceval's second period of education. Perceval not merely sends the knights he has bested to King
Arthur's court but does so out of deference to Gornemant's lessons.
Not once but three times Chrétien attributes Perceval's silence
before the lance and Grail to his thoughts about what he has
learned. In place of saying aloud, "My mother told me thus," the
knight is made to think to himself: "Thus Gornemant charged
me."

Gornemant's pedagogic method is first to ask questions of his
student in order to ascertain the extent of his ignorance ("Who
gave you this armor?" [1377]; "What do you do with your
horse?" [1384]) and to determine whether any previous learning
can be applied to practical problems ("In fighting a knight what
would you do if your lance broke?" [1511 f.]). He then teaches
by example.[21] Perceval's chivalric Instruction consists in copying
demonstrated techniques. Three times Gornemant mounts the
charger to teach proper handling, and three times Perceval is made
to mount to practice what he has seen (1505 f.). Similar to the
Advice offered by the mother, Gornemant's four dicta are specific,

20. Loomis, op. cit., on Belrepaire, pp. 363-73; on the Grail Castle, pp. 374-
414; on the Proud Knight Orilus de Lalander, pp. 395 f.
21. Teaching a young man the ways of knighthood by personal example is
the method of instruction of Gurnemanz in Wolfram's Parzival, of Johfrit in
Lanzelet, and of Tînas von Lîtan in Eilhart's Tristrant. It probably reflects
contemporary practices. A. Schultz, citing other examples, says: "Zog ihr
Herr in den Krieg, so beleiten ihn seine Knappen und lernten da das Kriegswe-
sen praktisch kennen''; Das höfische Leben zur zeit der Minnesinger (2 vols.;
Leipzig, 1889), I, 179.

separate, and concern the goals of a lifetime of chivalric courtesy—
in battling with knights, in speaking with other men, in aiding the
distressed, and in approaching God. Rather than stressing appearances, as Perceval's mother does, Gornemant's emphasis is upon
actions, particularly those which display honor. Although his
language is plain, as is the first tutor's, his sentences consist of
metaphors which he assumes his student comprehends ("Thus I
buckle the spur on you"); but their full significances are lost to
Perceval.

Yet, in practical chivalry, Perceval is anxious to learn, eminently able to learn, and quick to learn. "Ne querroit ja mes un jor
vivre/Ne terre ne avoir n'eüst/Mes qu'ausi feire le seüst," says
the hero about horsemanship (1460-63); he rides and thrusts his
sword superlatively "Car il le venoit de nature" (1480); once he
sees a feat performed he follows skilfully—as if he had always
done so (1474). He indeed exemplifies Gornemant's conception of
education:

> Il covient a toz les mestiers
> Et painne et cuer et us avoir:
> Par cez trois puet an tot savoir.
> (1466-68)

Perceval leaves Gornemant's castle with his Instruction and Advice
internalized, no longer stating whence his learning comes. Again,
however, he approaches his adventures with uncritical obedience
to his second tutor, with Advice for which he has but little preparation, and, as ever, with little discretion. Things learned by following example lead to results consonant with chivalry and with
reason; but from the Advice comes misfortune caused by one major
error: Gornemant's Advice is not tempered by Perceval's judgment. His utter dependence upon his mentor's word makes him
distrust his noble intuitions. In attempting faithfully to execute
what Gornemant advises, Perceval violates courtesy at Belrepaire
because of his initial silence; because of his failure to ask questions
at the Grail Castle, he violates his proper instincts of curiosity and
compassion. Gornemant's tutelage, then, makes out of the rustic
Dümmling the Neophyte Knight. Perceval's thoughtless obedience

is the excess of the neophyte who cannot yet apprehend *Omnia in mensura et numero et pondere disposuisti.* This Wisdom of Solomon could neither be taught nor learned in one night. Perceval's second period of education is significant not only for what and how he is taught, but by whom. Just as the chivalric Instruction and Advice seem to be Chrétien's invention, so is the character of the tutor Gornemant. He is the one major figure in the romance without an accepted derivation from Celtic or other tradition.[22] He appears in no other Perceval romance but Wolfram's, except by implication in *Sir Perceval* as the unnamed uncle to whose castle the hero goes before the Lufamor episode,[23] and in *Peredur* as the unnamed uncle who gives the prohibition against asking questions. In Gerbert's *Continuation*, Gornemant appears as a character with no attributes of the tutor.[24]

Gornemant's critical role in Chrétien's poem, his characterization, and his bestowal of knighthood deserve consideration. As the tutor to the youth who lacks nothing but nurture, as the one whose Advice is made the motivation for Perceval's failure to ask the compassionate question, and as the uncle of the besieged Blanchefleur, making him Perceval's kin by marriage, Gornemant is thus the only personage directly related to the three major topics of the romance: chivalry, religion, and love. Later, Wolfram develops these themes with relationship to the tutor by making him even more the spokesman of chivalry's ethics, by having him teach the hero religious ritual, and by giving Gurnemanz a daughter as well

22. Loomis, *op. cit.,* pp. 360-62. Griffith's theory on the "Red Knight-Witch-Uncle" theme, as a stage in the development of Perceval story, is fairly convincing. *Op. cit.,* particularly pp. 70 f.

23. Griffith, *op. cit.,* pp. 68-77.

24. Mary Williams (ed.), *Gerbert de Montreuil. La Continuation de Perceval, CFMA* (Paris, 1922-1925). Between adventures, Perceval meets two youths leaving a battlefield carrying their wounded father Gornement. Gornument entertains Perceval who vows vengeance upon Gornument's enemies; each night after their being killed, these enemies are resuscitated by a hideous hag. Perceval later meets her on a battlefield and is told that (1) he will never find the Grail while she lives; (2) her balm revives the dead; and (3) she wars against Gornument at the behest of the king of the Waste City because Gornument had made Perceval knight. Perceval decapitates her and is himself wounded. With her balm he revives and cures (1) his slain horse, (2) his worst enemy, for the purpose of killing him again, (3) himself, and (4) Gornument.

as a niece who is loved by the hero, thus bringing a woman in Parzival's life closer to Gurnemanz and, thereby, Gurnemanz closer to Parzival. Chrétien makes Gornemant the model of the hospitable host, a knight well suited to teach gentle arts and martial skills by example. As a romance character, he probably originated by a process of separation of qualities once belonging to a single uncle—in some early traditional form of Perceval story— and the attribution of those qualities to three different characters: Gornemant, the Fisher King, and the Hermit uncle.[25] His name could well have developed from the named tutor of another popular romance hero, Tristan's Kurneval.[26] Some forms of both names are remarkably close in spelling, Gournemaus–Cournevaus, for example. It would take only a change of one or two letters or the absence of a scribal stroke to make them identical. Chrétien might have intentionally kept enough of the name of Tristan's tutor for its helpful associations. The vivid and humorous contrast between learned young Tristan and ignorant Perceval must have been apparent to Chrétien and his audience.[27] Indeed, Wolfram says of his Parzival: "No Curvenal brings him up," "in zôch nehein Curvenâl" (144:20).[28]

25. Cf. Williams, *op. cit.*, pp. 109-17; Loomis, *op. cit.*, pp. 360-62.
26. It is possible that the proper name Kurneval itself (other versions of "Kurneval" are "Gurneval," "Guvernal") developed from the Old French common noun "go(u)verneur"—one who governs, leads, instructs, advises. (Cf. Modern French and English "governess"). The simple linguistic changes of metathesis and a type of dissimilation would account for the exchanges of "v" "n" and "r" and "l" in the variants of the tutor's name. It appears that, as so often in the history of language, the original form of a word returns in later centuries by means of a reverse of the very linguistic laws which once changed it; thus, the tutor of the hero in Malory's Book is "Gouvernail." Cf. also Hoccleve's *Governail of Princes*.
27. The Tristan story, in whatever version, was surely known to courtly audiences before *Perceval* was written, in *ca.* 1191; in addition, there is always the tantalizing possibility of a poem of Chrétien's own on "roi Marc et d'Ysalt la blonde" which exists today only in his enumeration of his past works in the introduction to *Cligès* (5).
28. Wolfram's statement might be a barb directed against Gottfried von Strassburg and have relevance to their *Literaturstreit*. But I suspect that the Curvenal reference has the broader implications of the Tristan-Perceval contrast. Studies pertinent to the Wolfram-Gottfried antagonism are W. J. Schröder, "Vindaere wilder maere, Zum Literaturstreit zwischen Gottfried und Wolfram," *Beiträge*, LXXX (1958), 269 f.; and W. T. H. Jackson, "Tristan the Artist in Gottfried's Poem," *PMLA*, LXXVII (1962), 372; to Wolfram's relationship to Eilhart's poem is H. Eggers, "Literarische Beziehungen des

Not only is Gornemant the tutor and a central figure in the romance but Perceval is knighted by him—in a rapid ceremony the morning of departure from the castle. Although Chrétien relates this knighting episode, his hero displays a strange ignorance of it. When asked who knighted him, Perceval replies, "King Arthur!" Upon his arrival at Gornemant's castle Perceval asserts, "Chevalier m'a fet li rois" (1369). And much later in the poem he still believes this; he instructs the Proud Knight of the Glade to say to the king that he was sent by

> celui
> Cui il fist chevalier vermoil
> Par le los et par le consoil
> Mon seignor Keu, le seneschal.
> (3960-63)

It seems unlikely that this inconsistency between the poet's "fact" and his hero's "impression" is an accident. Chrétien specifically characterizes Perceval as believing that the verbal allotment of arms is the bestowal of knighthood. In fact, young Perceval's concept of knighthood is reflected in his beliefs about armor. To him, armor is knighthood, and a knight is his armor.[29]

The poet gives several justifications for Perceval's misconception. First, armor and King Arthur are twice united in statements to the youth still in the forest. The knight who denies that he was born wearing hauberk and spurs says,

> N'a mie ancor cinc jorz antiers
> Que tot cest hernois me dona
> Li rois Artus, qui m'adoba.
> (288-90)

Parzival zum Tristrant Eilharts von Oberg," *Beiträge*, LXXII (1950), 39-51; and to the Perceval and Tristan poems is G. Ehrismann's commentary in his *Geschichte der deutschen Literatur* (München, 1918-1935), III, 322.

29. Chretién exploits the humor of this unity. At Perceval's first sight of chivalry, awestruck by the glitter and crashing of the knights' harnesses, he considers what he sees beautiful, desires it, and vows to achieve it; clutching the shining metal, he asks, "Were you born this way?" (282). Later, after killing the Red Knight, he cries in childish chagrin, "I'll have to cut him into pieces to get them off . . . they stick together so thoroughly that inside and outside must be all one piece" (1134 f.).

To the innocent youth, "knighted me" means nothing, but "gave this armor" means all. At parting, his mother enjoins,

Vos iroiz a la cort le roi,
Si li diroiz qu'armes vos doint.
De contredit n'i avra point.
(512-14)

Here again there is the union of the king and the arms. Secondly, Perceval interprets Kay's jest, "Take the arms, they are yours," literally. Thus having been "given" the Red Knight's arms he believes himself a knight. Third, Gornemant does not correct the hero's bumptious assertion that Arthur knighted him but answers with a sarcastic quip, "I thought Arthur had other worries than making knights" (1370 f.). More importantly, Gornemant never simply says to the hero, "I am making you a knight," but rather speaks indirectly, with metaphors (fastening on the spur, girding on the sword) not yet comprehensible to Perceval.

Et li prodon s'est abeissiez
Si li chauça l'esperon destre:
La costume soloit teus estre
Que cil qui feisoit chevalier
Li devoit l'esperon chaucier.
D'autres vaslez assez i ot;
Chascuns qui avenir i pot
A lui armer a la main mise.
Et li prodon l'espee a prise,
Si li çainst et si le beisa
Et dit que donee li a
La plus haute ordre avuec l'espee
Que Deus et feite et comandee:
C'est l'ordre de chevalerie.
(1624-37)

And before Perceval leaves the castle the nobleman suggests that rather than saying "My mother told me" to explain actions, he may say that "Li vavasors . . . Qui *vostre esperon vos chauça*/Le vos aprist et anseigna" (1686-88).

Interestingly enough, in every other version, if there is a knighting at all, it is King Arthur who dubs Perceval. It is possible that Chrétien gave the action of knighting to Gornemant but the hero's attribution of it to Arthur as a literary reconciliation of two traditions: the knighting of the Irish hero Cuchullain by his maternal uncle Conchobar,[30] with which the whole Gornemant episode shows some slight affinity, and the knighting of an Arthurian hero by the King of the Round Table. Most other romance heroes are knighted by kings; Lancelot and Gawain receive the accolade from Arthur, Tristan is dubbed by Mark. Chrétien's retention of this old Celtic formula or his purposeful adoption of such a tradition may have been a compliment to Count Philip of Flanders,[31] the patron for whom *Perceval* was written, a nobleman who made knights.

The hero's second period of education, then, has noteworthy features unattributable to tradition and consequently interesting to examine for the style of Chrétien's narrative art. It is apparent that Chrétien used both the mother's and Gornemant's educational periods for the characterization of his hero. These two times of tutelage also are parallel in structure; they thereby affect the total framework of the romance.

Only Chrétien has this striking structural parallel between the two sets of Advice in the *enfance*. Each series has four injunctions. Each of the mother's injunctions is related, in exact order, to each of Gornemant's. In both, the first statement concerns a basic chivalric tenet: the achievement of honor through mercy. The mother, a woman interested in Perceval's behavior with other women, and Gornemant, a knight concerned with conduct with other knights, emphasize that mercy to a woman in distress and mercy to a vanquished knight represent the knightly services in which honor

30. Loomis, *op. cit.*, p. 360.
31. Helen Adolf identifies Philip of Flanders with Perceval himself, believing that the count's failure at the court of Jerusalem is paralleled by Perceval's failure at the Grail Castle (*op. cit.*, chap. i). However, the "failure" of the Grail Castle adventure is traditional to the Perceval story and needs no influence from contemporary events for its explication. In addition, Chrétien's description of the *Dümmling* would make rather dubious flattery. Rather, the courtliness and generosity of Gornemant is in harmony with the description of Philip, the "Alexander" of the poem's prologue.

resides. The second dicta of Advice concern speaking to others. The mother advises her son to say enough to gain necessary information ("Le non sachiez a la parsome" [561]), while Gornemant exhorts him to beware of saying too much. From the mother's point of view, courtesy requires asking questions; from Gornemant's, courtesy demands refraining from queries lest something rude be said. The third subject is advice itself. The mother requests him to take advice, Gornemant tells him to give it. This parallel explains Chrétien's unusual use of the word "advice," "conseilliez," (1660) at this point in Gornemant's speech where "help" or "aid" offered to a needy person would be the natural concept and expression. The final injunctions concern practice of religion. Both advisors suggest going to a minster to pray. The goals of prayer in both are the same: honor in this life, help in the next; when viewed together they are seen to be stated in a chiasmic construction:

Alez proiier nostre Seignor   Proiier celui qui tot a fet
Qu'an c'est siecle vos doint enor   Que de vostre ame merci et
Et si vos i doint contenir   Et qu'an cest siegle terriien
Qu'a bone fin puissiez venir.   Vos gart come son crestiien.
         (569-72)   (1667-70)

In addition, Chrétien expresses the results of these two parallel Advice series in three similarly constructed incidents of Perceval's attempts to adhere to precept. Chrétien thus makes a triad of adventures follow each of the two periods of education.

As so often in Chrétien, the bravura of his style masks his rigid structure. These two closely related periods of education in the *enfance* also have a structural parallel in the third educational period later in the poem: Perceval's meeting with his Hermit Uncle. Having followed chivalry for five years without ever once remembering God, Perceval, directed to the Hermit by knights and ladies doing penance, removes his armor, humbly supplicates forgiveness and aid, learns of his relationship to the holy man, receives penance, and remains in contrition in the forest hut for two days (6238 f.). This third period, like the two in the *enfance*, is biphasic: Instruction is given for atonement, and Advice for salvation. The Instruction consists of means of penance and methods of worship, interrupted at mid-point by four dicta of Advice. These Advice statements when read only in their context, or when reread after examining Wolfram's Trevrizent scene, appear unsalutory and artistically wrong. But when considered structurally, they reveal an exact inversion of the two previous, parallel series of injunctions in the *enfance*.

The Hermit's first statement, like the fourth counsels earlier, concerns religious practice: go to a minster, believe in God, love Him, and worship Him (6439-58). The second defines relationships with other people: Honor good men and women (6460)—just as the earlier third dicta consider the give and take of advice with men and women. The Hermit's third relates to manners with men which form an impression and express an inner state of being. Perceval is to rise in the presence of a priest, for this displays "umilité" (6461-64) ; just as in the second precepts in the *enfance* he is to speak enough to display politeness but not speak so much as to appear rude. The Hermit's fourth concern is chivalric conduct in which honor is derived from mercy and service: "help a maid, widow, or orphan, for in this lies the highest service" (6465-69). Perceval's mother and Gornemant make honor through mercy to ladies and knights their first precepts.

Chrétien's structural use of all three educational periods is apparent in a consideration of features common to the three tutors, their different subjects, methods, and effects upon the hero, and the evident progression in theme from Perceval's learning with his mother, through Gornemant's tutelage, to the final education by the Hermit.

Each tutor, once active in the way of life for which he trains Perceval, rejects that life for comparative seclusion, recognizes and states Perceval's need for education (to which Perceval promises obedience), gives him shelter, comfort, Instruction and Advice, plus symbolic clothing, and sends Perceval out into the world of chivalry. Whereas Perceval's mother teaches by answering questions, giving verbal Instruction, and stressing appearances, and whereas Gornemant teaches by asking questions, demonstrating techniques, and emphasizing actions, the Hermit hears confession, participates with Perceval in religious ritual and in penance, and concerns himself with right beliefs. About his education with his mother, Perceval cares little: he comes to her arrogantly determined to have the "knighthood" he saw, demands food ("A manjier me doner!" [491]) after she speaks, and hears Advice for which he has absolutely no preparation. For Gornemant's education he cares far more ("There is nothing I wish more in the world, not lands ..." [1459 f.]); he is invited to eat at the host's opulent table, and has some small degree of preparation for the Advice he receives. The Hermit's education he cares for most: in dread of having offended God, in tears, kneeling and begging for the counsel for which he has such need, Perceval does not absently accept nor enthusiastically request but humbly entreats knowledge; he is commanded to eat penance food of greens and spring water; and he has the most preparation possible for the Advice he receives. Knighthood alone, all Perceval had wished for in the Welsh forest, has proved insufficient. His mother's and Gornement's tuition bring him to Arthurian perfection. His chivalric excellence among knights is evidenced by the sixty knights he sends as captive to King Arthur's court (6233). His courtly finesse with women is exemplified first by the splendid scene in which a narrative conceit becomes a habit of mind—the knight, thinking of his beloved, stands in a trance of love at the sight of red drops of blood on newly fallen snow (4164 f.); second, by his fulsome and courteous greeting to Guinevere (4582 f.); and third, by his gentle kindness to the maiden who laughed (4596 f.). However, something beyond the mother's and Gornemant's education becomes necessary. Hence, the symbolic return is to learning in a forest of hornbeam trees.[32]

32. The only trees mentioned in Chrétien's descriptions are hornbeams and oaks, and these appear at dramatic junctures. Hornbeams and oaks are the trees of the Welsh forest in which Perceval lives with his mother; the young woman (Wolfram's Sigune), who mourns her headless lover, sits beneath an oak; Perceval ties his horse to a hornbeam in front of the Hermit's dwelling. It is entirely likely that these trees have symbolic significance. Information may be found in F. Cabrol (ed.), *Dictionnaire d'archéologie chrétienne et de liturgie* (Paris, 1907-1932); and E. Droulers, *Dictionnaire des attributs, allégories, emblèmes, et symboles* (Turnhout, 1950). Wolfram, interestingly enough, substitutes linden trees for Chrétien's hornbeams. No specific trees are mentioned in the *Waldleben*; Sigune sits beneath a linden; Gornemanz does

The three periods of education thus form a progress of culminations. The mother's education is the culmination of the *Waldleben*,
Gornemant's of the rustic *Dümmling's* existence, and the Hermit's
of the chivalric life unalloyed by Christianity. While *Perceval* is
not an *erziehungsroman*,[33] it is a romance of education.[34] Chrétien's hero does not learn from experience but, rather, is made to
experience the learning of which he had been deprived in the forest.
The careful construction of each educational incident and the
subordination of common romance episodes to exemplify and
amplify these periods of tutelage are aspects of Chrétien's poem
generally overlooked but worthy of appreciation. If this romance
is not read as an educational progress, much of its humor is obscured, many of its anachronisms are overemphasized, and Chrétien's evident architechtonic design is ignored.

However, the moral and religious possibilities of the *Dümmlingsmotif* are not truly developed by Chrétien. His Preceval has
no real spirituality, though he learns the manners of religion. His
religious education consists more in descriptions of churches and
learning of fixed prayers than in the realization through ritual of

so as well; and a linden tree is associated with Trevrizent. This tree, so
familiar to German fairy tales and to *Minnesang*, is surely symbolic. Such
symbolism is considered in A. T. Hatto's fascinating discussion: ''The Lime
Tree and Early German, Goliard, and English Lyric Poetry,'' *MLR*, XLIX
(1954), 205 f.

33. Often used to describe medieval literature, this term is entirely inappro-
priate to it. Originally coined to categorize psychological novels, the epithet
serves no purpose in medieval criticism. Professor W. T. H. Jackson's important reminder about the medieval view of character bears repeating:
''Character was determined by the presence or absence of virtues or vices, and
by a combination of them.'' As for the medieval hero, ''Events call forth the
virtues within him, and in many cases, the vice is purged from him by experience and suffering, but the interest lies in the full realization of the potential
character with which he is born.'' *The Literature of the Middle Ages* (New
York, 1960), p. 16.

34. David C. Fowler's denial that *Perceval* is a romance of education but
rather a romance of opposites, a psychological ''inner quest,'' seems misguided. His application of the methods and terminology of modern psychology
and psychoanalysis in *Prowess and Charity in the Perceval of Chrétien de
Troyes* (Seattle, 1959), is not a propos to medieval romance; while ingenious,
the study reads better as ''psychoanaliterature'' (after Willard Gaylin,
Columbia University Forum [June, 1963]) than medieval criticism. On education in the romances and the didactic qualities of these romances of education, Friedrich Heer offers suggestive comment (*The Medieval World*, trans.
Janet Sondheimer [Cleveland, 1962], pp. 143, 144).

a spiritual condition. Only in the Hermit's scene is there some religious interest—there is essentially none at the Grail Castle— but even the Hermit stresses superficial adherences to Church routine rather than recognition of a true faith. The total education of the *Dümmling* hero, his two periods of learning in the *enfance* and the final one with the Hermit, does not initiate new uses of chivalry nor new definitions of love. What Chrétien might have done with the many strands left loose in this unfinished poem will never be known, but the work as it exists, with Perceval's adventures ending at the Hermit's hut, gives no hint of a deeply devotional nor moral conclusion.

The latent themes and inherent beauties in Chrétien's subject have their consummate statement in Wolfram von Eschenbach's *Parzival.* In Wolfram's poem the goal of chivalry is Christian fellowship, and the aim of life is fruitful marriage. The education of the hero, which occupies most of Book III of *Parzival,* accentuates the differences in poetic intentions and in artistic methods of the French and German poets. While Chrétien must have been Wolfram's "main source,"[35] other Perceval versions[36] and other romance traditions[37] may have contributed. But Wolfram's own predilections seem to have been the catalysts for this new compound of familiar elements.

Parzival, like Perceval, has two periods of education in the *enfance,* one with his mother, Herzeloide, the other with Gurnemanz de Graharz. Each of these periods, also like Perceval's, has two separate phases, one of Instruction and one of Advice. In comparing Wolfram's with Chrétien's romance, subtle differences between the first periods of education and the more dramatic dif-

35. Otto Springer, "Wolfram von Eschenbach's *Parzival,*" in *ALMA,* p. 224. Cf. J. Fourquet, *Wolfram d'Eschenbach et le Conte del Graal* (Paris, 1938); G. Weber, *Wolfram von Eschenbach, seine dichterische und geistesgeschichtliche Bedeutung* (Frankfurt, 1928), I, 1-152; and Ehrismann, *Geschichte,* III (1927), 237-46.

36. F. Panzer, *Gahmuret: Quellenstudien zur Wolframs Parzival* (Heidelberg, 1940); M. F. Richey, *Gahmuret Anschevin* (Oxford, 1923). Cf. B. Mergell, *Wolfram von Eschenbach und seine französischen quellen* (Münster, 1936).

37. Since Books I, II, and great parts of IX, in addition to much incident and characterization in the other books, have no suggestion in Chrétien but affinities with particular literary and historical examples, Panzer's hypotheses for Wolfram's eclecticism are convincing (*op. cit.*).

ferences between the second periods mark Wolfram's moralization
of the Perceval-Grail theme.

Raised by his Queen Mother in the Forest of Soltane, Parzival is
permitted but one pastime of his royal heritage: hunting—and this
only by crossbow and gabylôt. He displays his noble sensitivity
and spiritual yearnings by his childhood sorrow at the song of
birds. Seeing the distress the birds cause her son, Herzeloide commands their deaths, until Parzival, in even greater anguish and
mystification at this cruelty, demands peace for them; in his
mother's admission that she cannot alter the eternal order, he
learns about God and the Devil (119:17-28). To Herzeloide's sub-
missive, "Wes wende ich sîn gebot/der doch ist der hoehste got?"
(119:13-14), Parzival asks the question: "Ôwê muoter, was is
got?" (119:17). He is taught that God is brighter than daylight,
that God must be prayed to when there is trouble—"sîn triwe der
werlde ie helfe bôt"—and that the "Master of Hell" who is black
and faithless must be shunned, and so must be "zwîvels," incon-
stancy and wavering (119:26-29). "Sîn muoter underschiet im
gar/daz vinster und daz lieht gevar" (119:29-30). Armed only
with this religious Instruction, Parzival encounters knights in the
forest whom he believes God(s) because of their "bright shining,"
—calls them "ritter got," "got," "helfericher got," even after
their denials of divinity—and from them learns that knighthood is
bestowed by King Arthur. Returning to his mother, he begs leave
and a horse, and receives, in addition to a bad mare and fool's garments, four dicta of Advice: (1) On untrodden paths beware of
dark fords; where it is light, ride boldly in; (2) Be polite and give
people greetings; (3) Follow the teaching of a man grey with age,
if he is willing to counsel "zuht"; and (4) Take a woman's ring
and greeting; "ez tuot dir kumbers buoz." Kiss her and clasp her
tight in your embrace; that will bring happiness and high spirit,
"op si kiusche ist unde guot." Herzeloide also reveals that a certain knight, Lähelîn, murdered Parzival's father and wrested
away his three domains. The youth promises vengeance with his
gabylôt (127:11-128:12).

The differences between this first period of education and that
in Chrétien are many. Whereas Chrétien presents the religious

Instruction as background revealed in dramatic action, Wolfram
makes the Instruction a separate scene. While every other version
except Chrétien's also has an Instruction incident, Wolfram moti-
vates it by the delightful vignette of the bird song and Parzival's
sorrow, which serves first to introduce immediately the theme of
the hero's inborn nobility (of heart and compassion) and to make
the youth's question, "was is got?" meaningful. This question, not
present in Chrétien and long a matter of learned dispute,[38] surely
is traditional to Perceval story. Testimony to this is its presence in
the crude English romance of *Sir Perceval*, which represents one of
the earliest forms of Perceval's adventures.[39] This metrical
romance—without Grail, without Grail company, without the
demise of the hero's mother, and replete with witches, magic oint-
ments, and burning of enemies—could hardly have been influenced
by Wolfram's poem;[40] but intermingled with the bizarre traditional elements[41] is the hero's very question: "Whatkyns a God
may þat be?" That Wolfram fully realized in the traditional
question the possibility for display of pure innocence (not folly,
as it appears in the other versions), that he so exquisitely motivated
it, and that he let it return at Parzival's spiritual crises—these display the excellence of Wolfram's meaningful transformation of old
themes. Recognition of such emendation, consistent as it is with the
poetic methods of the whole poem, gives better insight into Wolfram's art, than, denying the evidence of other poems, assertions of
Wolfram's "invention."[42] The mother's answer to the question,

38. Springer maintains that the question "was created by Wolfram and no
one else. Why should we continue to hunt for dubious parallels and unknown
sources to which to credit all artistic talent and invention that we find in a
work such as *Parzival?* Why not rather credit such talent and invention to the
poets well known to us?" (*ALMA*, p. 227). Agreeing with this interpretation
are Mühlhausen, in *ZRP*, XLIV (1924), 465-543, and Mergell, *op. cit.* However, the other Perceval poems, which have too many parallels to this question,
its antecedents, and its aftermath to be the result of chance, surely cannot be
considered "dubious parallels" or "unknown sources." The points of similarity between these poems and Wolfram have been amply and undeniably documented by Miss Weston, *op. cit.*, pp. 85 f.; Strucks, *op. cit.*, pp. 8-28; and
Griffith, *op. cit.*, pp. 14-39.
39. Griffith, *op. cit.*, *passim*; Weston, *op. cit.*, pp. 92-93; Strucks, *op. cit.*,
pp. 8-28, 74 f.
40. Griffith, *op. cit.*, p. 27.
41. *Ibid.*, pp. 116-31; Loomis, *op. cit.*, pp. 338, 364, 403, *et passim*.
42. Cf. Springer, *ALMA*, p. 227; Mergell, *op. cit.*; and Mühlhausen, *op. cit.*

however, is more significant than the query itself. Parzival, unlike Perceval, learns nothing about angels, either malign or good. Two apects of her Instruction, which have no mention in Chrétien, are important as the initial statements of basic themes of the whole romance: the attribution of fidelity, "triwe," as God's characteristic, and the antithesis of it, "untriwe," as that of the Devil;[43] and the emphasis upon white and black, light and dark, both as descriptive characteristics and as symbols.[44]

Herzeloide's Advice in Wolfram's poem differs from the mother's in Chrétien's more than does the Instruction. This Advice may also illuminate a few otherwise unexplained features in Chrétien's poem and suggests the common tradition from which both Chrétien and Wolfram drew. Like the Chrétien Advice, that in Wolfram has four dicta. But there is no religious interest here, nothing to correspond to Chrétien's fourth counsel concerning church-going. Wolfram's first injunction, with its characteristics of folk tale[45] and of the Irish *geis*,[46] is advice against crossing dark fords.[47] Wolfram's second counsel, to be polite and give greeting to

43. Wolfram specifically makes "triwe" the signal attribute of Herzeloide, and also of Parzival her son. There is an intimation in the characterization of Gahmuret in Books I and II that although he possesses "manliche triwe" (107:25), he does not possess spiritual "triwe" because he aspires too high and becomes the ultimate victim of his own need for reknown (I, 7:28-30; 9:26-28; 13:12-14; II, 109:23). Herzeloide says of him: "den nam mir sîn vrechiu ger" (II, 109:23). A sympathetic and masterly study of Wolfram's characterization of Gahmuret is M. F. Richey, *Gahmuret Anschevin*.

44. The light and dark symbolism in this poem is striking and has often been recognized. On its relationship to Biblical symbolism, see Wapnewski, *op. cit.*, pp. 55 f. Again and again, Wolfram couples his references to light and dark with "magpie" imagery—in the "Vorgeschichte," "blame and praise both come to the dauntless man's spirit, which is black-and-white-mixed, like the plumage of the magpie" (3-6); Belacane's name, she whose special quality of character is "triwe," means "magpie-colored"; the skin of Feirefis is black and white like the magpie's coloring (XVI, 805-806). I know of no discussion of symbolic references to magpies, although there are several studies of other bird symbolism, such as that of the goldfinch and eagle. (H. Friedmann, *The Symbolic Goldfinch, its History and Significance in European Devotional Art* [Washington, 1946]; and G. Ferguson, *Signs and Symbols in Christian Art* [New York, 1960], pp. 13-14.)

45. See S. Thompson, *Motif-Index of Folk Literature* (6 vols.; Bloomington, 1958) Chapter "H" on "Tests" and Chapter "C" on "Tabu"; and Aarne, *op. cit.*, Nos. 1691 f.

46. See J. R. Reinhard, *The Survival of 'Geis' in Medieval Romance* (Halle, 1933).

47. Although there is no such prohibition in Chrétien's poem, yet the hero

those met, may correspond to the second in Chrétien, which is to be polite and ask the names of people met. The third principle, to follow the teachings of an elderly man, is identical to that in Chrétien except for phraseology. Wolfram's fourth dictum represents a significant departure from Chrétien's and is one which receives even more emphasis in Parzival's second period of tutelage. Herzeloide's Advice about behavior with women, superficially corresponding to the first proposition of the mother in Chrétien, specifies the object of Parzival's affections and predicts the effects of love upon him. Her emphasis upon chastity and goodness as the woman's necessary qualities returns again in Gurnemanz' Advice about women and marriage, and still later appears as the special qualities of Parzival's beloved and wife, Conduiramors.

Another difference between the mothers' Advice in the two versions is the presence in the German of the vengeance motif, which has no place in the French. Wolfram presents the subject of Lähelîn several times again: Sigune speaks of him (141:7); Parzival accuses the Red Knight whom he is about to kill, "du maht wol wesen Lähelîn/von dem mir klaget diu muoter mîn" (154:25-6); and Trevrizent later asks Parzival, "Hêrre, sît irz Lähelîn?" (474:1). The presence of this *Rachemotif* in the *enfance* removes some of the senseless barbarity from Parzival's murder of Ither the Red Knight by implying vengeance as the hero's mistaken motive; more probably than not, this motif was present in the earliest versions of Perceval story,[48] and Wolfram, finding it, retained it and put it to use, whereas Chrétien rejected it entirely. Interestingly enough, Parzival's promise of vengeance, his last words to his mother after the four dicta, corresponds to Perceval's promise to go to church to pray, also the final words after the mother's four counsels. It would not have been impossible for Chrétien to have substituted conventional religious practice for

---

twice avoids crossing black rivers into which he "dares not descend" even though he believes the object of his quest, his mother, to be on the opposite shore. Before coming to Gornemant's castle and before the Grail Castle, Perceval fears to cross the dark fords (1305 f.; 2985 f.).

48. Strucks, *op. cit.*, pp. 46 f., 74; Griffith, *op. cit.*, p. 126; Loomis, *op. cit.*, pp. 394-414.

the original vengeance quest, and then the promise to adhere to religious manners for the promise to avenge a death.

Herzeloide's Instruction and Advice lead Parzival to the same humorous attempts, as in the French poem, to put counsel into action. The religious Instruction affects the encounter with the knights, and the Advice causes the three incidents of blunder, those of the tent, King Arthur's court, and Gurnemanz' castle. The differences between the two versions, however, are not only in narrative details but also in emphases. In Chrétien, the hero's three errors of mistaken identifications, mistaken applications, and mistaken expectations of functions are discernible in each adventure and gain force and humor from an almost incremental repetition. Chrétien delights in his hero's rustic incongruities and constructs each such example in similar fashion. Wolfram, on the other hand, while maintaining the episodes, while embellishing them with even more hilarious details, while emphasizing his hero's literal interpretation of what he hears and his repetitions of "Thus, my mother told me," yet does not dwell upon similar structures nor multiple errors. Only the mistaken applications (of behavior with ladies, acquisition of armor, and use of horse and arms) are congruent. There is no *pater noster* to the tent nor prayer for food, no misinterpretation of Kay's jest nor erroneous expectation of armor (for Arthur does "give" Parzival arms), and no mistake of hospitality at Graharz for anything more than it is. The single dictum of Advice which is repeated in young Parzival's misapplied obedience is his giving of greetings to all whom he meets. (The counsel possibly comparable in Chrétien—to ask names of those met—is there used only once.) Thus, the lady of the tent (132:23), people on his path (138:7), Signe (138:25), all knights, all merchants (145:9), the members of the Round Table (148:4), and the king and queen (148:14 f.), are greeted and told, "sus riet min muoter!" In fact, his mock-heroic threat to Ither the Red Knight, if he denies Parzival his armor, is: "widersagt sî dir mîn gruoz/ob du mirz ungerne gîst!" (154:8-9).

The qualities of Instruction and Advice in the two poems are similar, but Wolfram gives them different setting and in so doing transforms them. Herzeloide's tutelage is concerned with appearances and is given in simple yet symbolic language. By fuller characterization of both tutor and son, by reduction of Chrétien's emphasis upon foolish behavior in the attempts to use the education, and by specifying what is briefly suggested in Chrétien, the significance of inherited characteristics, Wolfram changes the intention and the effect of these *enfance* scenes.

Herzeloide, "ein stam der diemüete" (128:28), the paragon of women, is nobler, more resourceful, more the woman of conflict than Perceval's mother. Even discounting Wolfram's earlier characterization of Herzeloide in Books I and II of his poem, her characteristics within the *enfance* period are made specific—and later made to live in her son. Fidelity is her spiritual name. Pity is her signal expression of heart. But her instincts toward pity are distracted by a selfish desire. Her strangling of the birds to keep her son from anguish (118:23 f.) is an example; it parallels her attempt to stifle Parzival's chivalric heritage and destiny as a Christian knight. In both episodes her "triwe" and "pity" make her submit, after protest and reconciliation, to the inevitability of God's plan. Her final protest is purposefully to send Parzival out of the forest into the world of chivalry dressed, not as a Welshman, as he is in Chrétien, but as a fool—his horse is a thoroughly bad one (126:22-23), his clothes are in the square cut of the "tôren Kleider" (126:26-127:5)—in the hope that mockery may drive him home again to her. Her final reconciliation is in her death (128:17-22), which significantly differs from Chrétien's version. Parzival is not told in detail of her sorrow at his departure, and, not having seen her death swoon, he is not guilty, as is Chrétien's Perceval, of a youth's spiritual failure of compassion.

Wolfram's characterization of Parzival also is not so dependent upon the qualities of the tutelage and the qualities of the student as is Chrétien's. Wolfram portrays his hero not merely as rustic but as the prince as rustic. The numerous descriptions of the more opulent *Waldleben*[49] and, especially, the poet's epithets for his hero stress nobility. Whereas Chrétien indicates that his naïve hero

49. Examples include Herzeloide's extensive lands, the large number of her servants, and the jewelry of her ladies in waiting. See Weston, *op. cit.*, p. 86, and Griffith, *op. cit.*, p. 21.

has a heritage of noble blood, Wolfram consistently calls Parzival "le fils du roi," "the prince," "the noble youth," "the high born lad," and portrays him as leaving the forest imbued with two noble heritages. On the one hand, from his father, Gahmuret, Parzival inherits chivalric nobility without its refinements of spirit. Like his father, Parzival has all the physical capabilities of a superlative knight, but he also has a "wavering," "inconstant"[50] temperament. (Volatile and quick to anger, Parzival kills Ither in a paroxysm of rage at being struck [155:1 f.] ; at the Grail Castle he clenches his fists until blood flows, when he believes himself the butt of a joke he does not understand [229:1 f.] ; he leaves the Grail Castle shouting and shrieking in anger when he finds the halls deserted [247:1 f.].) So too, Gahmuret's flaw is a too pervasive arrogance (I, 9:26-28; 13:12-14; II, 109:23). From his mother Herzeloide, on the other hand, Parzival inherits "triwe," that fidelity of spirit which permits pity of undeserved suffering. Indeed, it is the paired characteristics of fidelity and pity—those same which are united in Herzeloide's definition of God and in Wolfram's description of Herzeloide—which are temporarily obscured in Parzival's spiritual progress.

Whereas Chrétien's *enfance* episodes are strictly structured to demonstrate the results of education, Wolfram uses the theme of inherent qualities similarly to inform a symmetrical frame. In the *enfance* Wolfram presents six scenes which represent the conflict between the two heritages from Parzival's parents. Of these six, three episodes intimate Herzeloide's legacy, three, Gahmuret's. The first triad is constructed around a single theme: young Parzival's sensibility to undeserved suffering and his desire to alleviate it. The incident with the birds in the forest demonstrates this pity as a profoundly personal trait, the sensitivity of the child untouched by learning. Second, the meeting with his cousin Sigune mourning over her slain lover Schionatulander indicates Parzival's pity for a vassal and kinsman, slain and unavenged because of himself, and evokes his chivalric rectitude and respect for family. Third, his pity for Cunneware and Antenor, unjustly dishonored at court because of him, exemplifies his laudable instinct in a courtly situation.

50. Book I, 7:28-30; 9:26-8; Book II, 90:28; 90:3, 4; 96.

Counterbalancing these three episodes displaying pity are three incidents in which Parzival's inherent tendency is distracted by desires for knighthood. First, his desire to become a knight overcomes his affection for Herzeloide and her wish for him to remain in the forest; second, his arrogant will for Ither's red armor violates chivalric honor and bonds of kinship; finally, Parzival's pity for Gurnemanz and affection for his daughter Liaze are deflected by his desire for knightly trial and fame.

These three incidents of pity distracted by desire parallel in type the previous three displays of pity: the first, a personal lapse, the second, a violation of chivalry and kinship, and the third, an imperfection in courtly behavior. In all six incidents Parzival causes undeserved suffering to those with whom he comes in contact; each of the people, either Parzival's blood relative or prospective kin by marriage, sustains punishment for the chivalric life. Thus, in incidents following the first period of education, Wolfram portrays his hero's double heritage of Gahmuret and Herzeloide in conflict— each heritage causing episodes of merit or fault, and each leading to a triad of encounters demonstrating a personal, chivalric, or courtly characteristic.

Just as noteworthy as this structural balance of inherited characteristics centered about the first learning period is Wolfram's portrait of Parzival as a child. While Chrétien insistently calls his hero a youth, Wolfram makes him behave like one. In the scene with the birds, young Parzival, so overwhelmed with beauty and sadness, is unable to explain his grief to his concerned mother—"ern kunde es ir gesagen niht/als kinden lîhte noch geschiht" (118:21-22). Before meeting the knights, he is seen delighting in the child's pleasures of investigating natural things, as when he breaks a leaf for the whistle that it makes (120:13). Neither example is found in Chrétien. In the scene comparable to the meeting with the knights, Perceval is described as casting javelins hither and yon. Different from Chrétien's hero's too are Parzival's numerous references to his mother: his assertions of ingenuous bravery before the expected devils who are knights: "I'll stand up to them, although my mother would fear to"—"ich waene ir ellen sî verzagt" (120:22); his telling the hour of the day by his mother's time of awakening, she who, aging, "kan sô vil niht wachen" (166:9)! The latter example is original to Wolfram; in the earlier, Chrétien's Perceval says nothing about his mother's daunted courage. The changes Wolfram makes are small but characteristic of his realism in describing his rustic prince as a child.

In addition to his portrait of Parzival as a child, Wolfram has other child characters in the romance. All of these are without origin in Chrétien or in other direct literary source. "Kleine Obilot," for example, no matter what her ultimate prototype may be[51] and despite the fact that she serves as humorous "Mistress Little Sleeves" to amorous Gawain, is portrayed as a little girl whose first concerns are for her dolls and her friends (VII, 369:1 f.). The Gray Pilgrim's daughters (Book IX), who politely though insistently contradict their father and who entreat Parzival to join them in Good Friday penance, are young girls who, like children, are fond of their little dogs and who, like nubile adolescents, have eyes for a gallant knight (448:27 f.). Even Parzival's own son Loherangrin has the characteristics of the young boy whose ambivalence between obedience to parents and hesitancy to greet strangers makes him unwilling to kiss his dark-skinned uncle Feirefis: "dô der was swarz unde wîz/Der knabe sîn wolde küssen niht" (805:30-806:1).

Not only does Wolfram depict these children realistically but he makes reference to children in analogy and in narrative detail. The analogy to the dangerously swaying bridge at Belrepaire is to children swinging: as children swing in swings, and we do not want to stop them, so swayed the bridge, but without a rope: "diun was vor jugende niht sô geil" (181:7-10). At King Arthur's court, not only are the expected courtiers and entertainers present, but children of the castle run forth to stare at the awkward young Parzival and noisily mill round him (147:12). This presence of children and child characters in medieval romances is unusual, and their realistic representation is even more rare in the works of Wolfram's contemporaries.[52] In narrative and in lyric poetry,

51. See W. Stapel, "Die kleine Obilot," Deutsches Volkstum., XVIII (1936), 108-14.
52. An interesting consideration of child themes and characterizations in

children usually appear as symbols of innocence, guilelessness, purity of emotion, or of specific theological virtues.[53] Only in later medieval writers can there be found children portrayed realistically.[54] Wolfram's portrait of Parzival as a child and his inclusion of other references to children are consistent with his tendency toward realism in the romance and are indicative of the difference in moral temper between Chrétien's celebration of courtly love, in which children have no place, and Wolfram's exaltation of courteous love within the frame of marriage.

The differences in moral intention and artistic expression between Chrétien and Wolfram are even more striking in the

medieval German literature is F. C. Arnold, *Das Kind in der deutschen Literatur des XI-XV Jahrhunderts* (Griefswald, 1905).

53. Random examples are Heinrich von Morungen's ''Mirst geschen'' to exemplify the use of child reference in lyric; and the characters of Galahad in the *Vulgate Queste*, and Pearl in the English alliterative poem which bears her name, as romance and narrative instances.

54. For example, the English Isaac of the *Brome MS* play; Chaucer's child characters (Maurice in ''Man of Law's Tale,'' Virginia in ''Physician's Tale,'' Hugolino's sons in ''Monk's Tale,'' the ''little clergeoun'' in ''Prioress' Tale,'' and Griselda's children in ''Clerk's Tale''); and in French national epic, William's delightful nephew Guiot in the *Chançun de Guillaume*. F. Fellinger, *Das Kind in der altfranzösischen Literatur* (Göttingen, 1908), considers the references to children in about ninety Old French texts.

A recent book which summarily ignores Wolfram, as well as almost all medieval literature, in its judgments about medieval ''child concepts'' is Philippe Ariès, *Centuries of Childhood: A Social History of Family Life* (New York, 1963). A ''demographic historian,'' Ariès claims that the Middle Ages cannot even be considered the opposite of ''child centered'' since it lacked any distinct conception of childhood. See D. Wrong's review of this in *Scientific American* (April, 1963), pp. 181 f.

Medieval representation of children has excited the interest of psychologists, anthropologists, and folklorists. Suggestive studies which have bearing upon the *enfance*—works which frequently are more significant for their documentation than their conclusions—include: A. Morillot, ''De la condition des enfants nés hors mariage dans l'antiquité et au moyen-âge,'' *Revue historique du droit français et étranger*, XII (Paris, 1866); P. Saintyves (pseudonym for E. Nourry), *Les vierges mères et les naissances miraculeuses* (Paris, 1908); Lord Raglan, *The Hero, A Study in Tradition, Myth, and Drama* (London, 1949); Joseph Campbell, *The Hero with a Thousand Faces* (New York, 1956); C. Jung, *Das göttliche Kind* and *Das göttliche Mädchen* (both, Amsterdam, 1941); H. Ploss, *Das Kind in Sitte und Brauch der Völker* (Leipzig, 1884); A. F. Chamberlain, *The Child and Childhood in Folk-Thought* (New York, London, 1896); M. B. Ogle, ''The Discovery of the Wonder Child,'' *American Philosophical Association, Proceedings and Transactions*, LIX (1928), 179-204; and H. Scherb, *Das Motif vom starken Knaben in den Märchen der Weltliteratur* (Tübingen, Stuttgart, 1930).

second period of education, the Instruction and Advice of Gurnemanz de Graharz (162:1-179:12). While this long scene is cer-
tainly modeled upon Chrétien's, the changes made by Wolfram are
almost as significant as his transformation of the later "Hermit
Uncle" scene into the Trevrizent episode. Close examination of the
French Gornemant and German Gurnemanz scenes makes it difficult to join the scholarly consensus proclaiming their essential
similarity.[55] The French and German incidents differ basically in
two aspects: the order and content of the education, and the characterization of the tutor. The education of Wolfram's Parzival
gives counsel for a type of love that is not courtly, and for a type
of chivalry that is not selfish—not merely proof of individual
prowess—but social in intention and in achievement. The role of
Gurnemanz is augmented by his fuller characterization, by an attendant personage, his daughter Liaze, and by realistic detail.

Riding clumsily in his ill-gotten armor, Parzival approaches the
dignified, gray-haired Gurnemanz, tells of his mother's Advice
about elderly men and greetings, and asks a night's hospitality.
After having removed his armor, only after much coaxing, Parzival
stands awkward yet radiant in his fool's garments. After Gurnemanz' momentary hesitation to be host to a fool, Parzival is invited
to mass, at which he receives religious Instruction; then, to dinner,
after which he receives a long series of Advice dicta; and finally, to
ride horseback, at which time he receives Instruction in chivalry
and then distinguishes himself in chivalric games. Gurnemanz
instructs his daughter Liaze to tender to their guest's every wish,
which she does with sweetness and propriety; he then offers her to
Parzival as bride, along with the kingdom which might have been
left to his three sons, whose deaths in jousts he laments. Although
recognizing his host's sorrow, Parzival, refusing both wife and
domain until he can prove himself in combat, leaves Graharz after
a fourteen-day stay.

Narrative components appearing in Wolfram's version emphasize the development of the three relationships between the hero

55. Springer, *op. cit.*, p. 229; G. Keferstein, *Parzivals ethischer Weg,
Ritterlicher Lebenstil im deutschen Hochmittelalter* (Weimar, 1937), pp.
35 f.

and his second tutor which are observed in more rudimentary form
in Chrétien: their bonds of religion, chivalry, and love. In Chrétien, there is no mass and no religious Instruction; only the fourth
Advice injunction concerns religious practice. Wolfram's Parzival
is taught to make the offering and the sign of the Cross and thus
foil the Devil—"der wirt zer messe in lêrte/daz noch die saelde
mêrte" (169:17-18); the Advice, however, unlike Chrétien's, contains nothing regarding religious practice. Gurnemanz' task is the
instruction of the hero in practical applications of religious belief
(just as it is in the chivalric), as opposed to Herzeloide's more
general and descriptive approach to religion. Chrétien, in a simpler
narrative scheme, gives the hero's mother both of these functions.
Wolfram's attribution of religious Instruction to Gurnemanz may
have prompted him to invert the order of the educational phases
as they had appeared in Chrétien, for Wolfram makes chivalric
Instruction follow Advice and in so doing changes the nature of
both of these phases. The Advice, long and complex, and with
specific structural importance, will be considered separately. In
Wolfram and Chrétien the Instructions in practical chivalry concur in teaching the youth how to spur a horse and to carry a shield.
While Chrétien's Perceval learns to hold the lance and pennon,
Wolfram's Parzival is taught to urge the horse to the charge and to
properly lower the spear. While both tutors instruct the hero by
example, Wolfram's Gurnemanz does not teach by asking questions,
does not state an educational theory about nurturing the noble
nature, and does not request his student to practice thrice the
skills demonstrated. Rather, Parzival is made to display dramatically his father's heritage of chivalric aptitude by taking the
prize in the bohurt organized for his instruction (173:13-175:11).
   The duration of the second period of education in Chrétien is
but a single night, whereas Parzival's is two weeks long. Rather
than Perceval's desire to return to his mother, Parzival gives a
chivalric justification for leaving his host. Most importantly, although Wolfram heightens the chivalric detail and incident in this
section of the *enfance*, Gurnemanz nonetheless does not knight
Parzival. Book IV opens with a description of the hero as bearing
"ritters site und ritters mâl" (179:14), and as having lost his

"tumpheit" (179:23). But there is no "swertleite." A final narrative component found only in Wolfram is the new character,
Liaze.[56] She and the purity of her love foreshadow the perfection
of Parzival's next encounter with a woman, his beloved Conduiramors, and his marriage to her. Liaze tightens the tie between her
father and his student by making Gurnemanz (not only eventual
uncle, but) Parzival's prospective father-in-law, thus giving the
older knight the hope of the successor and son for whom he yearns.

The content of the education period with Gurnemanz has been
seen to differ from Chrétien in the Instruction phases, but the
differences between the Advices are much more. The French Gornemant's four dicta are concise and concern chivalric honor, speaking
with others, advice, and religious worship. Wolfram's, with its far
greater length, its discursive charm, and its anomalous sentence
structures which make it difficult to see where exposition ends and
amplificatio begins, oddly has been neglected by critics and dismissed as a mere copy of Chrétien. But the Advice of Gurnemanz
states, in theory, concerns of the poet which appear later in characterization and in action; in the guise of an intelligent "father's"
wise words to his "son," Gurnemanz' Advice sententiously expresses the conceptions of love and chivalry which differentiate the
German from the French poem.[57] A close reading reveals both a

56. Springer, *op. cit.*, p. 229, and Mergell, *op. cit.*, pp. 64-66, believe Enite
of Hartmann's *Erek* to be the prototype of Liaze, but there are only vague
similarities between the two ladies. Griffith, *op. cit.*, pp. 70, 77, suggests
that Liaze is remotely related to a female relative of the hero who appeared
in some early version of Perceval story. "Wolfram did not invent Liaze;
she was an integral part of his source" (p. 70). This theory, suggesting that
a female character may have been joined to the hero at an early point in his
adventures, but not that Wolfram's characterization of her has traditional
origin, has merit.

57. Numerous critics have considered Wolfram's conception of ideal chivalry, but, while examining Books VI and IX in detail, they have given little
emphasis to Gurnemanz and his teachings in Book III. There has been no
study of the specific contents, literary function, or structure of this Advice
section. Some discussion on Gurnemanz is found in F. Lichtenstein, "Zur
Parzivalfrage," *Beiträge*, XXII (1897), 10 f.; W. Mielke, *Die Characterentwicklung Parzivals* (Gartz, 1904); A. Misch in *DVLG*, V (1926), 213; G.
Keferstein, *op. cit.*, pp. 35 f.; W. Mohr, "Parzivals ritterliche Schuld,"
Wirkendes Wort, II (Feb.-March, 1952), 151 f.; W. J. Schröder, *Der Ritter
zwischen Gott und Welt: Idee und Problem des Parzivalroman Wolframs von
Eschenbach* (Weimar, 1952), pp. 191-92; and M. F. Richey, *Studies of
Wolfram von Eschenbach* (London, 1957), pp. 115 f., and especially pp. 127-29.

definite structure for the whole Advice section and a progression
in types of counsels which represent noteworthy variation upon
Chrétien's Advice pattern.

In Gurnemanz' attempt "to tame a wild will" (170:8), there
are twelve dicta. Separation into injunctions is not so easy as it is
in Chrétien's simpler scheme, for most counsels are either prefaced
or followed by comment or *amplificatio*. However, the following
reading may be proposed. Instead of Chrétien's four statements,
Wolfram has twelve which compose four successive categories.
First comes a triad of ethical and spiritual counsels: (1) Never
lose your sense of shame "ir sult niemer iuch verschemn," for the
shameless man is always molting, always shedding his honor; (2)
Have compassion for the needy, particularly the poor man of good
birth, for his shame is the hardest to bear; and thus: "swenne ir
dem tuot kumbers buoz/sô nâhet iu der gotes gruoz" (171:3-4);
and (3) As a lord, be both poor and rich appropriately; make
"maze" your rule. Then follows the statement, somewhat anachronistic in its position, "I see that you need Advice." Such
statement of the hero's deprivation of knowledge is traditional to
almost all versions.[58] The four counsels which follow it form the
second category of Advice, concerning polite behavior directly ap-
plicable to daily life. (4) Leave "unfuoge," bad behavior, to its
own quarrel (171:16); (5) Do not ask too many questions; (6) Do
not ignore thoughtful answers; (7) You can see, hear, taste, and
smell; let these senses bring you wisdom. Third is a pair of chivalric injunctions, the first theoretical, the second, practical. (8)
Let mercy accompany daring. "Sus tuot mir râtes volge schîn"
(171:26). Let the surrendered knight live; and (9) After you
wear armor, wash off the rust from your face, "sô wert ir min-
neclîch gevar." The fourth category consists of a triad of rules for
behavior with women. (10) Be manly and cheerful, for this brings
honor and praise from ladies; (11) Let women be dear to you; do

58. For example, the hero in *Peredur* is said to be so ignorant that he cannot differentiate between goats and hinds; in *Sir Perceval*, he knows "neither
nurture nor lore"; Carduino believes that only the animals, his mother, and
himself are the whole of creation; in the "Bliocadran," the hero is said to
have "very little sense."

not waver from their service; lies may deceive many of them, but
true love is not based upon deception;

dâ wirt der slîchaere klage
daz dürre holz ime hage
daz pristet unde krachet
der wahtaere erwachet;
(172:17-20)

and finally, (12) Know that husband and wife are united as are
the sun and the day; they are inseparable; both blossom from one
seed. At this conclusion, Parzival bows his thanks and stops talking about his mother, "mit rede, und in dem herzen niht; als noch
getriwem man geschiht" (170:12-173:10).

These four categories were probably modeled upon Chrétien's
four dicta. Each of Chrétien's injunctions can be found in Wolfram, but two of them in significantly changed form. Chrétien's
first, regarding mercy to vanquished knights, is paralleled by
Wolfram's eighth; the French second, against too much talking,
by the German fifth. Chrétien's enjoining of "advice" to women
in distress does not specifically appear, but similar strictures on
conduct with women are Wolfram's tenth and eleventh enjoinders.
But Wolfram's twelfth, dealing with the perfection of marriage,
has no suggestion in Chrétien; the French Gornemant advises only
for courtly love. In place of Chrétien's fourth counsel concerning
church and worship, Wolfram has the first triad of ethical precepts[59] in which state of soul and man's relationship to God are
the like subjects differently treated. Where Chrétien discusses the
outer expressions of ritual, Wolfram dwells upon the moral achievements of *humilitas, misericordia,* and *mesura.*

This triad of ethical virtues, significant for its position as
Gurnemanz' introductory counsels as well as for its content, is
directed not only to Parzival as new knight but to Parzival as

59. Hermann Heckel in *Das ethische Wortfeld im Wolframs Parzival*
(Würzburg, 1939), discusses all the words of ethical import in the poem, their
number, type, and meaning for the romance. Cf. Schröder's exceptions to
Heckel's interpretations, in *Der Ritter,* pp. 193 f. Fascinating ancillary
material on ethical statements, on sententious sayings, and on their traditional
backgrounds is found in Blanche Colton Williams' *Gnomic Poetry in Anglo-
Saxon* (New York, 1914), pp. 1-81.

prince. These dicta contain reference to his position as leader of men—"ir mugt wol volkes hêrre sîn" (170:22)—and his consequent responsibilities of personal morality and social justice. Similar configurations of moral statements are common in early medieval *miroirs de princes*[60] and in the works of clerical theorists of the day.[61] They are most unusual in the *enfance* of a knight, and no other romance text has a comparable interest, except the *Prose Lancelot*, which will be discussed in the next chapter. The function of these three enjoinders appears to be twofold. First, they form an early theoretical statement of Parzival's ultimate achievements after trial, which are displayed later in the poem as a dramatic progress. Second, this group of virtues, proposed as attainments not merely for personal salvation[62] but as achievements in a social context, adumbrates the specific qualities required of the prince who is to become king of the Grail Fellowship.

60. Examples include Isidore of Seville, *De Principis Honestate*, in *PL*, LXXXII-LXXXIV; Jonas of Orléans, *De Institutione Rego*, ed. J. Reviron, *Les idées politico-religieuses d'un évêque du IXᵉ siècle* (Paris, 1930); and Hincmar of Rheims, *De Regis Persona et Regio Ministerio*, in *PL*, CXXV. Analyses of these and other earlier and later *miroirs* may be found in L. K. Born, "The *Specula Principum* of the Carolingian Renaissance," *Revue belge de philologie et d'histoire*, XII (1933), 583-612, and the same author's Introduction to his translation of Erasmus' *The Education of a Christian Prince* ("Columbia University Records of Civilization," No. 27 [New York, 1936]); A. Werminghoff, "Die Fürstenspiegel der Karolingerzeit," *Historische Zeitschrift*, LXXXIX, 193-214; E. Booz, *Die Fürstenspiegeln des Mittelalters bis zur Scholastik* (Freiburg, 1913); F. von Stromer-Reichenbach, *Der deutsche Fürstenspiegel* (Dresden, 1925); K. Bartsch, "Das Fürstenidel des Mittelalters im Spiegel deutscher Dichtung," *Gesammelte Vorträge und Aufsätze* (Freiburg, 1883); and J. Röder, *Das Fürstenbild in den mittelalterlichen Fürstenspiegeln* (Münster, 1933). Possible relationships between the *miroirs* and the romances will be discussed in chap. iv. (These titles are listed under chap. iv in the Bibliography.)

61. This subject will also be considered in chap. iv. Some examples are John of Salisbury, *Policraticus*; Giraldus Cambrensis, *De Principis Instructione*; William Perrault, *De Eruditione Principum*; Aegidius Romanus, *De Regimine Principum*, and Thomas Hoccleve's *De Regimine Principum*. L. K. Born, "The Perfect Prince," *Speculum*, III (1928), 470-504, discusses the "pattern of the perfect prince" in the thirteenth- and fourteenth-century works, as does W. Berges, *Die Fürstenspiegel des hohen und späteren Mittelalters* (Stuttgart, 1938). Cf. A. Werminghoff, "Drei Fürstenspiegeln der 14 und 15 Jahrhunderts," in *Studien . . . A. Hauck* (Leipzig, 1916). (These titles appear under chap. iv in the Bibliography.)

62. Other views are expressed in B. Mockenhaupt, *Die Frömmigkeit im Parzival Wolframs von Eschenbach* (Bonn, 1942); Schröder, *Der Ritter*, pp. 216 f.; and Schwietering, *op. cit.*

The second group of injunctions is directed to Parzival the boy. The dramatic intensity of the prohibition against questions (interestingly enough, the shortest precept here, the longest and most emphasized in Chrétien) is toned down by the succeeding statement against disdaining answers. The four as a group are the simplest and most direct of the twelve; they have the gnomic quality of *Märchen* advice and come closer than anything else in Gurnemanz' speech to the elements of the *Ratschläge*.[63] The hero as new knight is the subject of the Advice of the third category.[64] The lover who is a devoted husband is addressed by the final triad. These tenth, eleventh, and twelfth dicta, while counseling courtesy to women, stress the need for that unwavering devotion and lack of deceit which characterizes fidelity in love. There is no interest in abject service, unrequited affection, nor furtive extramarital relationships. On the contrary, rather than an initiation into courtly love, which this speech is generally called,[65] Gurnemanz introduces Parzival to the glories of married love;[66] Wolfram here states in principle what occurs later in the dramatization of Parzival's and Conduiramors' courteous love.

The final remark of Gurnemanz, on marriage, and his first, on the sense of shame, state the two themes in which Wolfram's poem radically differs from Chrétien's and which are central to *Parzival*: the progress of the hero through *zwîvel*,[67] and the achievement of love within marriage.

This apparent structure—with its spiritual counsel for the

63. Cf. Ramondt, *op. cit.*, p. 19 and Sparnaay, *op. cit.*, pp. 82 f.; fuller references are in note 11 of this chapter.

64. Regarding the practical instruction in chivalry which Parzival receives, a fascinating study of the origin and growth of chivalric dislike for javelins and arrows—with particular interest for Parzival's slaying of Ither—is A. T. Hatto, "Archery and Chivalry: A Noble Prejudice," *MLR*, XXXV (1940), pp. 40-54. (One wonders whether there might be some symbolic meaning to the enjoinder concerning washing off of rust).

65. Springer, *op. cit.*, p. 229; Mielke, *op. cit.*, *passim*.

66. K. Boestfleisch, in *Studien zum Minnegedanken bei Wolfram von Eschenbach* (Königsberg, 1930), gives little attention to Gurnemanz' precepts and their later development; nor does Schröder credit it, *op. cit.*, pp. 172 f.

67. See W. T. H. Jackson, "The Progress of Parzival and the Trees of Virtue and Vice," *GR*, XXXIII (1958), 118-24; Snyder, *op. cit.*, chap. iii. Cf. Helen Adolf, "The Theological and Feudal Background of Wolfram's 'Zwîvel,' " *JEGP*, XLIX (1950), 285-303.

young prince, practical advice for the boy, chivalric tutelage for
the new knight, and statements of courteous amenities for the man;
and these enclosed by the first injunction for the Christian prince,
and the last, for the husband with "triwe"—is borne out by
numerical analysis of the Advice of Gurnemanz. Entirely consistent with Wolfram's fondness for arithmetic constructions,[68] this
important section of the poem has the following numerical structure.

The total Advice is offered in 84 lines—from 170:13 through
173:6. A break at the forty-second line (171:24) separates the first
two Advice categories of ethical and practical precepts from the
third and fourth categories of injunctions pertaining to chivalry
and love. The first category, consisting of a triad of statements,
encompasses 31 lines; the second, with its four counsels, consists of
11 lines; the third, with two precepts, takes 12 lines; and the final
triad consists of 30 lines. These groups are susceptible to further
separation according to numbers of lines. In the first category, the
three moral counsels have the constitution of 8 lines (170:13-20),
16 lines (170:21-171:6), and 7 lines (171:7-13), with an inner
structure[69] of 1, 7, 16; 4, 3; the first line of this category is an invita-

68. Discussions of Wolfram's numerical structure of the whole romance
include H. Eggers, "Strukturprobleme mittelalterlicher Epik dargestellt am
Parzival Wolframs von Eschenbach," *Euphorion*, XLVII (1953), 260-70;
W. J. Schröder, "Der Dichterische Plan des Parzivalromans," *Beiträge*,
LXXIV (1952), 160-92; G. Ehrismann, *Geschichte*, III, 264 f.; and P. Wapnewski, *op. cit.*, pp. 115 f., 123 f.
69. In part, this inner structure depends upon where one places the semi-
colons and periods in the poetic paragraphs. Since no two editors agree on this,
I have punctuated according to meaning, separating, for example, *sententia*
from *amplificatio*—such as in the eleventh injunction, (172:9-28): lines 172:9-
12 and lines 172:13-28 make the four-line, sixteen-line "inner structure" of
the twenty-line whole:

172 9   und lât iu liep sîn diu wîp:
          daz tiwert junges mannes lîp.
          gewenket nimmer tag an in:
    12   daz ist reht manlîcher sin.
          welt ir in gerne leigen,
          ir muget ir vil betriegen:
          gein werder minne valscher list
          hât gein prîse kurze vrist.
          dâ wirt der slîchaere klage
          daz dürre holz ime hage:
          daz pristet unde krachet:

tion to listen to the Advice to follow: "habt iuch an mînen rât."
An inversion of this numerical configuration composes the fourth
category, of love Advice. Its three injunctions are composed of 2
lines (172:7-8), 20 lines (172:9-28), and 8 lines (172:29-30–173:1-
6), with an inner structure of 2; 4; 16; 7; 1, the final line being an
exhortation to take to heart the Advice given: "des nemet künste-
clîche war." The second category, of practical words to the youth
emerging from the forest, consists of the two-line preface, "ich pin
wol innen worden/daz ir râtes dürftic sît" (171:14-15), followed
by injunctions of these lengths: 1 (171:16), 1 (171:17), 4 (171:18-
21), and 3 (171:22-24), of which the second single line is the shortest in the whole Advice section: "irn sult niht vil gevrâgen." The
12 lines of the third category are devoted to chivalry, 6 to its
theory (171:25-30), and 6 to its practice (172:1-6). The total
Advice of Gurnemanz thus has the neat numerical structure of 1, 7;
16, 4, 3 // 6, 6 // 2; 4, 16; 7, 1.

The results of Gurnemanz' Advice when put into action
represent subtle differences from Chrétien's version. The incidents
are the same, and Parzival's literal application of learning is made
his motivation for errors of judgment. But at Belrepaire he sits
silent in the presence of Blankefleur not only because he has been
counseled against questions unless they are "discreet ones" but
because of his love-longing for Liaze, whom this lady so closely
resembles. The natures of the two battles to free Belrepaire are also
changed. Fighting against the seneschal Kingrun (Chrétien's
Anguingeron), Parzival receives his guarantee of surrender, but
although accepting it after first refusing, he says nothing about
Gurnemanz' teachings about mercy. However, the second battle
against Clamide (Chrétien's Clamadeu) is a "real test" of the
Advice—the "real trial" of learning (171:26) that Gurnemanz

---

der wahtaere erwachet.
ungeverte und hâmît,
dar gedîhet manec strît:
diz mezzet gein der minne.
diu werde hât sinne.
gein valsche listeclîche kunst:
swenn ir bejaget ir ungunst,
sô müezet ir gunêret sîn
28   und immer dulten schemeden pîn.

had proposed in his eighth counsel. While Chrétien fully describes the battle against the seneschal and invokes *occupatio* to neglect describing the second (2678-81), Wolfram portrays both fights but gives more detail and significance to the second. Parzival remembers Gurnemanz' counsels only reluctantly, after a begging lament by the conquered knight, for, since Parzival is husband as well as defender of the besieged lady, he is much less anxious than in Chrétien's version to grant amnesty. "Mîn wîp/mac nu belîben vor dir vrî/nu lerne waz sterben sî" (212:30-213:2), says Parzival, ready to kill. In reversing the incidents of begging and granting mercy, Wolfram gives better motivation for them than does Chrétien, whose concern, among other things, is to display the hero's adherence to the second tutor's Advice. So too the similar incidents at the Grail Castle are motivated differently. Only once, instead of Chrétien's triple reference, does the knight soliloquize, "mir riet Gurnamanz . . . ich solte vil gevrâgen niht" (239:11-13); the beauty of the Grail bearer and his memory of Gurnemanz' excellent hospitality in which "all questions were answered without questions being asked" (239:16) are quite as important as the remembered prohibition in preventing Parzival from making the compassionate gesture. At the Grail Castle, as at Belrepaire (186:1-5), he is made to wash off his armor rust—as the ninth precept demands—to restore him to love's color (228:1-6). Finally, in the joust against the Proud Knight, Orilus de Laländer, Wolfram makes no reference to Gurnemanz' teaching in Parzival's ultimate grant of mercy to the vanquished knight, whereas Chrétien does. Where Chrétien makes his hero dismount at a critical point in this battle because Gornemant had not instructed him in swordfight on horseback (2224 f.), Wolfram reverses the intent of the incident by specifically emphasizing this mounted swordfight as an extraordinary skill.[70]

In these attempts to follow Advice, Wolfram emphasizes

70. Helen M. Mustard and Charles E. Passage (trans.), *Wolfram von Eschenbach, Parzival* (New York, 1961), p. 143, n. 18. See S. Painter, *French Chivalry* (Ithaca, 1957), pp. 46-48; Schultz, *op. cit.*, II, 106 f., 154 f. Much valuable material on swords and their uses is available in V. Schirling, *Die Verteidigungswaffen im altfranzösischen Epos* (Marburg, 1887); W. Boeheim, *Handbuch der Waffenkunde* (Leipzig, 1890); and G. F. Laking, *A Record of European Arms and Armour* (London, 1920).

inherent chivalric capabilities and inherited qualities of character
rather than specific qualities of the education. To recapitulate the
qualities of the second period of tutelage: it is quite different from
that in Chrétien in content, in emphases, and in characterization of
the tutor. The many counsels are directed not to a courtly lover
but to a courteous husband, not to a neophyte knight's personal
salvation but to a prince whose new knighthood and spiritual progress culminate in the highest earthly fellowship. Just as in the
first period of education, Chrétien's Perceval the rustic is portrayed
in Wolfram as the prince as rustic, so too Chrétien's neophyte
knight becomes the prince as neophyte knight. Chrétien's original
character, the tutor Gornemant, who is the pattern of chivalric
knowledge and courtesy, is in Wolfram a man of greater discipline
and greater sorrow. The French Gornemant, though superficially
more courteous, is less intimately interested in his charge. Gurnemanz, direct and strict, bridles a foolish tongue with insult
(170:10); his tutelage is called the "training of a wild will"; its
necessary discipline saves Parzival from mishap better than the
"swankel gerte" which tears the skin of wayward children (174:7-
9). His request for Parzival to remain at Graharz is not an interest
in a young fighter who might become the best in the world (as
Gornemant's is in Chrétien) but an aggrieved man's desire for
another son to prevent his " 'trey' of sorrows," "des fürsten
jâmers drîe," from increase. But that "trey" becomes a "four"
when Parzival leaves his second tutor to seek proof through adventure of knighthood's rewards. From Gurnemanz, and like him, he
learns that knighthood has a knotted whip of sorrows as its tail—
"ir zagel ist jamerstricke haft."

Unlike Chrétien's Gornemant scene, Gurnemanz' education of
the hero has little apparent structural parallel to the first educational period with the mother and only vague structural relationship to the episode with the hermit uncle. It is possible that Wolfram may have attempted some structure of Instruction and Advice
for his Trevrizent scene but abandoned this idea in favor of his
elaborate cyclic construction, which better suits the purpose of
relating to Parzival his heritage and his destiny. Again unlike
Chrétien, the theme of education, with its three periods of tutelage,

is not merely a progress of culminations but a dramatic representation of the ethical and philosophical implications of each educational period. Out of the education with Herzeloide, Wolfram
develops the theme of innocence as insufficient for salvation.[71] Out
of the Gurnemanz episode, Wolfram makes an exposition of moral
knighthood which may be an achievable goal,[72] but one for which a
special preparation of the elect is required.[73]

The total education of Parzival sets forth multiple views of
chivalry. Not only can Wolfram's poem be read as a spiritual progress[74] but also as a chivalric progress from destructive chivalry to
chivalric nobility. Viewed from the forest, knighthood means loss,
pain, and disaster to Parzival's mother; to himself it is that
"bright shining" innocently confused with divinity. Viewed from
Graharz castle, Gurnemanz personally finds it sorrow, while his
chivalric ideal, expressed in his Advice, represents one of the
Middle Ages' most perfect moral justifications for the chivalric
temper. Parzival, divested of *tumpheit* by Gurnemanz but not yet
armed with the *humilitas* he counsels, seeks to prove chivalry joy.

71. Weber, *Der Gottesbegriff*, proposes an 'Augustine-Aquinas-shift' to explain the inconsistency between Wolfram's exposition of predestination early in
the poem, and the need for good works later in the romance. Cf. Rachbauer, *op.
cit.*, and Schröder, *op. cit.*, pp. 216 f.
72. Critical studies pertaining to the moral "value system(s)" of chivalry
are interesting to examine in the light of Wolfram's Gurnemanz scene. E.
Naumann, "Der Streit um das ritterliche Tugendsystem" in *Erbe der
Vergangenheit: Festschrift für K. Helm* (Tübingen, 1951), reviews the
scholarly battle between Ehrismann's theory of the Ciceronian "three"
values, set forth in "Die Grundlagen des ritterlichen Tugendsystems," *ZDA*,
LVI (1919), 137-216, and Curtius' devastating denial of it in his *European
Literature*, pp. 519 f. Suggestive materials bearing upon the subject of
chivalric ideals, with the scholars' references to antiquity, Welsh tradition,
and medieval history, include F. W. Wentzlaff-Eggebert, "Ritterliche Lebenslehre und Antike Ethik," *DVLG*, XXIII (1949), 47 f.; T. P. Ellis, "Urien
Rheged and his Son Owain," *Welsh Outlook*, XVIII (1931), 121-23, 157-60,
183-85; U. Kühne, *Das Herrscherideal des Mittelalters und Kaiser Friederich
I* ("Leipziger Studien auf dem Gebiet der Geschichte," V [Leipzig, 1898]),
pp. 4 f., 57 f.; and G. Mathew, "Ideals of Knighthood in Late 14th-Century
England," *Studies in Medieval History Presented to F. M. Powicke* (Oxford,
1948). Of great interest also are E. Eberwein, *Zur Deutung mitteralterlicher
Existenz* (Bonn, Cologne, 1933) pp. 27 f.; and F. Preissl, *Hroswitha von
Gandersheim und die Entstehung des mittelalterlichen Heldenbildes* ("Erlanger Arbeiten zur deutschen Literatur," XII [1939]).
73. Weber, *op. cit., passim*; Wapnewski, *op. cit.*, pp. 192, 216 f.
74. W. T. H. Jackson, "The Progress of Parzival," pp. 118-24; and J.
Schwietering, *op. cit.* Cf. Mergell, *Wolfram von Eschenbach.*

Parzival's chivalry seen by Trevrizent is sin—since Gahmuret's heritage of chivalric excellence has not yet been tempered by Herzeloide's legacy of spiritual "triwe." By revelations of religious truths and by self-sacrificial acceptance of Parzival's sins, Trevrizent helps reconcile his nephew's two conflicting heritages. Thus, chivalry viewed from the Grail Castle by its destined king is the "bright shining" of his youthful impression, now intelligently interrelated with God's gift of the "brightly shining" Grail.

Slowly wise, Parzival achieves through education the balance between *staete* and *unstaete* which compose his nature. The periods of education mark the hero's progress. He grows in wisdom after each time of counsel, shedding his insufficient beliefs, his restrictive symbolic clothing, and his too-full adherence to the ideals of either of his two heritages. The Instruction and Advice of Herzeloide and Gurnemanz in the *enfance* are freighted with moral and religious implications of the insufficiency for salvation of innocence, election, or good works alone, with chivalric enjoinders for nobler goals than battle for a woman's sake or for its own, and with conceptions of love admitting physical and spiritual unity within marriage. In Chrétien, though these themes of religion, chivalry, and love are components of the hero's tutelage, they remain separate and superficial: the religious element consists in routine devotional practice, the chivalric aspect, in exercise of prowess, the love interest, in courtly behavior. Through his tutor spokesman, Wolfram enjoins the moral reconciliation of the three themes, when chivalry and love, each and together, are bound with religion.

Both Chrétien's and Wolfram's poems are distinguished by striking structural uses of the periods of education, first within the educational phases and then in the relations of these phases to one another. Their presence in Wolfram is more dramatic because of his heightened characterizations of the tutors and his new emphases within the subjects taught. Though serving similar narrative functions to those in Chrétien, the tutors in Wolfram are also ennobled by sorrow. Although Trevrizent's difference from his model in

Chrétien[75] and Herzeloide's tenuous relationship to her French counterpart[76] are well known, even more noteworthy is the transformation of Chrétien's original character Gornemant into Gurnemanz. In this characterization and in the precepts given him to speak, Wolfram's artistic and ethical standards are discernible, entirely distinct from concerns about the Grail or ulterior traditional figures. The poet's moral interest and his care for poetic symmetries are evidenced by the structure of the Advice speech, by the prefiguration of Parzival's wife in Gurnemanz' daughter Liaze, and by the specific emphases, order, and content of this education of Parzival. The hero himself, in the two educational periods, differs in characterization in the French and German poems. Chrétien creates Perceval the rustic and then the neophyte knight by emphasizing the qualities and effects of each learning adventure. Wolfram makes his hero's heritage more noble and his destiny more selfless. He stresses Parzival's double inheritance of Herzeloide's Grail lineage and Gahmuret's (Angevin) chivalry and the conflict of these two during the hero's youth. "Trachlîche wîse," Wolfram's hero is first Parzival the prince as rustic, and then, the neophyte knight who is the Grail prince.

The excellence of Chrétien's and Wolfram's emendations of the *Dümmlingsmotif* is made most vivid by comparison of these poems with the less sophisticated romances of *Peredur, Sir Perceval, Carduino, Tyolet,* and the "Bliocadran's Prologue." These five works concur in giving little significance to the educational periods, in possessing no Gornemant, and in characterizing young Perceval by the omniscient-humorist-technique as amusing *Dümmling* and bungling knight.

Radically different from the education of Tristan, Perceval's tutelage does not make him a learned gentleman, artistic musician, or sensitive lover. His destiny is not ultimately so selfish. Rather than achieving artistic cultivation which serves only one queen and the knight himself, Perceval is destined to serve all chivalry and Christianity through the winning of the Grail. Rather than reject-

75. Rachbauer, *op. cit.*; Ehrismann, *ZDA*, XLIX (1909), 442-49; Keferstein, *op. cit.*, pp. 155-245; Schröder, *op. cit.*, p. 192; and Richey, *Gahmuret.*
76. Richey, *Gahmuret*; and Panzer, *op. cit., passim.*

ing chivalry and mocking its canons, as the Tristan poets do in their creation of the learned artist, the poets of Perceval, Wolfram particularly, exalt knighthood by placing it in the service of morality. Rather than making death the escape from the impossibility of perfect human love on earth, as Gottfried does, Wolfram makes marriage, and its ultimate fulfillment in children, the moral compromise between adultery and abstinence. The educations of Tristan and Perceval within their *enfances*—one a display of intellectual precocity, one a progression from *Dümmlingheit* to potential wisdom—adumbrate the different literary functions of these knights and dramatically demonstrate the opposing artistic intentions of their poets.

Chapter III

The Education of Lancelot

✑ Altar, Bower, and Sword

Obest plerumque iis qui discere volunt
auctoritas eorum qui docent.

—Cicero

*L*ancelot is one of the world's symbols for the lover. Unlike Tristan's love for Isold and Perceval's for God, both of which are affected by the heroes' *enfances*, Lancelot's fatal longings for Guinevere are not directly determined by his youthful learning. The most important of the several Lancelot versions, Chrétien's *Chevalier de la Charette*, has no youthful portrait of the hero.[1] Only two Lancelot romances have *enfances*; each of these possesses qualities well worthy of study. The first *enfance* appears in the Swiss *Lanzelet*,[2] by Ulrich von Zatzikhoven, which is composed of 9,444 lines of ingenuous, exuberant, though rambling and often incoherent, High German verse. Magic, mists, and marvels, naïve exhortations to morality, and accidental characterizations all commingle in what is a poor Arthurian romance but a remarkable Arthurian document. A late twelfth-century "translation" of a lost Anglo-Norman poem,[3] *Lanzelet* preserves the most primitive versions of many of Lancelot's adventures and therefore is exciting material for the study of sources and traditions.

The other *enfance* of the hero has been denied its deserved consideration not because of its quality but because of its enormous bulk. The early thirteenth-century *Prose Lancelot*[4] of the

1. Several probable vestiges of Lancelot's early history appear in Chrétien's poem: his name "du Lac," his possession of a magic ring, and his position "in the forest" before the rescue of Guinevere. All three of these details are supplied in full narrative in *Lanzelet* and in the *Prose Lancelot*. For Chrétien there was no artistic necessity and, probably, no artistic interest in portraying the hero's early life.

2. K. A. Hahn (ed.), *Ulrich von Zatzikhoven. Lanzelet* (Frankfurt, 1845). Out of print and owned by very few libraries, this edition is extremely difficult to obtain. Therefore almost all the quotations in this chapter are from the translation by K. G. T. Webster, revised by R. S. Loomis, *Ulrich von Zatzikhoven, Lanzelet* ("Columbia University Records of Civilization Sources and Studies" [New York, 1951]), hereafter referred to as *Lanzelet*.

3. H. Sparnaay, "Hartmann von Aue and his Successors," *ALMA*, pp. 436-39; *Lanzelet*, pp. 6-8.

4. H. O. Sommer (ed.), *The Vulgate Version of Arthurian Romance* (Washington, 1913), III. Other and superior editions of parts of the *Prose Lancelot* appear in *Marburger Beiträge zur romanischen Philologie*, II (1911), VI (1912), VIII (1912) by G. Bräuner, H. Becker, and H. Bübinger. While many readings in these are superior to Sommer's, his is yet the only complete

Vulgate Version of Arthurian Romance, accessible in quarto
volumes totalling nearly one thousand pages, and characterized by
the ingenious though unwieldly *entrelacement* technique,[5] more
often must be viewed as a romance repository than as a work of art.
But it is infused with a spirit of Christianity in delicate balance
with the dilemmas of chivalry; its characterization of the knight
and the queen whose love causes the Arthurian cataclysm is unmatched for sophistication and humane sympathy. Lancelot's education in these two *enfances* demonstrates a development from
simple recitation of traditional exploits to dramatic exposition of
theories of learning. The comparison between callow Lanzelet's
fairy training and noble Lancelot's education with its reflections of
"humanism"[6] indicates better than the versions of any other hero's
youthful adventures the progression in romance from "féerique"
to "humanistique."[7]

In Ulrich's poem, Lanzelet, the son of contentious King Pant
von Genewis and his beautiful, compassionate Queen Clarine, re-

and accessible text. In addition, for the material used in this chapter, the
differences between texts are minimal; they affect no quotation and no conclusion. All page quotations are therefore from Sommer's version. The German *Prose Lancelot* is an exact translation of the French romance and will not
be discussed (R. Kluge [ed.], *Lancelot, Deutsche Texte des Mittelalters,* XLII
[Berlin, 1948]). The *enfance* section of the Middle Dutch translation is lost
(W. J. A. Jonckbloet, *Roman van Lancelot* [Gravenhage, 1846-1849]).

5. This term describing the romance structure of "interlacing" adventures
—in which one episode interrupts another: a second begins before the first
reaches its climax, only to be interrupted by a third and fourth, which in turn,
make way for the conclusion of the earlier ones—was coined and analyzed by
F. Lot, *Étude sur le Lancelot en prose* (Paris, 1918; new ed., 1954), especially
pp. 17-28.

6. J. Frappier discusses the "humanism" and possible influence of the
Prose Lancelot enfance upon later scenes of pedagogy. " 'L'Institution' de
Lancelot dans le *Lancelot en prose,*" *Mélanges de philologie romane et de littérature médiévale offerts à Ernst Hoepffner* ("Strassburg Université Faculté
des Lettres, Publications," No. 113 [Paris, 1949]), pp. 269-78. "Il n'a rien
écrit de comparable, on s'en doute, à l'*Émile,* ou à *Télémaque,* ou à l'essai sur
l'*Institution des enfants* ou aux chapitres xxi-xxiv du *Gargantua*" (p. 269).
My own discussion of the prose version of Lancelot's education shows its
debt to Frappier's paper.

7. E. Philipot makes a distinction between "enfances féeriques" and
"enfances humaines" (*Romania,* XXVI [1897], 296-300). A third stage in
the progression of romance *enfances* is possible to discern and useful to
distinguish: that is, the "enfances humanistiques," such as the French prose
Lancelot exemplifies.

mains in the care of his mother until he is just over one year old, when his father's malign ways are repaid by insurrection by his nobles, by loss of his domain, and by his death. Lanzelet is abducted by the Fairy Lady of the Lake who raises him in isolation from chivalry in her watery realm of ten thousand ladies. In the Lake he is educated by the ladies in courteous achievements and by "mermen" in sports; at fifteen years of age, "wise and manly" (29), though ignorant of his parentage, name, and all chivalry, he begs permission to depart for the world of tourneying and fighting. He requests instructions, promises vengeance upon his fairy foster mother's enemy Iweret, receives armor, a horse, and advice before parting from her, and concludes the first of his two periods of education riding clumsily on a horse, trusting only to luck and the saddlebow. His second period of tutelage is with the nobleman Johfrit de Liez. From him Lanzelet learns the chivalry which had been denied him in the Lake. Detailed consideration of these two educational periods and their results, first in terms of their import for this romance and then in relation to other romances, suggests a hitherto little emphasized relationship between Ulrich's work and Wolfram's *Parzival* and also distinguishes the tradition represented by *Lanzelet* from that exemplified in the *Prose Lancelot*.

In Lanzelet's first period of education in the underwater fairy world which admits no winter, no aging, and no men, he is taught honorable conduct by the Lady: "to be faithful, well-mannered, and well-disposed" (28). When he has some notion of what is good and suitable, he is turned over to the ladies by whom he is taught to be polite in behavior and speech with women, to keep silent at the proper time, to harp, fiddle, play all types of instruments, and to sing "confidently" (28). At his own request, "mermen" are brought to the castle to instruct him in use of the sword and buckler, the game of prisoner's base, jumping, wrestling, hurling the stone, throwing darts, and still-hunting, hawking, chasing with the full pack, and shooting with the bow. Lanzelet's departure from the Fairy is marked by his statement of shame at all the time "I have wasted here" (29), his promise to avenge her upon Iweret—"Give me all the advice that you can, for I am eager to get at him!" (30) —and her advice on board the ship when they part: Lanzelet is to treat everybody honorably, be steadfast, and do the best that he can. The fairy qualities of this first period of Lanzelet's education are not disguised. The Fairy's mists, the timelessness of her abode, her golden castle on a crystal mountain enclosed by a diamond gate, the "merwunders," the gift of white armor and horse, and the Lady herself[8]—"ein wisiu merminne/diu was ein kuniginne" (v. 180-81)—have long heritages in the Celtic past. These many fairy elements make acceptable the supposition of the ultimate origin of the whole Lancelot tradition in a tale, probably Celtic, of a king's son abducted by a water fay.[9] But within this otherworld setting are subjects of education and a pattern of incidents which are not supernatural. They represent commonplace *enfance* motifs and resemble the learning periods of other literary heroes,[10] the Tristans of Eilhart and Gottfried[11] and, particularly, Wolfram's Parzival. Reminiscent of Tristan's education is the age, seven, at which teaching is begun (*Lanzelet*, p. 28, *Tristan* 23-25); a second resemblance is the curriculum consisting of music, both instrumental and vocal, followed by physical training in feats of sport and then hunting; and a third is the hero's statement of shame for having wasted so much of his life before entering the chivalric world: Lanzelet makes this recognition at fifteen years of age, Tristan at fourteen!

The resemblances to Wolfram's Parzival are more comprehen-

8. On the Celtic origins of all of these, the most comprehensive discussions and bibliographies are found in the notes to *Lanzelet*, pp. 157-65.

9. J. Weston, *The Legend of Sir Lancelot du Lac* (London, 1901); L. A. Paton, *Studies in the Faery Mythology of Arthurian Romance*, rev. R. S. Loomis (2nd ed.; New York, 1960). Professor Loomis argues for Lancelot's origin in the Irish king's son, Lug, known to later romancers by means of a Welsh intermediary, Lluch: *Lanzelet*, pp. 15-18, 163-65; and *Arthurian Tradition and Chrétien de Troyes* (New York, 1949), pp. 188-95.

10. Many other heroes are fairy fostered and have comparable education periods; see M. Kaluza (ed.), *Libeaus Desconus* ("Altenglische Bibliothek," V [Leipzig, 1890]); Renaut de Beaujeu, *Le Bel Inconnu*, ed. G. P. Williams (Paris, 1929); Von der Hagen and Büsching (eds.), *Wigamur*, in *Deutsche Gedichte des Mittelalters* (Berlin, 1808), I; F. Castets (ed.), *Maugis d'Aigremont* (Montpellier, 1893); Harry F. Williams (ed.), *Floriant and Florete* (Ann Arbor, 1947); and Wirnt von Gravenberg, *Wigalois*, ed. F. Pfeiffer (Leipzig, 1847). All these may reflect a common tradition or some possible literary influence. This point will be considered again later.

11. Richter discusses the relationships between Ulrich and Eilhart, and Ulrich and Gottfried in *Der Lanzelet des Ulrich von Zatzikhoven*, "Deutsche Forschungen," XXVII [Frankfurt, 1934]), pp. 22 f., 260 f.

sive and form a surprisingly detailed pattern. Both Lanzelet and Parzival have these many elements of their first educational periods in common: the youth, who has never mounted a horse, so longs for chivalry that he leaves his "mother's" domain, in which he had lived and learned until his teens, in ignorance of his name and of his heritage as a ruler's son. His "mother," distressed at his departure, recognizes and points out his insufficient preparation to protect himself from harm in the world beyond her own. Telling the hero of her need for vengeance upon one who has wronged her, she receives his promise to avenge her and offers him several dicta of advice before they part. Wearing the clothing and riding the horse bestowed before departure, the youth, mounted for the first time, rides all day long in the new world, not knowing how to sit his horse properly, nor how to hold his weapons, nor how to use the reins or bridle.

Parzival's first period of education, as the preceding chapter suggests, results in three incidents which display his courtly "tumpheit." Lanzelet's fairy fosterage leads to two incidents of courtly blunder: the encounter with the Dwarf of the Castle of Pluris and the meeting with his chivalric tutor, Johfrit de Liez. These two incidents, immediately following the departure from the Lake, demonstrate the hero's *Dümmling* character. With the first education period preceding them and the second education period following them, these episodes of ineptitude form one of the only parts of *Lanzelet* in which there is an apparent attempt at a dramatic structure of cause and effect.[12] With his horse's reins dangling about its ears, Lanzelet rides in blithe disregard of the Pluris Dwarf's whipping first the horse and then the hero himself. So callow is the youth that only upon smarting from the whip's slash does he change from the belief that whipping is "proper behavior" to violent anger at this insult. In the second incident

12. There are a few other demonstrations of a rudimentary plan in *Lanzelet*, but these are not scenes or incidents, but rather, part of the fairy "machinery." The magic tent, the mutable mantle, and the gift of the net and sword return again after their first representation. Only at the conclusion of the Pluris Castle incident is there reference to the episode of the Pluris Dwarf: "to this conclusion the whip stroke led with which Lanzelet had been struck" (pp. 100-1). With these few exceptions, the *enfance* offers the only structural design in Ulrich's episodic poem. See also note 20 to this chapter.

which follows Lanzelet's fairy upbringing, his unguided horse carries him to a broad field where he meets with the young, courteous nobleman Johfrit, who considers Lanzelet's ridiculous riding, coupled with his noble bearing, a gesture of courtly "penance" for a lady's sake. Johfrit offers friendship, hospitality, and instruction in chivalry by his own example. Lanzelet's stay at Johfrit's castle constitutes his second period of education.

Lanzelet's encounter with the Pluris Dwarf is similar to Parzival's meeting with Ither the Red Knight both in its position in the narrative and in its portrayal of the hero's display of violent anger. Just as Parzival, coming from the forest, is insulted by the first male character he encounters, immediately preceding his meeting with his nobleman tutor in chivalry, so Lanzelet, coming from the Lake, is whipped by the Dwarf immediately before his period of tutelage with Johfrit. And just as Parzival displays fury and hatred because of the buffet he receives and vows revenge, so Lanzelet angrily promises to avenge himself for his hurt. Granted that these are only general resemblances, they are significant for the similar narrative positions which the Dwarf[13] and Ither adventures occupy in *Lanzelet* and *Parzival,* and for their similar displays of the hero's ignorance of courtly behavior and his volatile manner when physically attacked.

Lanzelet's meeting with his tutor in chivalry and his second period of education, however, are so similar to Parzival's that separate descriptions of each would result in virtually identical paragraphs. Some of these resemblances—between Lanzelet's tutelage by Johfrit and Parzival's by Gurnemanz—have been noticed before.[14] The total similarity, however, has not been recognized previously nor has a suggestion of possible influence of Wolfram's narrative upon Ulrich's been accepted.[15]

13. On the Celtic origin of the Dwarf, see *Lanzelet,* p. 162, n. 12; Helaine Newstead, *Bran the Blessed in Arthurian Romance* (New York, 1939); and Vernon J. Harward, Jr., *The Dwarfs of Arthurian Romance and Celtic Tradition* (Leiden, 1958).

14. W. Hertz (ed.), *Parzival von Wolfram von Eschenbach* (7th ed.; Berlin, 1927), pp. 440 f.; W. Foerster (ed.), *Christian von Troyes . . . IV, Der Karrenritter* (Halle, 1899), Introduction; A. C. L. Brown, "The Grail and the English 'Sir Perceval,'" *MP,* XVII (1920), 361 f.; and *Lanzelet,* p. 168, n. 29.

15. Miss Weston was the first to suggest that Ulrich knew Wolfram's poem, *op. cit.,* pp. 25-29.

For both Lanzelet and Parzival, the meeting with the chivalric master and the elements of his tutelage form a detailed common pattern. Clumsily riding, the horse leading the way, the shield held askew, the hero meets by chance a courteous knight who is not only hospitable but trains the youth, who, just having left his education by women, is eager for knighthood but ignorant of its ways. Meeting upon a broad field, the prospective tutor, whose name is immediately revealed by the author,[16] recognizes the hero's nobility on the basis of physical beauty and brilliant armor and considers the disparity between courtly demeanor and foolish behavior the result of knightly penance for an offense against a lady. Asking the hero's name and home, he pledges friendship and hospitality. After alerting those at his castle of the hero's arrival, he and his female relative affectionately entertain the youth, who reveals his ignorance of his heritage and name and proves his innate courtesy in his conduct with the lovely lady. Instruction in proper horsemanship and in bearing weapons by emulation of the tutor's example is so succesful that the earlier bungling behavior would appear to have been an act. At a bohurt arranged in the hero's honor for the purpose of instructing him in chivalric methods, he distinguishes himself as if he had always so excelled. Thus improved, the hero is eager to be off; and leaving his host, he, now with knightly bearing, but not "knighted," rides a day's journey on a long straight road near a dark forest.

There are divergent details in the midst of this startling congruence. Ulrich's Johfrit is a young man in his prime whereas Wolfram's Gurnemanz is grey with venerable age; Johfrit's female relative is his mother whereas Gurnemanz' is his daughter Liaze. Johfrit considerately rides ahead of his guest to alert the castle to the hero's coming whereas Gurnemanz sends a sparrowhawk as messenger. The penance excuse for the hero's initial chivalric awkwardness is offered by Johfrit himself whereas a knight in the retinue of Gurnemanz makes the explanation for Parzival. Although Lanzelet's education consists of instruction in chivalry and advice, it is not strictly of the biphasic composition of Instruction

16. In Chrétien, the revelation of the tutor's name is delayed until much later in the scene (1.1548, *Perceval*).

and Advice as is Parzival's. And the length of time of this second period of education is not specific in Ulrich—the bohurt takes three days to play[17]—whereas Parzival remains at Graharz for two weeks. But the outline otherwise is valid for both works. The striking correspondences in the *Dümmling* characteristics of the heroes and the particulars of their displays of foolish qualities, the characterizations of the tutor, his family, and his methods of teaching, and the total transitions in the heroes' natures from chivalric awkwardness to knightly excellence because of this chance castle visit surely cannot be accidental.

Both Lanzelet's and Parzival's first periods of education with women cause incidents which display the youths' *tumpheit* and make them bear the epithet "foolish young man." But although their second education periods are remarkably similar, the results of their chivalric learning differ. At the close of the second tutors' instructions, the two narratives cease to correspond. At this same juncture Ulrich's rudimentary dramatic structure of cause and effect breaks off. Whereas Parzival's second period of education, just like his first, leads to three incidents in which his new learning is applied, for Lanzelet the effect of the second period of tutelage is nil. Hereafter, incidents concatenate—the battle with Kuraus, the adventures at Galagandreiz' castle, Limors, King Arthur's court, Dyoflê—each follows the other by momentum of narrative, not planned structure. Neither the first learning period, which creates the *Dümmling* in courtly affairs, nor the second, which initiates his chivalry, has any later reference in this romance. The theme of a *Dümmling* hero refined by a courtly tutor does not seem integral to the Lancelot story in Ulrich's poem or in any other Lancelot version;[18] the *Prose Lancelot* has no suggestion whatever of this theme.

In *Lanzelet*, then, the total effect of the two educational periods

17. Another tournament at which the hero competes is arranged by a knight named, interestingly, Gurnemanz, at Dyoflê: *Lanzelet*, pp. 8, 14, and 186, n. 93. Fascinating examinations of this type of tournament are J. L. Weston, *The Three Days' Tournament, a Study in Romance and Folklore* (London, 1902); W. Richter, *op. cit.*, pp. 52 f.; and P. Schütze, *Das volkstümliche Element im Stil Ulrichs von Zatzikhoven* (Griefswald, 1883).

18. Miss Weston comes to the same conclusion in *Legend of Sir Lancelot*, pp. 98-99.

is insignificant. Whereas Tristan uses his youthful learning to ennoble his adventures and his love, and whereas Parzival's life is an
educational progress completed only after his third period of learning with his Hermit Uncle, Lanzelet's youthful training has no effect
upon his later characterization. The crudeness of this portrait is
made humorous by Ulrich's juxtaposition of Lanzelet's bungling
behavior with insistent attributions of courtliness and intelligence
to his hero. Equally clumsy characterization is exemplified by
rough and crude Lanzelet's nice wit in bed with his succession of
innamorata.[19] But despite the hero's courtly exertions and Ulrich's
insistence, Lanzelet is not a learned hero nor a progressively en-
lightened Christian knight.

The very combination in Lanzelet's education of the *Dümmling*
motif with the program for courtly education (which Lanzelet
receives from the Lady of the Lake) displays Ulrich's misunder-
standing, misreading, or misapplication of both of these separate
themes. Neither the *Dümmling* theme nor the theme of the knight's
courtly cultivation are integrated into this work. Two distinct
enfance traditions—one, the adventures of the naïve and foolish
young hero, the other, the exploits of the precocious and learned
youth—are ineptly joined in this romance document which emphasizes action as opposed to motivation and ingenuous vigor of
movement as opposed to reasoned outline of plot. The education of
the hero in *Lanzelet* exemplifies the single excellence of this crude
romance: its unembellished documentation of stock Arthurian
motifs.

Although the total education does not affect the characterization
nor structure of *Lanzelet*, one personage of the *enfance* is yet significant throughout the poem. While the chivalric tutor Johfrit
disappears from the poem after his instruction of the hero, the fairy
instructress, the Lady of the Lake, reappears several times. Her

19. Bedroom scenes with much pillow-talk are a striking characteristic of
many courtly romances and of other medieval narratives which possess romance
qualities. I am preparing a short study listing and analyzing these bedroom
dialogues—their types, their qualities, and their significances for the works
in which they appear—in such works as *Sir Gawain and the Green Knight*,
Roman de la Rose, Chrétien's *Erec*, and *Perceval*, Wolfram's *Parzival*, *The
Nibelungenlied*, and Chaucer's *Troilus*, and Tales of the Wife of Bath, Clerk,
Merchant, Shipman, and Nun's Priest.

repeated influence in her protégé's series of adventures is the single binding theme in this episodic poem. Either the Lady or her fairy messenger comes riding to Lanzelet at crucial moments.[20] In a sympathetic analysis, the whole romance might be viewed as the working out, in adventure, of the predetermined plan of a fay.[21]

Since the fairy fosterage is clearly traditional in origin,[22] and is among the incidents earliest connected with the hero,[23] it is

20. The Lady of the Lake tells Lanzelet that her shame can be assuaged only if Iweret the Strong is overcome; this, indirectly, leads to the adventure at Iweret's castle in the Beautiful Forest and to the winning of Iblis; this in turn offers the background for the triumphant return to Dodone, at the end of the hero's adventures. The Lady maintains contact with Lanzelet through a messenger maiden who first reveals Lanzelet's heritage and name, and later, rides to King Arthur's court with the magic mantle.

21. The theme of a fairy's raising and training a young hero for the purpose of becoming her lover, or for some special task of vengeance, or for finding his own father (usually the mortal lover of the fairy) undoubtedly underlies the Lancelot *enfance*. Considerations of this subject include Paton, *op. cit.*, pp. 167-95; and *Lanzelet*, pp. 159-62. The fairy fosterage motif is very often bound with two other themes, those of the "father quest" and the "father and son combat"; examples include: *Ridder metter Mouwen, Yder, Wigalois, Richard li Biaus, Sir Degarre, Gregorius, Historia Meriadoci,* and *Morien.* The most comprehensive discussions of these motifs and their literary expressions are: Murray A. Potter, *Sohrab and Rustem: The Epic Theme of a Combat between Father and Son* . . . (London, 1902); A. van der Lee, *Zum literarischen Motif der Vatersuche* ("Verhandelingen der Koninklijke Nederlandse Akademie van Wetenschappen, Afd. Letterkunde, Nieuwe Reeks," Deel LXIII, No. 3 [Amsterdam, 1957]). Other pertinent studies are J. L. Weston, *The Romance of Morien* (New York, 1901), Introduction; P. Federn, *Die Vaterlöse Gesellschaft: Zur Psychologie der Revolution* (Leipzig, Wien, 1919); J. Witthoff, *Das Motif des Zweikampfes zwischen Vater und Sohn in der französischen Literatur* (Nürnberg, 1921); L. Radermacher, "Söhne zweier Vater," *Forschungen und Forschritt,* VII (1931), 172 f.; C. H. Slover, "Sir Degarre: a Medieval Hack Writer's Methods," *University of Texas Studies in English,* IX (1931), 5-23; and H. Rosenfeld, "Das Hildebrandslied . . . ," *DVLG,* XXVI (1952), 431 f.

22. See P. Märtens, "Zur Lanzelotsage," *Romanische Studien,* V (1880), 557 f.; Weston, *Legend of Sir Lancelot,* pp. 21-29, 89-99; and *Legend of Sir Gawain,* pp. 65 f.; C. H. Carter, "Ipomedon, an Illustration of Romance Origins," *Haverford Essays in Honor of Gummere* (Haverford, 1909), pp. 248-55; *Lanzelet,* Introduction and Notes; and R. S. Loomis, "Objections to the Celtic Origins of the 'Matière de Bretagne,' " *Romania,* LXXIX (1958), 57-62. For the Irish Lug's fosterage with Tailltiu, see T. P. Cross and C. H. Slover, *Ancient Irish Tales* (New York, 1936), pp. 13 f.; and for Cuchulainn's with Scathach, R. Thurneysen, *Die irische Helden- und Königsage bis zum siebzehnten Jahrhundert* (Halle, 1921), pp. 396-403.

23. Weston, *Legend of Sir Lancelot,* p. 21; Paton, *op. cit.,* p. 183; A. Mennung, *Der Bel Inconnu des Renaut de Beaujeu in seinem Verhältnis zum Lybeaus Disconus, Carduino, und Wigalois* (Halle, 1890), pp. 44 f.; W. Scho-

likely that in the development of the Lancelot story the motif of the hero who leaves the fairy world for the chivalric one would need or invite augmentation by a theme of education of the hero in the behavior proper for his new existence. Some knightly tutor would thus be an artistic necessity. Either one of the two types of male tutors represented in the educations of romance heroes might be, as it were, "invited into the Lake." The first type of instructor is the professional tutor who, introduced by the youth's (foster) parent, undertakes all aspects of the hero's education; examples are Tristan's Kurneval and the tutor of Lancelot in the *Prose* version. The second type of tutor is the courteous host, met by chance, who instructs the hero in that part of his education which had been denied him during his early isolation with women, most usually with his (foster) mother; such are Gornemant and Gurnemanz of the Perceval poems and Johfrit of *Lanzelet*. It would seem that in the same manner in which other adventures of other heroes were adapted to Lanzelet by Ulrich or his source,[24] a tutor in chivalry, of the Gurnemanz type, was adopted not merely as a general pattern for a master but as an exact model for Johfrit.

This tutor character, the detailed correspondences already noted between the two education periods of Lanzelet and Parzival, similarities between the parents of the heroes, internal indications in *Lanzelet* that Wolfram's Gurnemanz was known to Ulrich, and philological evidence that Ulrich and Wolfram are related—all these strongly suggest that Ulrich borrowed the elements of his *enfance* of Lanzelet, both in incident and in characterization, from Wolfram's education of Parzival. This, however, is not accepted opinion. There are several other suppositions for the origin of Lanzelet's *enfance*. First, it has been stated that the hero's education may be based upon tradition specific only to Lancelot.[25] A

---

field, *Studies on the Libeaus Desconus* (Boston, 1895), pp. 145 f.; *Lanzelet*, p. 159, n. 6, p. 161, n. 10.

24. *Lanzelet*, Notes, *passim*; K. G. T. Webster, "Ulrich von Zatzikhoven's 'Welsches Buoch,'" *Harvard Studies and Notes in Philology and Literature*, XVI (1934), 203-28; W. Richter, *op. cit.*; and his "Der literarische Raum des *Lanzelet*," *ZDA*, LXXV (1938), 33-39. Cf. Schütze, *op. cit.*

25. G. Paris, "Études sur les romans de la Table Ronde: Lancelot du Lac," *Romania*, X (1881), 471-96, and XII (1883), 459 f.; K. G. T. Webster, "Walter Map's French Things," *Speculum*, XV (1940), 272; *Lanzelet*, pp.

second supposition is that the education features may represent a common tradition to which other heroes as well as Lanzelet belong.[26] A third point of view is that any of the Perceval versions, not specifically Wolfram's, could have been the origin of the incidents as Ulrich preserves them.[27]

As far as Lancelot's "tradition" is concerned, his romance heritage is remarkably short. Even though his ultimate prototype may be the Irish god Lug,[28] his figure as romance hero first appears only in the twelfth century. This valorous knight, unknown to Geoffrey of Monmouth and mentioned as the knight third in significance in Chrétien's *Erec*,[29] has adventures and characterizations demonstrably adapted from those of other heroes.[30] With few exceptions, he has little adventure he can call his own.[31] Yet, if the education of Ulrich's Lanzelet represented only Lancelot tradition, one might expect some further reference and development in *Lanzelet* of the education of the *Dümmling*. But the elementary dramatic structure of education periods followed by incidents which display "learning" is precipitately abandoned after the second period of education. More importantly, one might expect this theme of the *Dümmling's* education to appear in some other Lancelot version, particularly, the *Prose*. But, as the rest of this chapter will indicate, it does not; the *Prose* intimates a markedly different tradition.

The second proposition—that Lanzelet's *enfance* belongs to a

15-19, especially correspondence nos. 4, 5, 6; p. 163, n. 14. Cf. J. Bächtold, *Der Lanzelet des Ulrich von Zatzikhoven* (Frauenfeld, 1870).

26. G. Paris, *Romania*, XV (1886), 1-24; A. Mennung, *op. cit.*, pp. 44 f.; E. Philipot, *op. cit.*

27. W. Foerster, *op. cit.*, pp. xx f., xlv f.; J. D. Bruce, *The Evolution of Arthurian Romance from the Beginning Down to the Year 1300* (Göttingen, Baltimore, 1928), I, 210 f.

28. *Lanzelet*, pp. 15-17, 159-64.

29. M. Roques (ed.), *Erec et Enide* (Paris, 1955), 1.1674.

30. *Lanzelet*, pp. 15-19, 159-64, *et passim*, and other references in note 24 of this chapter.

31. Even his passion for Guinevere is itself a traditional theme attributed, in part, to other heroes. The best discussions are, Gertrude Schoepperle, *Tristan and Isolt: A Study of the Sources of the Romance* (2nd ed.; 2 vols.; New York, 1960), II, 531-39; T. P. Cross and W. A. Nitze, *Lancelot and Guinevere: A Study in the Origins of Courtly Love* (Chicago, 1930); and K. G. T. Webster, *Guinevere: A Study of Her Abductions* (Milton, Mass., 1951).

special hero "type"—is more credible. Correspondences to the educations of heroes, notably those of the Fair Unknowns[32]—including Bel Inconnu, Libaeus Desconus, and Wigalois—are noteworthy and not easily discounted. But as Schofield demonstrated long ago,[33] the *enfances* of the *Libaeus Desconus* cycle originated in the Perceval story.[34]

Closest to the conclusions of this chapter is the third proposition, that a Perceval variant, perhaps even Chrétien's poem, could have contributed to Ulrich's. However, it is Wolfram's *Parzival* with which Ulrich's *Lanzelet* is most clearly allied. Ulrich's agrees with Wolfram's in the very details in which Wolfram's poem differs from Chrétien's. It would be hard to believe that Ulrich independently and accidentally hit upon the same changes from Chrétien's *Perceval enfance* that Wolfram also arrived at in his *Parzival*. Examples of these include: the "mother's" vengeance motif, the revelation of the chivalric tutor's name, the character of the female relative of this tutor, and the bohurt he arranges for the hero's martial instruction.

Against the concept that *Parzival*, or any romance not pertaining to Lancelot, is partial source for Ulrich's work is his own statement that his poem is a translation (151). But how close a translator is he? His references to "authority" have been analyzed and reveal his use of material traditional in origin.[35] While these references demonstrate that Ulrich did not make things up *ex nihilo*, they do not indicate out of which nor out of whose tradition he drew. In addition, many liberties of this "translator" have been ascertained: his learned references to lapidary lore, his attribution of the imperial crest to Lanzelet's shield, and, most important of all, his familiarity with and use of Hartmann von Aue's *Erek*, and probably *Gregorius*, have been established.[36]

If Ulrich's additions to his source book are accepted, is it not

32. References are listed in notes 10 and 23 of this chapter.
33. *Op. cit.*, pp. 145 f. Miss Paton concurs, *op. cit.*, p. 178.
34. Philipot's vigorous denial of this thesis does not invalidate Schofield's basic contention that the Perceval legend is the origin of the other *enfances* (Philipot, *op. cit.*, pp. 296 f.).
35. Webster, "Ulrich von Zatzikhoven's 'Welsches Buoch,'" pp. 203-28.
36. Samuel Singer, *Aufsätze und Vorträge* (Tübingen, 1912), pp. 144 f.; Richter, *Der Lanzelet*, pp. 22 f., 47 f.; *Lanzelet*, p. 4.

possible that the *enfance* section of *Lanzelet* may have an origin not credited by this "translator" of the "welsches buoch"? It seems justifiable to return to Ulrich's and Wolfram's poems for suggestion. The total *enfance* of Lanzelet and, most significantly, the two periods of education demonstrate characterizations, incidents, and a structure akin to those of Wolfram's Parzival.

Even before the Lady of the Lake abducts Lanzelet, two small details of his biography are revealed which are not meaningful in themselves but which seem to reflect characteristics of the parentage of Wolfram's Parzival. The first is the character portrayal of the pairs of parents. Lanzelet's father Pant von Genewis, just like Gahmuret, is an arrogant warrior whose bellicosity is the ultimate cause of his death;[37] in direct contrast is his wife Clarine who, like Herzeloide, is gentle, steadfast, beautiful, humble of spirit, and beloved by all people for her noble heart. Secondly, Clarine, like Herzeloide (and unlike almost every other romance mother who puts her newborn child in a nurse's care),[38] cares for her infant son herself and suckles him at her own breast.

The detailed similarities, previously listed, between Lanzelet's upbringing in the fairy Lake and Parzival's in the waste forest and their comparable departures for the world of chivalry, are most notable. After the first period of education, the incidents which display the hero's *tumpheit* and lead to the second education venture represent both a structure and a characterization which are foreign to the total *Lanzelet* poem but integral to Wolfram's romance of *Parzival*. The second education periods present even more and even closer parallels than the first. Ulrich's characterization of Johfrit and the components of the education episode

37. See chap. ii and chap. ii, notes 43 and 50. Interestingly enough, Lanzelet's and Parzival's fathers have been derived from the same, ultimate, Welsh prototype. See Helaine Newstead, ''Perceval's Father,'' *RR*, XXXVI (1945), 3-31; and R. S. Loomis, *Arthurian Tradition*, pp. 347-55. Other derivations of the characters are suggested by E. Brugger, in *Aus romanischen Sprachen und Literaturen, Festgabe für H. Morf* (Halle, 1905), and F. Lot, ''Celtica,'' *Romania*, XXIV (1895), 335.

38. A. Schultz, *Das höfische Leben* (2 vols.; Leipzig, 1889), I, 149 f.; M. Richey, *The Story of Parzival* (Oxford, 1935), p. 30; on literary mothers, children, nurses, as well as other related considerations, useful material is found in Fellinger's *Das Kind in der altfranzösischen Literatur* (Göttingen, 1908). See also *Lanzelet*, p. 158, n. 5.

represent the Gurnemanz scene stripped of the grandeur of Wolfram's conception. Indicative that Parzival's tutor in chivalry, Gurnemanz, was known to Ulrich is yet another character in *Lanzelet* called by the tutor's very name, Gurnemanz (61), who arranges a bohurt, as does Wolfram's Gurnemanz, at which the hero is eminently successful.[39] This character is given the same epithet by which Wolfram's Gurnemanz is known, "den wîsen fürst."

These many congruities of narrative suggest what Miss Weston concluded at the beginning of this century: Ulrich must have known Wolfram's poem.[40] Indeed, careful philological analyses by Singer[41] and then Richter[42] demonstrate Ulrich's debt to Wolfram's style, particularly that of the first six books. Leitzmann[43] also has shown Ulrich's familiarity with the language and style of certain *Parzival* Books, including Book III, the *enfance* of the hero. These philological studies, approaching the problem from another direction, serve to bear out the suggested influence that consideration of the narrative features of the two works portends. Detailed examination of Lanzelet's and Parzival's educations suggests that Ulrich was influenced by Wolfram's story—its characterizations, its incidents, and its structure of the *enfance*—as well as by Wolfram's style. Study of Lanzelet's education within the *enfance* thus illuminates the origin of this portion of the most primitive version of Lancelot's adventures.

Between the ingenuous marvels of the Swiss Lanzelet's *enfance* and the Christian humanism of the *Prose Lancelot's*, the separation in time is small but the gulf in quality is tremendous. So different are narrative elements, emphases, and characterizations within the *enfances* of these two works that they intimate not merely the *Prose* writer's superior artistry and artistic intent but also his use of an

39. Such a doubling of character is frequent in Arthurian romance, as Professor Loomis has often noted (*Arthurian Tradition*, pp. 50 f., and Index *sub* Morgan).

40. *Legend of Sir Lancelot*, p. 27.

41. *Op. cit.*, pp. 144 f.

42. *Der Lanzelet*, p. 204, and again in "Der literarische Raum," pp. 33 f.; see also Wallner's scathing though unsuccessful rebuttal to Richter in *Anzeiger für deutsches Altertum*, LIV (1935), 171 f.

43. A. Leitzmann, "Zu Ulrichs Lanzelet," *Beiträge*, LV (1931), 293-305. Cf. Sparnaay, *ALMA*, p. 437.

entirely different tradition for the education of the hero. First, much of the fairy setting of *Lanzelet* is rationalized in the prose, and some of the stark characterization is mellowed. The Swiss Fairy fosters Lanzelet in her otherworld home as the instrument of her vengeance. The French Lady of the Lake, although she was once Merlin's beloved and from him learned much magic, and although one of her retinue is her fairy messenger, yet raises the hero with no interest in vengeance; her "Lake" is but a mirage, and she is portrayed as a gentlewoman who retains but little of the mantic art. While Lanzelet's father is portrayed as a fiery, contentious king, Lancelot's is an elderly, sympathetically portrayed monarch whose death in grief represents the first tragedy to attend the hero's youth.

Secondly, most of the characterization in *Lanzelet* is incidental to and dependent upon the action of the episodes—the hero is a good knight because he releases besieged damsels and removes enchantments—whereas characterization in the *Prose* is intentional and carefully controlled: the youth's qualities of character are enumerated by the author, displayed in action, and revealed in Lancelot's speeches. Third, *Lanzelet's* structure consists of a biographical concatenation of the hero's own adventures, but the *Prose* *entrelacement*[44] structure affords interruption of Lancelot's exploits by adventures of other characters, such as his cousins Lionel and Bohort, who represent important parallels and contrasts to the hero.

Most significantly, aspects of characterization and structure in the education section reveal that the *Prose* differs from *Lanzelet* in precisely those places where *Lanzelet* corresponds to *Parzival*. The *Prose* appears completely free from contamination with the Perceval story. While Ulrich's Lanzelet has two periods of education, the first in the Lake with the Lady and "mermen," and the more important second period in the chivalric world with noble Johfrit, and whereas Lanzelet's first period leads to incidents displaying his *Dümmling* nature, the French Lancelot has two educa-

44. F. Lot, *Étude*, pp. 17-28, J. Frappier, "The Vulgate Cycle," *ALMA*, pp. 298 f. Cf. A. Micha, "Symmetry in the *Prose Lancelot*," *ZRPh*, LXVI, pp. 369-71.

tion periods, only the first of which is significant. There is no incident and no characterization of *tumpheit* in the *Prose* version.
Lancelot's male tutor works in the Lake during the first education
period. He is a master of the Kurneval type, not the chance, chivalric host who teaches by example, the Gurnemanz type, such as
Johfrit represents; and Lancelot's tutor differs from both Kurneval
and Gurnemanz in qualities of heart. Not only is Lancelot's master
incapable of improving his student but he shows himself so inadequate to his task that he must be dismissed. His characterization
is unlike any other tutor's in a romance text. His student is far
from being a callow youth, such as Lanzelet is, isolated from
chivalry, horses, and men during the first period of education.
Lancelot, taught the origin, meaning, and responsibilities of
knighthood, instructed in horsemanship, and educated with the
companionship of his peers, is a precocious union of prowess and
wisdom. The education of Lancelot has its emphases in development
of character, uses of introspection, and obedience to personal
honesty. It is a dramatic discussion of teaching methods—imposed authority versus mutual affection—and the functions of
education—the following of instinct versus obedience to authority.
Indeed, the medieval controversy between Nature and Nurture, as
displayed in the thirteenth-century moral theorists,[45] is no where
better examined than in the *Prose* scenes of Lancelot's education.

Once the interlaced threads of narrative are untwined and the
adventures which are not Lancelot's are postponed for later discussion, the total education of the hero (Sommer's, vol. III, p. 3-128)
consists of two periods, the first, in the Lake of the Lady (pp. 3-
124) and the second, at King Arthur's court (pp. 124-28), immediately after departure from fosterage. This short second period,
with Ywain as tutor, lasts but a day and is significant not for what
little is learned but for what earlier learning is practiced. The
long and complex first education period, which occupies the youth's
years from abduction to readiness for knighthood, has three

45. This subject will be considered in chap. iv. As Langlois says, ''La
proverbe 'Nature passe Nourriture' est un des plus souvent cités au moyen-
âge'' (*Les Origines et les sources du Roman de la Rose* [Paris, 1891], p. 286,
n. 14038).

phases.[46] In the first phase, Lancelot resides with a nurse and master[47] until he is three years of age. The second phase, lasting through the early teens, brings specific studies and violent conflict between tutor and student. Third is an educational idyll in which, without formal tutor, guided by his own noble instincts and the affectionate remonstrances and explanations of the Lady of the Lake, Lancelot, at eighteen, prepares for knighthood.

Cherished by the nurse whom the Lady provides for him, Lancelot lives contentedly until he no longer needs her care and then is given over to a master who instructs him in gentle ways. Adored by his foster mother and all her court, he is called "beaus fils," "riche orphelin," "fils du roi," and thrives in body and mind in these three years as any other child might in five; so excellent is his demeanor that he appears to be three times his age (22, 33). Significant in this first phase of Lancelot's education are his early manifestation of extraordinary gifts and his namelessness. As in the *enfances* of Tristan and Alexander, the heroic babe precociously displays an aptitude for courtesy. The use of epithets for the hero in place of his own name makes him correspond to the Fair Unknowns, such as Perceval, Parzival, and Lanzelet, who are *Dümmling* figures. The *Prose* writer emends the traditional *tumpheit*[48] of the nameless heroes by endowing his hero with early promises of perfection in behavior, which are fully realized in the second and third phases of the first educational period.

Hunting with the bow and arrow, horseback riding, chess, drafts, and "all manner of games" are taught Lancelot by a master

46. These "phases" are not imposed upon the education text for the purpose of criticism but are integral to the romance; each of the three phases is interlaced by other episodes, such as the fate of Lancelot's mother and the educational adventures of Lionel and Bohort in the care of Claudas and Pharien. These interlaced episodes separating Lancelot's educational phases will be discussed later.

47. This *maistre* is mentioned only this once and no more. He is not to be confused with the incompetent tutor of the second educational phase who is a significant figure in the *enfance*.

48. An interesting comparison is the "Schöne Feigling," the subject of numerous papers by E. Brugger: *ZRPh*, LXI, (1941), 1-44; LXIII, (1943), 123-73, 275-328; LXV, (1949), 121-92; LXVII, (1951), 289-433. Cf. also, R. Ackerman, "Arthur's Wild Man Knight," *RP*, IX (1955) 115-19; and H. Meyer, *Der Typus des Sonderlings in der deutschen Literatur* (Amsterdam, 1943).

engaged to teach him and to demonstrate the conduct of a gentleman (33). Unparalleled in these accomplishments, and of perfect
physique and character, Lancelot displays himself the gentlest,
most debonair of young men, fierce against the felonious and
gracious to the gentle; but when angered, he is not easily appeased.
Separated from his master one day while hunting, Lancelot meets
a young knight leading a bony nag and lamenting the loss of his
war horse. To prevent the knight from dishonor (he must ride to a
joust to defend his name), Lancelot generously exchanges mounts
with him. Immediately thereafter, Lancelot politely greets an aged
vavasour and offers him the venison caught on the hunt; in return,
the elderly knight, recognizing the youth's nobility, gives him a
lithe and beautiful brachet. When the master again sees his student, now poorly horsed and without venison, he demands explanation. To Lancelot's defense of his two actions and assertion that
his new dog is worth two such horses as he earlier owned, the
master, willful and infuriated, strikes him from his horse. Only
when the wrathful tutor strikes the brachet, upon Lancelot's repetition of his judgment of the dog, does Lancelot lose his restraint and
break his bow upon the master's head. Each returns separately to
the Lady of the Lake to make complaint; Lancelot announces himself ready to be his own guide and, the Lady concurring, dismisses
the tutor.

Compared to Lanzelet, who learns polite behavior, harping,
fiddling, instrument playing, sword-play, wrestling, stone-throwing,
and hunting, among many other accomplishments, and compared to
all other heroes for whom there is an education text, Lancelot's curriculum is meager. Music is particularly striking in its absence
from the course of study, but remarkable for its presence in the
character portrait of the hero. Lancelot sings marvelously, but
not often; "for he never expresses joy without good reason:"

Nus ne pooit estre tant iolis ne tant enuoisies que il asses plus ne
le fust · & disoit maintes fois quant il estoit en sa grant ioie que
riens nule ses cuers noseroit emprendre · que ses cors ne peust
mener a fin · tant se fioit en la ioie qui de mainte grant besoigne le
fist puis au dedus venir · Et par che quil em parloit si suerement li
fu il atornei a mal de mainte gent qui quidoient que il le deist par
beuban & par uantise · Mais non faisoit · ains le disoit par la grant
seurte quil avoit en che dont toute sa ioie venoit. (35)

This passage is the first expression of two themes which return many times in the romance: music's power to express exultation, and more importantly, Lancelot's faith in his ability to accomplish the "impossible" when his heart has "grant ioie."[49]

Emphasis in this second educational phase is not upon what Lancelot learns from his master but how he is taught. The tutor's methods, from his earlier competence to his later impropriety, are carefully delineated. His early method is that of a good professional educator who gradually increases the difficulty of assignment as the student's strength and skill progress. His teaching of hunting is an example. The master first makes Lancelot a small bow with light arrows, befitting his stature, and teaches him to shoot at a target; then, upon Lancelot's achieving skill in this, the tutor strengthens the weapons and teaches him to shoot small birds in the forest; and when might further increases, he makes the bows and arrows even stronger, so that Lancelot may shoot hares and larger animals and birds (33). But although this early pedagogical rule is satisfactory, the tutor, under duress, reveals himself of insufficient character for teaching a truly noble man. This master's function, according to the Lady of the Lake, is to "garder de folie & ensegnier les boines oeures" (40), and "ensegna & monstra comment il se deuoit contenir a guise de gentil homme" (33). However, in the two episodes which lead to his dismissal, he not only misunderstands Lancelot's generosity for "folie" and wrongly advises about "boines oeures," but he cannot teach by example. He lacks the cardinal quality of *mesura*. Guilty of spite and willfulness, he attempts to reassert his power over the boy who has acted according to his own good judgment: he knocks Lancelot from his mount because he wishes to prove his rule over him (38); he is infuriated that Lancelot has acted according to his "own pleasure" (38); and he strikes the brachet because Lancelot has spoken "contrary to his will" (39).

49. Elsbeth Kennedy, "Social and Political Ideas in the French *Prose Lancelot*," *Medium Aevum*, XXVI (1957), 90-106, says, "Lancelot is enabled to perform great exploits because of his *love*," and uses this passage on "joie" as the example from the text. Although in Provençal and Old French lyric poetry "joie" refers to love and may be a synonym for it, in the *Prose Lancelot*, the meaning can only be "joy" or "exultation," and not love. The context here singing and the inner state of being expressible through music.

Thus, whereas other romance tutors, such as Lanzelet's Johfrit
and Parzival's Gurnemanz, are suited to their tasks of improving
their charges by specific instruction and by their own example, and
whereas a Kurneval's learning and moral worth is made Tristan's
by a virtual *translatio*, Lancelot's unworthy master abrogates his
responsibility. He is not a "gentil homme"; and, in a romance in
which almost every character is named, he does not even have the
dignity of a name. Lancelot's natural nobility is made to overcome the nurture of this incompetent instructor. Such consideration of authority appears in no other romance text and dramatically demonstrates in the *Prose* the conflict between two methods
of learning—by imposed order or by natural judgment.

More remarkable than the conflict of authority is the emphasis,
in this second phase of education, upon Lancelot's independence of
spirit. As Frappier puts it, "sa véritable nouveauté consiste dans
l' apprentissage de la réflexion personnelle."[50] Again and again
the young hero is described as unswerving in his obedience to the
dictates of his own intelligence. If he has the desire to do a deed
which seems in his heart to be "boine & raisounable," nothing can
dissuade him (35). He fears his master in nothing nor cowers
before him (35). Neither quick to anger nor quick to joy, but once
in a rage, he is mindful only of the injustice that causes his
wrath,[51] and once joyous, he can, in his exultation, do the greatest
deeds (35). His dependence upon personal judgment and his
confidence in his own nature are signs of his inherent nobility—
in Lancelot's own definition and that of the Lady of the Lake.
"Cuers domme ne puet a grant honour venir qui trop longement
est sous maistre" (40), says Lancelot, with the intent of dismissing
the tutor. To this the Lady agrees: "Be your own master, since you
know what is proper and good. You have not lacked the heart of a
king's son" (40). Such sentiments concerning the strength of
noble character gain significance later in the romance when Lancelot accepts the Lady's challenge to chivalry, and still later, when he
determines his special relationship to King Arthur and Queen

50. " 'L'Institution,' " p. 277.
51. The remarkable description of Lancelot in a furious rage (III, 34) is
reminiscent of the "riadstradh" of Cuchulainn (Cross and Slover, *op. cit.*,
p. 151).

Guinevere. In the second phase of the first educational period, then, Lancelot establishes his independence of all but just authority; he enters the third phase his own master.

The Lady of the Lake is not sorry to see the tutor go. Fiercely proud of Lancelot's noble sentiments, she determines to make the gifted youth, now without official master, a perfect Christian knight. The third phase of Lancelot's tutelage contrasts with the second and differs markedly from Lanzelet's education and from any other knight's.

Having invited his cousins Lionel and Bohort to live and learn with Lancelot in the Lake, the Lady, recognizing that it would be sinful to deprive the eighteen-year-old hero of the privilege of knighthood, sets forth the functions of chivalry, the qualities of the knight, the symbolic significance of his armor, and his heavy duties and responsibilities. Given the option of accepting or rejecting this difficult prospect, the young hero expresses his faith in his abilities and his willingness to succeed. He then departs from the Lake for King Arthur's court with the Lady, Lionel, Bohort, and a large entourage. On the way, the Lady instructs Lancelot in the way to conduct himself at court and specifically commands him to receive knighthood, in the armor she has given him, on St. John's Day. Having gained King Arthur's promise to grant these unusual requests and having given Lancelot a magic ring, she departs in great grief from the youth she has fostered.

The teaching methods of the Lady of the Lake are the opposite of the male tutor's of the second educational phase. Her rule is mutual love, not physical force; her achievement, the guidance of natural abilities, not the imposition of arbitrary, external will. Teaching by challenge is her method. To Lancelot's assertion that he longs for knighthood more than anything in the world, she retorts: "Ie quit que se vous sauies com grant fais il en a cheualerie · que iamais ne vous prendroit talens de lencargier" (112). Also, "Ia nauries si hardi le cuer · que tout ne vous en tramblast" (113). After enumerating the necessary qualities of heart as well as obligations, she threatens any knight who fails in chivalry with dishonor in this world and damnation in the next (116), thus making it safer not to risk than to attempt and fail. Her concluding nettle is: "Ore si me dites que vous en plaist ou del prendre ou del laissier" (116). In this teaching episode Lancelot's own fierce pride and his belief in the justice of his own judgment are put to the Lady's aid in teaching her subject. So also does she cleverly make use of his ignorance of his name for his moral instruction;[52] and so too does she feign anger when, to a proud though gentle heart, quick insult works better than slow persuasion (40, 112). The best of teachers, the Lady of the Lake shifts the responsibility for learning from instructor to student.

Not only are there contrasts between the tutors of the second and third phases but there are differences in companionage. Other heroes, the Percevals, the Tristans, and Lanzelet, are educated without companions. In Lancelot's second phase of education, though surrounded by courtiers, he has no peers; in the third phase, not only Lancelot learns under the beneficent discipline of the Lady, but so do his cousins Lionel and Bohort. These he loves and treats as equals, while all others he considers his subordinates (57). From their first day together, the three companions eat from a single bowl and share one couch (57); such is their equality and Lancelot's delight in their companionship,[53] that with them he shares his symbolic rose wreath.[54] Their friendship represents a charming vignette of boyhood honor and foreshadows yet another friendship between Lancelot and a man (Galehaut),[55] in which a woman's love (here, the Lady of the Lake's, later, Guinevere's) first ties and then severs their affectionate bond.

The most significant aspect of the third educational phase is the instruction in chivalry. Whereas Lanzelet, like Perceval and Par-

52. Frappier, " 'L'Institution,' " p. 277; Kennedy, *op. cit.*, p. 103.

53. A brief consideration of the significance of companionship as an epic theme is Dorothy Sayers' "Nurture and Companionage," in her translation of the *Song of Roland* (Middlesex, 1957) p. 37. The significance of Lionel and Bohort to Lancelot as a character, and to the romance in which they all appear, lies between the two opposing interpretations of Miss Paton, who considers the presence of the brothers merely a means by which the *Prose* writer lengthens an already too long work (*op. cit.*, p. 192, n. 7) and Miss Weston, who considers their presence the indication of the evolution of a "secondary branch" of romance, in which Bohort and his son become the chief characters (*Legend of Sir Lancelot*, p. 92, n. 1).

54. Frappier, " 'L'Institution,' " p. 277.

55. Sommer's edition, III, 201 through IV, 156.

zival, must wait until he is beyond the tutelage of his "mother" in order to learn what knighthood is, Lancelot's initiation into its meaning comes while still in the Lake. And whereas Lanzelet, just like every other hero whose education has two periods, is instructed by a knight, or a chance, courteous host who dispels the callow youth's ignorance, Lancelot's chivalric tutor is a gentle lady. While Lanzelet's instruction consists in carrying arms, bearing himself well on horseback, and riding a bohurt, Lancelot's is concerned not with technique but with theory, not with the simplicities of action but with the motivations and obligations of all chivalry. Whereas Lanzelet is prepared to be any lady's knight, Lancelot's prospective function is to maintain justice and protect the Christian Church. No love, except for justice and Holy Church, is demanded of this bachelor knight.

Maintaining that chivalry began when might gained the power to triumph over right, the Lady of the Lake symbolically explains that just as the knight's shield and hauberk protect his body, so must the knight be the protection and defense of the Church; just as his helmet is the "highest" of his garments, so must he act as watchtower for religion; and just as the lance is the most feared weapon, so must the knight be the Church's instrument of fear. The sword is three ways harmful to iniquity. Since the sword— "de toutes armes la plus honoree & la plus haute · & chele qui plus a dignite" (115)—can kill with either of its two edges or with its sharp point, the knight, as servant of God and of His people, must use one edge against God's enemies and one edge against mankind's. Obedience is the significance of the sword's point: "Car ele point · Ne nule riens ne point si durement le cuer ne perte de terre ne dauoir com fait obeir encontre son cuer" (115). The knight bearing such armor must have two hearts. One must be hard and firm as diamond, one, soft and yielding as heated wax. Diamond-hearted, stern, and cruel to the iniquitous, the knight must be gentle, compassionate, and merciful to the good.

This great charge of defending justice and religion to which the Lady of the Lake challenges Lancelot has three interesting aspects—its position in the romance, its correspondences to ex- amples of thirteenth-century chivalric theory, and its relationship to other romance expositions of knighthood, such as Gurnemanz' in Wolfram's *Parzival*. First, the two symbolic definitions to which the Lady gives most emphasis are those of the sword and of the double hearts. Their emphasis demonstrates the skill with which the explanation of chivalry, which might otherwise be an inartistic didactic tirade, is integrated into the total *Prose Lancelot* by means of dramatic motivations and dramatic repercussions. The symbolism of the sword's point—nothing so sorely pricks the heart as forced obedience—is particularly significant to the youth who has known and rejected just such forced authority during the second phase of his education; the superlative honor to which the weapon is said to be entitled makes Lancelot's later *swertleite*, in which he requests the queen and denies the king the bestowal of the sword, all the more dramatically sound. The symbolism of the two hearts of the knight is adumbrated by the earlier enumeration of Lancelot's own qualities of character (35) and has its after-image in Lancelot's double-hearted relationship to King Arthur, in which his militant feudal loyalty is joined to adulterous, personal betrayal.

Secondly, these same two emphases upon the sword and hearts are the points of differentiation betweeen the Lady of the Lake's symbolic interpretation of chivalry and those found in such writers as John of Salisbury, Étienne de Fougères, Alanus de Insulis, and Philippe de Beaumanoir.[56] Although the Lady's complete explanation is not original (St. Paul's letter to the Ephesians, sixth chapter, is the ultimate source) and although she undoubtedly expresses current, thirteenth-century ideas,[57] these detailed explications of the sword and hearts are not similarly stressed in contemporary accounts. These emphases are, however, in noteworthy

56. John of Salisbury, *Policraticus*, ed. C. C. J. Webb (Oxford, 1909); Étienne de Fougères, *Le Livre des Manières*, ed. J. Kremer (Marburg, 1887); Alanus de Insulis, *Anticlaudianus*, ed. Migne, *PL*, CCX; Philippe de Beaumanoir, *Les Coutumes de Beauvaisis*, ed. A. Salmon (Paris, 1899-1900). Kennedy considers these thirteenth-century writers' concept of the functions of chivalry, *op. cit.*, pp. 100-6. Étienne de Fougères' conception is also discussed by Ch.-V. Langlois, *La vie en France au moyen-âge d'après quelques moralistes du temps* (Paris, 1925), pp. 13 f. (These titles appear under chap. iv in the Bibliography.)

57. Kennedy, *op. cit.*, pp. 100 f.; Langlois, *La vie en France . . . d'après quelques moralistes*, pp. 15 f.; Lot, *Étude*, p. 160. Cf. A. Adler, "The Education of Lancelot: 'Grammar'-'Grammarye,' " *BBSIA*, IX (1957), 101-7.

consonance with the other moral ideas dramatized in Lancelot's education: his commitment to personal judgment of good and evil, and his individual responsibility for justice.

Finally, the Lady of the Lake's exposition of knighthood may be compared with that of Wolfram's Gurnemanz in form, content, and intention. While Gurnemanz' numerous dicta of Advice are expressed literally, the Lady's symbolism attempts to reveal the light within the lamp. Gurnemanz suggests the best ways of becoming a knight and the Lady explicates what becoming a knight means. Whereas the knightly tutor is concerned with morality, daily behavior, practical chivalry, and courteous love, the Lady's only subjects are justice and Church, with no concern with love whatsoever. And while Gurnemanz' speech justifies and enjoins the personal perfection of a Christian knight, the Lady of the Lake invites the universal perfection of a Knight of Holy Church, who joins in eternity and replaces in the present the Biblical figures who achieved the honor she describes (116-17); such is one who can, like St. John,[58] "trespasser de bonte & de cheualerie tous les cheualiers qui ore sont" (118). This benediction concludes the Lady's chivalric explication and the third phase of Lancelot's first education period. Armed with his Lady's gifts, his pride, and his independence of spirit, cultivated by his remarkable education, Lancelot leaves the Lake for the world of the court. Only the Lady and, to a lesser degree, Guinevere, later, know Lancelot to be so proud and so orgulous that he values nothing in comparison to his heart (112).

Lancelot's second period of education has no phases, no subject matter, and lasts no longer than a day. At Camelot, Ywain is named Lancelot's tutor by King Arthur. He is to instruct the youth in courtesy by his own fine example. "Ywain ie le vous commant le vallet. Car nus ne li sauroit enseignier miex de vous comment il se doit contenir" (124). But, in this second educa-

58. The specific interest of the *Prose* writer in St. John [the Baptist?] may have some significance which has not yet been discovered. St. John is the only saint mentioned repeatedly, throughout the complete romance; this frequent reference may offer a clue to the author's monastic interests. On the Cistercian influence upon the *Queste*, for example, see A. Pauphilet, *Études sur la Queste del Saint Graal* (Paris, 1921).

tional period just as in the first, Lancelot, rather than learning, teaches what the compassion of nobility is. Just as in the earlier period, there is a conflict between pity and authority. Here again, the hero disregards all rules and all advice except those of his conscience.

When he should have been still learning under Ywain's tutelage, Lancelot demands knighthood of King Arthur on the next day after his arrival at court, St. John's Day, as the Lady had commanded. To Ywain's polite "Hadn't you better wait until you know more about arms?" (124), and to King Arthur's unwillingness, Lancelot is unmoved. Having met the Knight of the Truncheons—who lies at Camelot helpless, injured, and in need of an avenger, but ignored by all the knights of the Round Table because of the impossibility of the justice he demands[59]—Lancelot, having been warned and prohibited, yet promises to undertake the challenge. To the chagrin and sorrow of Ywain, the king, and the queen, Lancelot removes the truncheons from the knight's wounds, thereby taking on the quest at the very moment that King Arthur completes the ceremony of knighting by girding the sword upon all the new knights except Lancelot. He wishes his sword bestowed by the exquisite queen whom he had earlier met and immediately loved. Thus incompletely knighted, his education at a close, Lancelot demands and receives his first Arthurian adventure, the aiding of the besieged Lady of Nahoat.

This second educational period is significant neither for the courtesy Lancelot learns nor for the advice he heeds, since he flouts both in the incidents of the *swertleite* and of the Knight of the Truncheons. Ywain's advice to postpone the ceremony of knighthood and his injunctions against aiding the entruncheoned knight make him as insufficient a tutor for the hero as is the master of the

---

59. The knight demands that his avenger must avenge him on all who liked him less than the one who wounded him (p. 126). Whatever this outrageous condition might mean to the individual knight undertaking the task, the Knight of the Truncheons appears at court to test the truth of the Fellowship's reputation for honor and compassion. He cannot believe that at Arthur's court—where all aid is, where all the brave are (pp. 119, 126)—he will remain unsuccored. But he is entirely ignored because of the fears of the Knights of the Round Table and of their king. His appearance, therefore, is as a messiah of cataclysm.

first period of education. Ywain, like the earlier tutor, owes allegiance to mere norms of authority but not to such extravagant moral excellence as Lancelot represents. Ywain therefore cannot teach Lancelot "comment il se doit contenir." But unlike the first tutor, Ywain's own nobility permits not resentment of Lancelot's fierce independence but recognition of what it prefigures and appreciation of the worth of passionate will. He submits to Lancelot with: "Car se vous vesquisies longement encore peusies venir a moult grant chose" (128).

In the *swertleite* incident, Lancelot—having been told by Ywain the importance of the sword, and previously having had its significance so stressed by the Lady of the Lake—states his firm intention to owe complete fealty to another than the king.[60] This disregard of King Arthur's right and responsibility to give the sword is later made the moral justification for Lancelot's amorous allegiance to Guinevere. In the episode of the Knight of the Truncheons, Lancelot demonstrates that pity rather than authority must determine actions. Just as in the first educational period, when Lancelot has compassion for the knight to whom he gives his horse and for the vavasour to whom he gives the venison, Lancelot's apprehension of a need for *misericordia* supersedes any obedience to authority. But whereas in the earlier examples Lancelot risks only his belongings and the affection of a tutor, in this later one he risks his life and countermands his king. This conflict between pity and authority re-echoes throughout Lancelot's later adventures in the *Queste del Saint Graal* and *La Mort Artu*.[61] In the education of the hero, the episode of the Knight of the Truncheons[62] along with the unusual knighting ceremony, are made the most dramatic of a series of

60. One does not have to be too careful a reader to recognize the *Prose* writer's emphasis upon Lancelot's purposeful intention to be fully knighted by the queen and not by the king. Three references exemplify this: pp. 130, 131, and 137. Cf. Frappier, *ALMA*, p. 298.

61. For example, vol. VI, 43 f.; VI, 300 f.

62. Because this knight and his adventure have been interpreted literally, instead of as the symbolic test of the moral turgor of the Arthurian fellowship, this episode has been described as ridiculous. However, Lancelot recognizes the shame the court will bear if the knight goes unaided. Thus, to protect the court from loss of reputation, and to satisfy his own compassionate instinct— "I felt such pity for him I could no longer endure it" (117)—Lancelot offers his pledge of help.

demonstrations of Lancelot's spiritual independence, an autonomy which the total education fosters.

Such an examination of this paragon courtly lover's two periods of education in the *Prose Lancelot* reveals a surprising interest in educational theory. The first period—with the youth's precocious promise of the first phase, his capabilities for self-rule and incompatability with his tutor of the second phase, and, in the third phase, his learning pressured only by love for the Lady and responsibility to his own nobility—presents dramatic contrasts between methods of teaching, demonstrates the importance of a tutor's character as a constituent of his teaching skill, and considers the dichotomy between instinct and authority. These ideas are all related to the broader question voiced in the first educational period concerning which deserves priority: Nature or Nurture. The three answers, that poor nurture cannot triumph over noble heritage, that a valiant nature needs little but gentle guidance of innate qualities, and that excellent nature can perfect itself by exercise (chivalry), are reinforced by the incidents of the second period of education. At King Arthur's court, under Ywain's supervision but his own authority, Lancelot accepts advice and prohibitions by ignoring them, orders the ceremony of knighthood to his personal needs, and obeys his instinct for compassion by offering succor beyond the selfish judgments of the best knights and their king. These two education periods emphasize two noteworthy elements. First is the portrait of the ultimate adulterer as a youth spiritually free, a characterization which at once forecasts and justifies his later arrogations as knight and lover. Second is the definition of the education itself, which, in elements and emphases, is not to be found elsewhere in the Middle Ages, either before or after the *Prose Lancelot*. Later, in such humanistic forays into education as Montaigne's, there is comparable concern with the young mind unfettered by unworthy authority, and similar faith in the capacities of youth for judgment and *joi*.

Such humanistic concern with the modes and results of education are distant indeed from the fairy qualities of *Lanzelet*. The *Prose* version's second education period has no prototype in the Swiss poem: Lanzelet's arrival at King Arthur's court occurs much

later in the narrative and much differently (59 f.). The first education periods are in no way congruent, except in that the Lady of the
Lake figures in each. But these fairies, the heroes as youths and
students, and the meanings of their educations are radically
different.

Innovations of the *Prose* writer extend beyond these dis-
similarities between the two works in subject matter, characterization, and presentation. By means of the *entrelacement*, the *Prose*
not only achieves dramatic discussions of pedagogical ideas but
also considers social and political theories in episodes of sound
drama. While Lancelot's childhood adventures are tinged with
these interests, it is mostly the exploits of others, with which
Lancelot's are interlaced, that represent discussions of feudal
loyalty, family honor, kingship, and chivalry in war.[63] These interlaced adventures briefly may be considered in their relationship to
the education of Lancelot. Subtly controlled in characterization,
these scenes present parallels and contrasts to Lancelot in matters
of family heritage and qualities of mind; the specific pattern of
their alternation gives a structural as well as a dramatic emphasis
to Lancelot's education in the Lake.

At the time of aged King Ban of Benowick's tragic death,
through Claudas' machinations and a seneschal's treachery, his
brother, King Bors of Gannes, dies of an extended illness. Ban
leaves his widow Elaine and infant son Lancelot, and Bors is survived by Evaine, sister of Elaine, and two sons, twenty-one-month-
old Lionel and nine-month-old Bohort. Elaine, after the abduction
of Lancelot by the Lady of the Lake, becomes the Queen of Many
Sorrows—"la roine as grans dolors" (15)—and endows a cloister
in which she lives and mourns her husband and son; she is later
joined there by her sister Evaine who, having lost her two sons to
Pharien, who is in league (at this time) with the usurper Claudas,
also laments her loss, achieving respite from grief only in death.
While Lancelot is in the first phase of his education in the Lady's
Lake, Lionel and Bohort are imprisoned in the tower of Gannes

---

63. While not attempting to establish precise sources for these ideas,
Kennedy (*op. cit.*) considers the *Prose* author's discussions of the relationship
between lord and vassal (pp. 90-96), of kingship (pp. 96-100), and of the
functions of chivalry (pp. 100-6).

along with Pharien (now the adversary of Claudas), and his
nephew, Lambeques, who act as tutors to the two young brothers.
During Lancelot's second phase, Lionel and Bohort learn of their
noble heritage, display their righteous hatred of their lot in aveng-
ing themselves upon Claudas by killing his son Dorin, and, with the
Lady of the Lake's messenger and magic aiding them, escape to the
Lake where they join Lancelot in this third phase of education.
They remain in the Lake after Lancelot, his tutelage in chivalry
complete, departs for court.

In the alternation of similar adventures between brothers,
sisters, cousins, and their tutors, there are purposeful contrasts.
Ban's death, an accidental fall from high estate, is more tragic than
Bor's ultimate submission to sickness. Of the sister queens, Lancelot's mother Elaine is the stronger emotionally and physically,
and whereas Evaine succumbs in piety and in grief, Elaine's
strength survives the rigorous cloister rule. Like Lancelot, the
young brothers Lionel and Bohort have intelligence, powerful wills,
and inborn nobility of character, with Lionel the more gifted of the
two. But they reveal themselves inferior to Lancelot's prodigious
temperament first in incidents preceding their coming to the Lake
—Lionel's two hunger strikes in the tower prison, for example
(51, 80)—and then in episodes within the Lake—such as Lionel's
tears of outrage, which are so gently yet so castigatingly re-
proached by Lancelot (88). Lionel is a delightful hot-head possessing Lancelot's independence of authority without his grandeur
of judgment. Contrasting too are the second phases of education
in which Lancelot must liberate himself from an incompetent professional tutor, whereas Lionel and Bohort learn by example from
their noblemen tutors Pharien and Lambeques, knights loyal to
morality, to feudal ties, and to the young princes themselves. In all
these interlaced contrasts, although the characters are related by
blood and are equal in feudal position, age, and physical attributes,
Lancelot's family is portrayed as superior.

When episodes tangential to this family chronicle[64] are excluded

64. The word "chronicle" is appropriate in two ways: first, as the record
of the exploits of the feudal family, and second, as the document of the time
sequence—even down to days and hours—in which these adventures occur.

(such as Merlin's life history, Claudas' relationship to his son, to King Arthur, to Pharien, and to Pharien's wife), the pattern of the *entrelacement* may be represented graphically. The life in the Lake marks the point at which the separate though converging family lines unite.

Feudal History of Benowick..Claudas..Feudal History of Gannes
King Ban.......Brothers United in Death.......King Bors
Elaine......Sisters United in the Cloister......Evaine

Lancelot....1st Phase of Education....Lionel and Bohort
    individual care in isolation
Lancelot....2nd Phase of Education....Lionel and Bohort
    individual recognition of heritages
    and liberations from oppression
Lancelot....3rd Phase of Education....Lionel and Bohort
    Cousins United in the Lake
    by the Lady of the Lake

These interlaced adventures contribute to the total characterization of Lancelot and his Lady mentor. The portraits in these episodes, entirely original with the prose writer, with no hint whatsoever in *Lanzelet*, reinforce the characterizations in the *enfance* sections pertaining directly to Lancelot. Whereas the Lady of the Lake in Ulrich's poem is a water fairy needing an avenger, in the French *Prose* version she is a gentle, intelligent woman who guides a vigorous mind with beneficent strength, who recognizes, maternally, that teaching certain amenities means teaching hypocrisy ("Your tutor is stupid and wrong, but courtesy demands that tutors not be contradicted nor slapped!" [40]), who fears the loss of her "son" to that very life for which she so excellently nurtures him, and whose own life thus borders upon bereavement. After the *enfance*, her influence is seen throughout the *Prose* narrative. The cleft in her gift-shield unites when Lancelot and Guinevere consummate their love (III, 305); her magic ring dispels enchantments for Lancelot (IV, 201); she twice cures him of madness (III, 415; IV, 155);[65] her marvelous influence dims only in the

Lot ignored this chronological construction of the *enfance*, beginning his consideration of the chronological *entrelacement* at the departure of Lancelot and the Lady from the Lake (*Étude*, pp. 29-62).

65. That Lancelot three times succumbs to madness is considered an

dawning brilliance of Christian asceticism in the *Queste*.

While the hero of *Lanzelet* is at first superlative in the courtly accomplishments taught him in the Fairy's land, he becomes a *Dümmling* figure as soon as he leaves for the chivalric world, needing a chance, courteous host, Johfrit, to instruct him for knighthood. Lanzelet is Parzival's shadow—the outline replicated, the perspective changed. The French Lancelot, on the other hand, precocious from infancy, fierce in pride, and insuperable in the cause of personally defined justice, is fostered in self-discipline. His humanistic education bears no relation to the mere list of subjects Lanzelet is taught. Lancelot's demonstrations of obedience to instinct (to pity, to love, to hatred) and his rejection of all authority save his own—displayed in dramatic considerations of teaching methods and education's functions—are not only at variance with the *Dümmling* characterization but seem unlikely to have developed from it.

The *enfance* selection of *Lanzelet* has an affinity with the *Prose*,[66] but only a very small portion of this *enfance*, a bare outline, is similarly present in both stories. Only these elements are common: the *enfances* are the beginnings of biographical Lancelot versions; the hero, after his father's death, is abducted by a water fairy and raised by her until ready for knighthood, remaining ignorant of

artistic blemish of the *Prose* author (Frappier, *ALMA*, p. 302). But there is a definite progression in the causes of these three periods of madness and in the efficacies of their cures. The first period follows Lancelot's imprisonment with the enchantress Camille; a second time, he wanders mad in a forest, distracted because of his loss of Galehaut. Each time, the Lady of the Lake finds him, keeps him in her company, and cures him. The third period occurs when both Lancelot and Guinevere become aware of the disastrous implications of their adulterous relationship. With the added burden of Guinevere's spurning him, Lancelot, who has already and unwittingly engendered Galahad, now goes mad again. This time the Lady of the Lake offers no balm, nor does she appear, as the reader expects from the previous episodes of madness. Now Lancelot suffers no mere loss of wits but the agony of questioning his faith to God, his spiritual and temporal alliances, and his eternal soul. At this point, only the Grail can heal him. The Lady of the Lake has disappeared from the story and returns no more.

66. Common aspects of *Lanzelet* and the *Prose* have been considered by Märtens, *op. cit.*; Paris, *Romania*, X (1881), 472 f.; Lot, *Étude*, pp. 166-69; Sparnaay, *ALMA*, pp. 436-38; and in *Lanzelet*, pp. 11-12 and notes to the translation.

his name. These general similarities, all traditional in origin,[67] all familiar to fairy mythology,[68] do not demonstrate literary influence. They indicate some common, possibly oral, lore attached to a popular hero. The numerous specific correspondences between Lanzelet and Parzival are strongly suggestive of Ulrich's use of Wolfram's poem. The lack of correspondence in the *enfances* between Lanzelet and Lancelot is most marked in those very incidents in which Lanzelet and Parzival agree. Examination of the Swiss poem's relationship to Wolfram's *Dümmling* characterization and consideration of the *Prose Lancelot's* humanistic concern with pedagogy and precocity indicate that the connection between the two versions extends but little beyond the hero's name.

Although the education of Lanzelet seems based on the *enfance* of Parzival, and the French Lancelot's appears to originate in other sources (probably the author's own concern with current humanistic thought and theory), comparison of the two extant texts of the hero's education permits an historical insight into the development of Arthurian romance. The progression in form from the education of Lancelot in the cruder earlier poem to the sophisticated prose romance marks a change in narrative pattern enforced by refinements in literary attitudes. Only rarely can such development be traced in literature. The educations of these two Lancelots transcend the specifics of their texts and excellently exemplify the romance progression from "féerique" to "humanistique."

67. *Lanzelet*, pp. 12-17, 159-65. Other references may be found in notes 21, 22, and 24 to this chapter.
68. The most important study of this subject is L. A. Paton's, *op. cit.*, pp. 167-203, and Professor Loomis' critique, pp. 291-4.

Chapter IV

The Education of The Arthurian Hero

ets Prevalence and Provenance

> A poines peut estre bon clers qui ne
> commance des anfance, ne ja bien ne
> chevauchera ne l'apprent jones.
> —Philippe de Novare

> Les sciences sont longues et la vie
> de l'omne si est brieve, il afiert
> que l'en commence en jennensce
> aprendre.
> —Aegidius Romanus

> Abroad in arms, at home in studious
> kind
> Who seeks with painful toil shall
> Honor soonest find.
> —Edmund Spenser

$\mathcal{CR}$ The education of the Arthurian hero within his *enfance* is an exceedingly malleable romance theme. The emphasis of the three preceding chapters has been upon the artistic utilizations of the hero's *enfance* and education. From this literary criticism it is appropriate to turn to the literary history of the idea. It is useful to consider the prevalence of this education theme both within Arthurian romance and in medieval romance in general. It is valuable also to inquire into the provenance of this theme. A brief review of the recurring features within the educations of Tristan, Perceval, and Lancelot will serve as basis for discussion of the education theme in other heroic stories. With this basis also it will be possible to indicate the frequency of the interest in the hero's education exhibited in other Arthurian romances as well as in such non-Arthurian material as the Alexander romances.

In examining the provenance of this remarkably prevalent romance theme, Celtic, classical, and medieval sources will be considered. While origin of the education motif is sometimes inseparable from that of the concept of the learned knight, distinction between the narrative details of the hero's learning and the philosophical concept of the educated hero often is illuminating. This chapter's purpose is to unify otherwise disparate material representing various literary forms of several epochs which have the education of the hero theme in common, to investigate the possible influences dictating this interest, and to suggest the literary factors which fostered this pervasive romance concern with the hero's youthful education.

The discussions of Tristan, Perceval, and Lancelot attempted to demonstrate the artistic elaborations and philosophical emendations of this theme, and they pointed to a general progression in its utilization, from simple listings of subjects within fairy settings (such as in *Lanzelet*) to complex portrayals of education within humanistic discussions of learning (such as in the *Prose Lancelot*). For the unskilled romancers, the education of the hero offered elements calculated to please the audience. *Sir Tristrem, Sir Perceval,* and *Lanzelet* detail the educations of their knights but present no development of the theme. Without a specific message to broaden common motifs, and without expert craftsmanship to transform them, the education texts in these cruder romances are merely lists of subjects taught by a tutor. Yet, in the mediocre but popular *Sir Tristrem, Sir Perceval,* and *Lanzelet,* the most striking aspect of the education theme is its presence. The hero's possession of at least one period of education appears to be as necessary to his total exploits as is his relief of at least one damsel and his victory over at least one dragon.

For the best romancers, the hero's *enfance* and education permitted a characterization of the knight which at once adumbrated and explained his adult qualities, which afforded a dramatic structure both within the *enfance* itself, and then, between the *enfance* and later parts of the romance, and which allowed an exposition of major concerns of the romance which received later development. Rather than cataloguing subjects, these texts explore the ramifications of the curriculum, the role of the tutor, and the effects of education upon the young hero. Thomas, Gottfried, Chrétien, Wolfram, and the *Prose Lancelot* writer portray their heroes as prodigious youths whose childhood learning demonstrably affects their later adventures, and thereby, the total romances which contain them.

The divergent artistic approaches and the varying achievements of the many romances of Tristan, Perceval, and Lancelot, notwithstanding, certain recurring qualities, thematic variations, and chronological relationships deserve brief comment.

Many such elements appear so frequently in the *enfances* of the major Arthurian heroes that a composite childhood can be established. Born the son of a ruler, the hero possesses inherited potential excellence which can be and is developed by education. This education consists of two or three separate periods. During the first period, the youth is cared for by a woman—his real or foster mother, or a nurse—who provides the necessary rudiments, courtly and religious, to make the infant a marvelous boy. He is next entrusted to a male tutor for a second educational period. Instructed in endeavors which cultivate both mind and body, he is given preparation for the world in which his later adventures will take place. The curriculum of this second period consists of "liberal arts," reading, instrumental and vocal music, law, hunting, exercise in sports, and tutelage in chivalry. The tutor, whose personal capabilities are delineated, is one of two types of masters: either a Kurneval type, a professional instructor employed to nurture the noble youth in all necessary courtly accomplishments, or a Gornemant type, a courteous knight met by chance, who, by virtue of personal desire and particular capability, instructs the young hero by example. Upon leaving this second period of education and having a childhood adventure in which his learning is displayed, the hero arrives at a king's court. Here, prior to the ceremony of his knighting, he either receives further education—his third period, under the tutelage of a courtier—or displays brilliant expertise which demonstrates his precocious refinement and readiness for knighthood.

The general configuration of this Arthurian *enfance*, as opposed to the *enfance* in other medieval literary forms,[1] consists essentially of the program of education and the display of youthful learning. Composed of more than one period and directed by more than one tutor, the youthful learning encompasses a curriculum of religious, moral, intellectual, physical, and chivalric content. Emphasis is laid upon the tutor's qualifications as well as upon his special qualities of character. The initiations into chivalry presented by the better romances are particularly detailed and elaborate. Beyond practical chivalric instruction, such heroes as Wolfram's Parzival and the *Prose* writer's Lancelot receive elucidation of the ethics of knighthood's craft—its personal, moral, and social implications. Once given the accolade of knighthood, the young hero dedicates the exercise of his prowess and the promise of his learning to women, Christianity, and justice. The commitments of the new knight, like the subjects of his education, are courtly, martial, Christian, and judicial.

The Perceval stories, with their portraits of a purposefully un-

1. Qualities of *enfances* in *chansons de geste* and Germanic epics will be considered later in this chapter.

educated youth, represent but a variation upon this pattern of educational periods, curricula, and tutors. Perceval's belated periods of learning, as Chapter II suggests, underline vital structural elements in those romances. In his delayed education, Perceval, unlike Tristan and Lancelot who are taught intellectual refinements of chivalry, is taught only its practical and moral essentials. Particularly in Wolfram's poem, the hero's destiny is so important and the trials of his election so frequent, there is no time for books, harping, hunting, or conduct for casual amours—which are instruments of chivalric leisure. Unlike Tristan's and Lancelot's educations, which cultivate some qualities of the *vita contemplativa*, Perceval's (Parzival's, most particularly) prepares the knight only for the *vita activa*; his is the formation of the *miles christianus* destined to become the *imperator christianus*. But these differences in the Perceval stories do not obviate the striking similarities in form among all the educations within the *enfances* of major Arthurian heroes.

French, German, and English versions of all three heroes' adventures contain education texts. None is earlier in time than the last quarter of the twelfth century; most versions are of the thirteenth and early fourteenth centuries. From the earlier to the later texts there is a progression from simple statement of education details, such as in Eilhart's *Tristrant* and Ulrich's *Lanzelet*, to complex development of the educational elements as well as to philosophical interest in the hero as educated, or learned, such as in Gottfried's *Tristan* and the *Prose Lancelot*.

For the major Arthurian heroes, then, an education appears to have been considered a necessary element in the hero's characterization. One might expect to find a similar presence of this theme and a similar progression in its utilization in other romances of the same eras. Indeed, it appears that in those romances which alone preserve the adventures of one hero, such as *Galeran*, *Wigalois*, *Wigamur*, and *Sone de Nausai*, as well as in other non-Arthurian romances which are preserved in several versions, such as those of Alexander and of the hero of the "Seven Sages," one finds the very same prevalence of the education theme—with similar narrative qualities and comparable artistic developments.

Just as for the major Arthurian heroes, so for the lesser heroes of romance: the theme of youthful education crosses boundaries of nation, time, and excellence. Of the enormous number of late twelfth- through fourteenth-century French and German romances, several have been selected to exemplify the frequency of the education theme. To give point to these examples, care has been taken to choose those which have no proved narrative relationship to romances of Tristan, Perceval, and Lancelot, nor any demonstrable interrelationships. These citations, simply indicating the presence and the similarities of the education theme in these unrelated texts, suggest the apparent literary necessity for this theme in the characterization of any hero within this literary form.

Galeran, in Jean Renart's Old French *Galeran de Bretagne*,[2] written between 1195 and 1225,[3] has a tripartite education for his prospective métier. As a ruler, he must be cultivated as both martial knight and refined courtier. Raised by his foster mother, the courtly Abbess Ermine, he is first cared for by a noble nurse.[4] He is then entrusted to his tutor, chaplain, and friend, Lohier, who instructs him during a second educational period in manifold arts of the hunt, horsemanship, languages, singing, and the games of chess and tables (1175-1208); by the age of fifteen, he is "courtois et bien apris et sages."[5]

> Par le conseil Lohier son maistre,
> Comment l'en doit ung oyseau pestre,
> Gerfaut, oustour ou esprevier,
> Faucon ou gentil ou lannier,
> Et l'aprint a laisser aller
> Et poursuïr et rappeller

2. *Galeran de Bretagne*, ed. L. Foulet (Paris, 1925).
3. *Ibid.*, p. xxxi.
4. There follows a long *excursus* on the qualities of nurses and the necessity (and difficulty) of matching the nobility of the nurse to the royalty of the charge. Romance concerns with heroes' nurses are surprisingly frequent and will be referred to again in versions of the "Seven Sages" and Alexander romances, as well as in the medieval *miroirs de princes*.
5. An interesting comparison to this educational period is that of Guillaume in Jean Renart's *L'Escoufle*, ed. [H. Michelant and] P. Meyer (Paris, 1894). Also, the education of Guillem de Nevers in *Flamenca*, P. Meyer (ed.), *Le roman de Flamenca* (Paris, 1901); and a new ed. and trans. by J. Hubert and M. Porter, *The Romance of Flamenca* (Princeton, 1962).

Et comment l'en le garde en mue
Et quant l'en l'oste et remue;
Des chiens sot, s'en ama la feste;
S'aprint a deffaire la beste,
Si sot de l'arbeleste traire
Et sot moult bien ung boujon faire;
Si sot de tables et d'eschecs. . . .
(1175-87)

In a third period before his knighting, the Abbess advises him of the functions and responsibilities of chivalry. Like Lancelot's Lady of the Lake, also an intelligent, forceful foster mother to an heroic youth with a noble sensibility, Abbess Ermine defines by challenge the ideal unity of noble body with noble heart:

Se li corps par le cuer ne pert,
Je vous tesmoing et si vous vant
Estre prodom cy en avant.
N'est riens a dire de biau corps
S'il a de maulvés cuer le mors;
Car neant plus ne vault l'escorce
Qui est sans moëlle et sans force,
Ne vault beauté de corps ne grace
Quant mauvaistié de cuer l'efface.
Biaux homs sans cuer vaillant et sage
Est tout aussi comme l'ymage
Qui d'or et d'argent est couverte
Et qui l'a par dedans ouverte,
N'i a fors fust ou pierre ou terre.
(24446-59)

Galeran's education, like Tristan's, cultivates accomplishments somewhat more suitable for courtly leisure than for martial honor. Also like Tristan with his master Kurneval, Galeran is instructed by a tutor whose own refinements make him particularly suitable to teach (910-32) : Lohier can expertly sing, read, "trouver lays et nouviaux chans," write French and Latin verse, play the harp and other instruments, and he excels in courtly games; thus, he is a mentor "Haux hons estoit, doulx et piteux" (934). Again like Tristan, the young Galeran loves a lady, Fresne, equally cultivated in her youth in intellectual pursuits and equally tempered by study and practice of art (1154-73; 1272-1312).

Of similar outline but different content and emphasis is the education of Wigalois in Wirnt von Gravenberg's Middle High German poem of the first decade of the thirteenth century.[6] Until the age of twelve, Wigalois spends his youth learning under the assiduous care of his "mother," "vrouwe Florie" and her multitude of lady attendants (1222-35).

> sîn reiniu muoter woldez nie
> von ir gelâzen einen tac;
> vor liebe si sîn selbe pflac
> und ander manic vrouwe hêr.
> in einem jâre wuchs ez mêr
> den ein anderz in zwein tuo.
> man lêrtez spâte unde vruo
> gewizzen unde güete.
> ouch was sîn gemüete
> zallen dingen veste;
> ez tet niwan daz beste;
> von rehte muosez saelic sîn.
>
> (1222-33)

In a second educational period, knights are invited to instruct him in riding, courteous speech, proper demeanor, sports, and chivalric crafts—"aller hande rîter spil," including:

> buhurdieren unde stechen
> diu starken sper zebrechen
> schirmen unde schiezen.
>
> (1235-60)

Returned once more to the ladies, Wigalois then seeks permission to try his fortune at King Arthur's court. Leaving his grieving mother, as Perceval does, and bearing a magical parting gift, as Lancelot does, Wigalois arrives at court, as Eilhart's Tristan does, for a final period of refining earlier instruction and preparing for

6. Wirnt von Gravenberg, *Wigalois*, ed. J. M. N. Kapteyn ("Reinische Beiträge und Hülfsbucher zur Germanischen Philologie und Volkskunde" [Bonn, 1926]). Cf. the older ed. of F. Pfeiffer (Leipzig, 1847). See H. Sparnaay, "Hartmann von Aue and His Successors," *ALMA*, p. 439.

knighthood. Here, his tutor is Gawain who transmits the best that he knows to the bachelor knight who is his son (1601-22).

> her Gâwein underwant sich sâ
> des knaben mit sîner lere;
> des gewan er vrum und êre.
> den besten was er undertân;
> mit rede hêt er den valschen man;
> ir deheinen er nie ze vînt gewan.
>
> (1601-6)

Wigalois, "sin manheit diu was harte grôz" (1617), lacks the youthful cultivation of intellect which the other heroes such as Galeran, Tristan, and Lancelot possess. The education of Wigalois devotes its emphasis to the moral probity requisite for a knight and to the necessary instruction and practice of warfare's skills.

Representing a slightly different series of qualities are the education texts in a later Middle High German romance, *Wigamur*, ca. 1250,[7] and an even later work in Old French, *Sone de Nausai*,[8] of the late thirteenth or early fourteenth century.[9] These poems, each of which is of less artistic significance than either *Wigalois* or *Galeran*, possess heroic educations which consist merely of subjects listed. However, just as with the cruder versions of *enfances* of Tristan, Perceval, and Lancelot, the attributed curricula achieve a better balance between subjects for the body and for the mind than do the education texts in superior romances.

Despite the humorous and fantastic incongruities of Wigamur's early history,[10] his education, after a period of fosterage with the Lesbia, is devoted to morals, music (singing, harping, composing), buckler-playing, running, wrestling, jumping, courtly games and sports; he thus learns in his "kintheit tugent and gefuoclicheit"

---

7. Von der Hagen and Büsching (eds.), *Deutsche Gedichte des Mittelalters* (Berlin, 1808), I. See *ALMA*, p. 441.

8. M. Goldschmidt (ed.), *Sone von Nausai* (Tübingen, 1899).

9. *ALMA*, p. 279; Joan Evans, *Life in Medieval France* (2nd ed.; London, 1957), p. 119.

10. Studies of the traditional content and quality of composition include G. Sarrazin, *Wigamur, Eine Literarhistorische Untersuchung* (Strassburg, 1879); O. E. Mausser, *Reimstudien zu Wigamur* (Munich, 1906); and G. Ehrismann, *Geschichte der deutschen Literatur* (München, 1918-1935), Part II, last vol., p. 57.

(342-593). However, in this second educational period, tutored, as is Ulrich's Lanzelet, by mermen, he learns nothing about chivalry.[11] Like Lanzelet and Perceval, he enters the world of knighthood anxious for its accolade but ignorant of its ways— and needing, as they do, a chivalric master of the Gornemant type to repair the damage of early isolation.[12]

In the tedious though sporadically delightful *Sone de Nausai,*[13] the education of Sone is directed by a total of four masters who first put him "to letters." By the age of twelve, proficient and refined, he has learned reading, writing, chess, backgammon, hawking and hunting, fencing, geometry, law, and singing (79-104). Before Sone's knighting, then,

> Plus biaus enfes n'estoit trouvés
> Ne nus enfes mieus ne cantoit.
> De tous biaus jus juër savoit,
> S'ot tel grasce que mout l'amoient
> Chil et chelles qui le vëoient.
>
> (100-5)

In *Galeran, Wigalois, Wigamur,* and *Sone de Nausai*—romances representing different countries, opposite ends of centuries, and different degrees of literary quality—the presence of the *enfances* and the general similarities of the education theme within them are noteworthy. Like the *enfances* of the major Arthurian heroes, the *enfances* of these lesser knights are also composed of descriptions of tutelage and displays of subjects learned. As with the major Arthurian heroes, the educations of these minor figures also consist of periods, tutors, and curricula encompassing moral, intellectual,

11. This first period of Wigamur's education has been considered to have been a derivation from Lanzelet's in Ulrich's poem. However, it appears more likely that this period in *Wigamur* is derived from a common tradition with the "Perceval-type" heroes. Mausser, *op. cit.,* proposes the influence of *Lanzelet* upon *Wigamur,* and Webster, among many others, denies it, *Speculum,* XV (1940), 272 f. Cf. chap. iii of this essay.

12. Comparable to these two periods of fairy fosterage and education by a knight are those in F. Castets (ed.), *Maugis d'Aigrement* (Montpellier, 1893), pp. 26-30, 29 f.; and in Harry F. Williams (ed.), *Floriant and Florete* (Ann Arbor, 1947), 1. 549-74, 753-64.

13. F. Hummel's two studies upon *Sone* are important, *Die Kulturhistorischen Element in Sone de Nausay* (Rostock, 1929); and *Zu Sprache und Verstechnik des Sone de Nausay* (Berlin, 1913).

physical, and chivalric subjects. The essential outlines of the educations of these minor Arthurian heroes are congruent with each other; they are similar as well to those of the major Arthurian heroes. In that the *enfances* of these minor heroes consist of educational programs and lists of curricula, they share with the major Arthurian romances a characteristic which is a distinguishing feature of this romance genre as opposed to other medieval literary types. Just as for Tristan, Perceval, and Lancelot, it appears that the romancers of Galeran, Wigalois, Wigamur, and Sone considered an education requisite to the characterization of their heroes and necessary components of their romances.

Within the romance genre after the end of the twelfth century this prevalence of the education of the hero is found as well for non-Arthurian figures. The hero of the "Seven Sages" romances[14] and Alexander of Macedon possess *enfances* recorded in several romance versions. These heroes' youthful exploits bear comparison in theme as well as in its artistic use to similar material in the major Arthurian romances.[15]

The extant Western medieval "Seven Sages" romances[16] include the metrical Old French *Roman des Sept Sages*, the Middle English metrical *Romance of the Seven Sages*, and the Latin prose *Dolopathos* by Johannis de Alta Silva.[17] Although Johannis'

14. Only in certain versions is this hero named, in others, not at all; and in those texts in which he is named, the names are different in each. Florentine, for example, is the hero of the English metrical romance, and Lucinius, the hero of the Latin prose *Dolopathos*.

15. Apollonius of Tyre deserves mention because the many versions of his "life" possess something of the ideal of an educated romance prince, even though they do not possess an *enfance* and education text. As with Chrétien's *Cligès*, even though periods of learning are not detailed, the display and practice of artistic ability is emphasized in the adventures recounted. Not only strength distinguishes Apollonius' nobility, but more so his musicianship and intellectual cultivation, which are the very qualities which mark the youthful exploits of Tristan, and which could have affected the concept of Tristan as learned. On the "Ur"-Apollonius, the best discussion is by Elimar Klebs, *Die Erzählung von Apollonius aus Tyrus* (Berlin, 1899), and on the relationship between Apollonius and Tristan, references are listed in chap. i, notes 18 and 26.

16. The clearest discussion of the Western versions and their possible relationship to the Eastern, is the Introduction to Killis Campbell (ed.), *The Seven Sages of Rome* (New York, 1907).

17. The Old French metrical romance is edited by J. Misrahi, *Le roman des Sept Sages* (Paris, 1933); the Middle English metrical, by K. Campbell, *op.*

Dolopathos, ca. 1184-1212,[18] represents the oldest extant Western version of this popular romance series,[19] the metrical French, though later in time, undoubtedly preserves the most primitive form and content of the "Seven Sages" story.[20] The whole frame tale of this romance—which consists of tales told by sages to vindicate their falsely accused student—is an *enfance* of the hero: a preparation for education followed by periods of learning under the guidance of tutors. Because the *enfances* of these heroes are such significant aspects of the romances, because the educations of these princes resemble those of Arthurian heroes, and because the popular "Seven Sages" heroes are literary contemporaries of King Arthur's knights, the developments of this education theme from simpler to more sophisticated forms are particularly interesting to consider.

The hero of the Old French *Sept Sages* has three periods of education, directed by a nurse, a "maistre," and seven sages named Bacillas, Lentulus, Cathons, Malquidas, Jesses, Damnas, and Berous. After elementary care by a nurse[21] until he is seven years old, the young prince is entrusted by his Emperor father to a "maistre," who inculcates rudiments of polite behavior:

> De trop mangier le gardera,
> A lui aprendre a parler
> Et gentil homme a honerer,
> Et od lui sera au couchier
> Et au vestir et au cauchier.

(350-54)

---

cit.; and the Latin prose, Johannis de Alta Silva, *Dolopathos*, is edited by A. Hilka (Heidelberg, 1913). Subtle changes from the Latin *Dolopathos* are found in the Old French metrical translation of Johannis' poem, by Herbert; C. Brunet and A. de Montaiglon (eds.), *Li romans de Dolopathos* (Paris, 1856), pp. 42-53.

18. Campbell, *op. cit.*, p. xix.

19. *Ibid.*, p. xviii.

20. Misrahi, *op. cit.*, p. xiv; Campbell, *op. cit.*, p. xviii. Cf. G. Paris in *Romania*, II, p. 501, and *Deux Redactions des Sept Sages*, ed. G. Paris (Paris, 1876), pp. 1 f.

21. Hereafter follows a long *excursus* (185 f.) on nurses, their qualities, and their acquisition.

He is then put to school in the "seven liberal arts" with the seven sages in Rome. His curriculum includes astronomy, "clergie," magic, geometry, astrology, rhetoric, and music:

> Les ars aprist d'astenomie;
> De tout son sens ama clergie.
> Il aprist l'art de ingremanche;
> Del aprendre forment s'avanche.
> Il sot tout courre des vens,
> Des estoiles les elimens,
> Et si gardoit bien en la lune
> Et si en disoit la fortune.
> Il sot de la dyaletike
> Et si sot les chans de musike.
>
> (371-80)

More than half of this Old French education text consists of the competition among the sages for the privilege of tutoring the prince; Bacillas, for example, promises the emperor to transmit all the good he knows during a period of seven years, and Berous would teach all knowledge in a single year but offers the compromise, "Aprenderai au valeton/Quanques entre nous siet savon" (333-34). Like the education texts in the cruder Arthurian romances, the education of this hero is essentially a list of studies. The tutors are not differentiated; their methods are unknown; neither the reasons for the prince's learning nor his achievements are discussed.

By contrast, the medieval English *Seven Sages, ca.* 1275-1370,[22] itself by no means a highly artistic work, develops the education theme. More than twice as long as the Old French version, the education of the English hero, named Florentine, maintains the basic outline but changes the details markedly. The seven sages still contend for the favor of instructing the seven-year-old prince, but like the tutors of Tristan and Lancelot, their physical and intellectual qualities are described; also, the curriculum and its inculcation are refined. Malquid(r)as, the fourth tutor in both texts, is not described in the Old French beyond his name and his promise to

22. Campbell, *op. cit.*, p. lix.

impart all knowledge in four years, but in the English version this mentor is an astronomer whose character is amusingly delineated.

> Of fifty winter was he alde,
> Quaint of hand and of speche balde.
> Him thoght scorn and grete hething
> Þat þai made so grete rosing.[23]
>   (89-92)

Descriptive detail in the Old French is made to serve the pedagogic method in the English. The French garden "tour asses plus blanche d'une fleur" upon which the "seven arts" are depicted becomes in the English version a hall surrounded by seven chambers richly painted with murals of Grammar, Musik, Astronomy, Geometry, Arithmetic, "Fisik," and Rhetoric. Thus, Florentine, ever studying, even when putting down his book, "On the walles wald he þan loke" (202). Not only does he learn these arts but he studies all in Latin: "Sone he concayued in Latin speche/Al þat his maisters wald him teche" (205-6). By the fourth year, rhetoric, grammar, and music are his own, by the fifth, astronomy; the sixth year's test proves his physical acuity (215-317); by the seventh year, the child's wit is so "wonder gode" that he surpasses his "maisters euerilkane" (250-52). Florentine's education thus achieves the goals of learning decreed by his father—there is nothing comparable to this in the French version—that he be knowing in "clergy" (46) and that there be none wiser under Heaven (153-54).

A further sophistication of the education of the "Seven Sages" hero is found in Johannis de Alta Silva's *Dolopathos*. In contradistinction to the Old French and Middle English versions, the youth is put to letters not by seven tutors but by a single master whose influence infuses the whole romance.[24] Virgil is Lucinius'

---

23. The changes in characterization are comparable in another tutor, Cato of Rome: *Roman de Sept Sages*, 315-18, and *Seven Sages of Rome*, 103-16.

24. Oddly enough, *Dolopathos* is the only Western version in which a single tutor instructs the prince. This feature relates the Latin poem to the Eastern versions in which one tutor, Sindibad, holds sway over the youth, not seven. As yet not satisfactorily explained, this phenomenon causes hypotheses of extraordinarily complex literary relationships, as Campbell has indicated (*op. cit.*, pp. xi-xxi).

tutor. In teaching method, subjects offered, and in ultimate friendship, Virgil resembles Tristan's Kurneval in Gottfried's poem.[25] Of the several versions of the "Seven Sages" story, *Dolopathos* represents the most artistically perfected and most humanistically inspired education. It exemplifies the malleability of the education theme, particularly in its possibilities for expression of individual writers' concerns.

At Virgilius ob reuerenciam et amiciciam regis puerum recipiens primo quidem ei litterarum tradidit elementa ac deinde blandiendo leniendoque, ut moris est magistrorum, sillabam ex litteris conficere et ex sillabis formare dictionem et ex dictionibus uero perficere orationem eum in augustia temporis perdocuit. Sicque paulatim proficiens puer iam per se et legere et utramque linguam, grecam uidelicet et latinam, proferre cepit. Lectabatur Virgilius et tantam in puero uelocitatem ingenii mirabatur spemque de eo concipiens meliorem ampliorem ei curam impendebat. Puer uero animum dictis magistri accomodans, qui naturaliter elegantis erat ingenii, quicquid semel audissit subtili statim ingenio intellectum uiuaci memorie commendabat, nec opus erat ei secundo super hoc requirere preceptorem. Vnde factum est, ut infra unius anni circulum consocios suos qui eum et etate precedebant iamque quinquennio uel septennio sub disciplina fuerant magistrorum, transscenderet rogaretque Virgilium quatinus eum altioribus instruere dignaretur. . . . Et primo quidem ei gramaticam que prima est et mater artium exposuit. . . . Dehinc ad dialectam uentum est. . . . Postquam igitur Lucinius omnium artium ex integro consecutus est scienciam, libros quoque poetarum ac philosophorum ab eodem Virgilio non omisit audire. . . .
(14-15)

The education of the hero of the "Seven Sages" versions appears more clerical than chivalric. The seven arts are the subjects of his learning; he has little of the martial and social educations of romance heroes. However, that so much of the frame tale is an *enfance* and specifically an education of the hero, that this education consists of separate periods guided by tutors offering a specific curriculum, that this theme is freely developed by each author, and that a progression is easily discernible from the simpler to the more artistically realized versions—these indicate a concern with

25. Professor W. T. H. Jackson notes a similarity between Tristan's and Lucinius' being put to the study of books by a wise man (*PMLA*, LXXVII [1962], 366).

the material and the manner of the hero's education analogous to that in the Arthurian romances.

Alexander of Macedon is another popular non-Arthurian medieval hero whose youthful exploits exemplify the prevalence of the theme of the romance hero's education. His youthful tutelage, as contrasted to that of the hero of the "Seven Sages," inculcates the unity between arms and letters which better approximates the educations of Arthurian romance heroes. Alexander's education is recorded in numerous medieval versions,[26] of which four of the most significant are: first, the twelfth-century, 105-line fragment of Alberic de Pisançon's Old French poem; second, a slightly later Old French decasyllabic version based upon Alberic's octosyllabics; third, another Old French adaptation of Alberic, and, perhaps, the decasyllabic version, preserved at Paris and referred to as "L"; and fourth, a Middle High German translation of Alberic by Pfaffe Lamprecht in the thirteenth century.[27] These four versions, like the several versions of major Arthurian heroes' educations, display similar progressions in content and quality from earlier to later versions.

Alberic's meager fragment, the first vernacular Alexander romance, is based upon Julius Valerius' work, which in turn belongs to the Pseudo-Callisthenes tradition.[28] Alberic's extant verses form a text of compression and variety which is almost en-

26. Accessible editions are, Paul Meyer (ed.), *Alexandre le Grand dans la littérature française du moyen-âge* (2 vols.; Paris, 1886), and Milan S. LaDu (ed.), *The Medieval French Roman d'Alexander* ("Elliott Monographs," Vols. 36-41 [Princeton, 1937 and on]). Other romances of antiquity which, indirectly, could have influenced knightly educations are the Troy stories; Professor R. M. Lumiansky suggested this interesting point in a letter considering this theme. Their effect, however, probably was more general than specific, and its demonstration would be more speculative than definitive. Dares and Dictys are newly translated in R. M. Frazer's *The Trojan War* (Bloomington, 1965); for Benoit, R. K. Gordon's *The Story of Troilus* (New York, 1964).

27. K. Sneyders de Vogel discusses these four versions in "L'Éducation d'Alexandre le Grand," *Neophilologus*, XXVIII (1942-1943), 161-71. Pages 169-71 of that paper give partial *enfances* texts. Complete versions, with the exception of Lamprecht's, are available in Meyer, *op. cit.*, II. Two editions of Lamprecht are obtainable, H. E. Muller (ed.), *Die Werke des Pfaffen Lamprecht* (Munich, 1923); and *Das Alexanderlied*, ed. F. Maurer (Leipzig, 1940; 2nd ed., 1964).

28. The best discussion of the sources of medieval Alexander versions is George Cary's *The Medieval Alexander* (Cambridge, 1956).

tirely an *enfance* of the hero. After initial care by a nurse, Alexander is instructed by five unnamed masters whose moral goals for their student in teaching "totas arz" are: "dignitaz," "conseyl," "bontaz," "sapientia," "onestaz," and "prodeltaz" (84-87). The first tutor trains him in four languages, Greek, Latin, Hebrew, and Armenian,[29] as well as "fayr a seyr et a matin agayt encuntre son vicin." The second tutor instructs in chivalric defense and warfare, the third teaches law, the fourth, instrumental and vocal music, followed by the fifth instructor's tutelage in geometry (or astronomy): "Li quinz des terra mesurar/cum ad del cel entro en mar." At this line the text breaks off.

Whether Alberic attributed to his hero more tutors, more subjects, and more facets of his learning can only be surmised from the other translations and adaptations of the poem.[30] The extant text, however, offers martial and judicial instruction requisite to the prince's future duties as king. Of the refinements necessary for a learned ruler, languages take precedence over all studies, and types of music are described as fully as practices of warfare (94-97):

> Li quarz lo duist corda toccar
> et rotta et leyra clar sonar
> et en toz tons corda temprar,
> par semedips cant adlevar.
>
> (100-3)

This concern with the development of both prowess and wisdom is Alberic's own invention upon the mere pairings of six tutors with six subjects which constitute the education of Alexander in Julius Valerius, Alberic's source.[31] Alberic's originality is defined

29. Armenian may have been considered necessary, and fashionable, for the prince's education because of the Crusades. See Sneyders de Vogel, *op. cit.*, p. 162.

30. That Alberic's text was fuller and included Aristotle as tutor is proposed both by Sneyders de Vogel, *op. cit.*, p. 167, and R. R. Bezzola, *Les Origines et la formation de la littérature courtoise en Occident, 500-1200* (Paris, 1944-1960), Part II, Vol. II, p. 522.

31. *Juli Valeri Alexandri Polemi res gestae Alexandri Macedonis translatae ex Aesopo graeco*, ed. B. Keubler (Leipzig, 1888); "paedagogus atque nutritor nomine Leonides, litteraturae Polynicus magister, musices Alcippus Lemnius, geometriae Menecles Peloponnesius, oratoriae Anaximenes Aristocli Lampsacenus, philosophiae autem Aristoteles ille Milesius" (Book I, p. 12).

by his achievement; "Aubri actualize, pour ainsi dire, l'éducation du jeune prince et combine d'une façon absolument nouvelle la formation scholaire avec la formation chevaleresque, la tradition de l'Antiquité, transmise par les clercs, avec la tradition guerrière qui est l'apanage des chevaliers."[32]

A remarkable variation upon Alberic's educational program is wrought by the poet of the decasyllabic version. Alexander is educated to be a twelfth-century courtier. During his first period of education with a nurse—from whom he refuses to suck until he is given an "orine cullier" (51)—he grows up with noble companions (32), displays brilliant promise, and grows more in those seven years than any other child "en cant" (54). Seven masters then undertake his education. Like the tutors in Alberic, these teach Alexander astronomy and law; but instead of specifying the languages and the music, instead of detailing instruction in warfare and horsemanship, the hero of the decasyllabic versions learns "seven arts plus *seven authors*" (68). Then he is initiated into courtly graces: magic, chess, tables, hunting ("d'esparviers et d'astors"), and to speak to women, courteously, of love. Particularly that last phrase, "parler a dames cortoisement d'amors" (71), represents a significant departure from Alberic. It characterizes Alexander as trained to "l'idéal de la société courtoise"[33] and exemplifies "la première fois que l'amour courtois apparaît dans la littérature au nord de la France."[34]

Even greater amplification and changes in curriculum are found in the "L" text. A first educational period, guided by a nurse (156-59), establishes rudiments of behavior:

> Si li donent tels maistres ki moult furent vaillant
> Selonc les elemens de la loi mescreant.
>
> (162-63)

The second period is overseen first by Nectanabus, who teaches astronomy and magic (167-76), and then by five sage masters who instruct in letters, Latin—"por mix entroduire le firent desputer"

32. Bezzola, *op. cit.*, p. 522.
33. Sneyders de Vogel, *op. cit.*, p. 168.
34. Bezzola, *op. cit.*, p. 525.

—"seven arts," many types of hunting, fencing, courtly games, chivalric horsemanship, weaponry, and music. These tutors encourage that fierce pride in nobility and justice which permeates the "alexandrine romance"[35] just as it does the *Prose Lancelot*:

> Et preudome à connoistre et chierir et amer
> Et le felon haïr et destruire et grever.
> Bien sot felon tolir et preudome doner,
> Et selonc lor maniere sot cascun honerer.
> (213-16)

In these strophes, intellectual endeavors, though present, are less emphasized than courtly pursuits of leisure; for example, hunting, just as in the later Tristan versions and in *Galeran*, becomes the most detailed study and the hero's special skill (195-204). However, a later strophe (xvi), anachronistically placed and derived from the "alexandrine" text,[36] gives back to Alexander the four languages attributed to him by Alberic (but substitutes Chaldean for Armenian!) and restores more qualities appropriate to a learned king, including knowledge of natural laws, astronomy, civil law, rhetoric, and the proper understanding and administration of justice.

Of these four Alexander versions, Lamprecht's poem is the most clearly "translated" from Alberic's, yet it emends the program of Alexander's education and gives it one specifically Germanic mark. Trebling the length of the Old French text, this Middle High German version changes the order of studies, placing languages and music in succession (as opposed to Alberic's first and fourth studies) and names Aristotle the tutor in astronomy and "alle de cundicheit."[37] Lamprecht also greatly expands the instruction in chivalric warfare, the use of weapons, the bearing of the shield, wielding of the lance, spear, and sword, and the proper handling of "sinen vîant" (238), which corresponds to Alberic's "vicin" (93). While Alberic's Alexander is taught law by his third master —"ley leyre et playt cabir/et dreyt del tort a discernir"—Lamp-

---

35. Sneyders de Vogel, *op. cit.*, p. 167.
36. *Idem.*, p. 164.
37. Aristotle's presence in Lamprecht is the justification for believing that Alberic portrayed the philosopher as Alexander's tutor.

recht's hero learns it from his sixth tutor. Alexander is taught to
administer justice like a Germanic king—"und lartin ze dinge
sitzen."[38]

> und lartin, wî er daz irdêhte
> wî er von dem unrehten beschiede daz rehte,
> und wî er lantreht beschieden kunde
> allen den er is gunde.
>
> (247-50)

These four Alexander versions display even better than the
"Seven Sages" romances the developments of the theme of heroic
education by individual writers. From Alexander romance to
Alexander romance, the variations of detail within the basic
framework—on an *enfance* that is essentially a recounting of youthful instruction characterized by several periods, tutors, and subjects of study—and the progression discernible between earlier and
later texts serve to reinforce the impression received by study of
the educations of minor medieval and major Arthurian knights:
the education of the hero is a prevalent medieval romance theme,
eminently susceptible to specific emendation.

These Alexander romances, or at least Alberic's, present a
problem in literary history. Could this "life" of Alexander have
directly influenced the Arthurian heroes' "biographies"? That
Alberic's fragment apparently dates from an earlier part of the
twelfth century[39] than the Arthurian romances which appear at its
end favors an affirmative answer to this question of influence.
However, Alberic's work is too fragmentary to permit valid com-
parisons between it and specific romance texts; its influence is
conceivable but not amenable to investigation. The adapters of
Alberic, the writers of the decasyllabic and "L" versions, and
Pfaffe Lamprecht wrote contemporaneously with the Arthurian
romancers; therefore these texts also cannot claim precedence.
Instead of their influencing the Arthurian romancers, the variations these writers contrived upon Alberic's text—such as the
interests in courtly games, hunting, and conduct with women—

38. Sneyders de Vogel says of this passage: "il nous montre Alexandre
. . . comme un roi germanique, entouré de ses barons" (*op. cit.*, p. 165).
39. *Ibid.*, pp. 162 f.

might well have been inspired by the qualities of Arthurian heroes' educations. More likely than any direct interrelationship, however, is their common reflection of a similar social and literary interest of the late twelfth and thirteenth centuries: that is, the physical and intellectual cultivation of a young prince for those exercises of body and dexterities of mind that his future duties would demand. This last possibility brings us to a consideration of the origin of the theme of the hero's education and the educational *enfance*.

The extraordinary prevalence in medieval romance of prefixing the hero's adult adventures with the education of his youth makes it necessary to inquire into its provenance. More than the mere phenomenon of literary development of the romance genre toward realism, didacticism, rationalization, and biographical content must be involved in this explanation. More also must be involved than is subsumed under the common medieval literary conception of chivalry and knighthood. For in no major definition of a ''knight'' is education emphasized or learning suggested. John of Salisbury's famous description of knighthood says nothing of prerequisites of learning, nor do the countless other definitions of the chivalric temper.[40] According to John:

Tueri Ecclesiam, perfidiam impugnare, sacerdotium uenerari, pauperum propulsare iniurias, pacare prouinciam, pro fratribus (ut sacramenti docet conceptio) fundere sanguinem et, si opus est, aninam ponere. Exultationes Dei in gutture eorum et gladii ancipites in manibus eorum ad faciendam uindictam in nationibus, increpationes in populis, ad alligandos reges eorum in compedibus et nobiles eorum in manicis ferreis. Sed quod fine? An ut furori uanitati auaritiae seruiant, an propriae voluntati? Nequaquam. Sed: Ut faciant in eis iudicium conscriptum; in quo quisque non tam suum quam Dei angelorum et hominum sequitur ex aequitate et publcia utilitate arbitrium (VI, viii).

The literary knight's education also ought not to be dismissed merely as a general reflection of the customs of the times. Investiga-

40. John of Salisbury, *Policraticus*, ed. C. C. J. Webb (Oxford, 1909, and London, 1932). See for example, St. Bernard's Rule for the Templars, *De laude novae militiae* (*PL*, CLI, 576); Alanus de Insulis, *Anticlaudianus* (*PL*, CCX, particularly pp. 186 f.); Étienne de Fougères' *Le Livre des Manières*, ed. J. Kremer (Marburg, 1887), ll. 537-40, 673-76; and Philippe de Beaumanoir's *Les Coutumes de Beauvaisis*, ed. A. Salmon (Paris, 1899-1900), XLV, 1453. Cf. G. Mathew, ''Ideals of Knighthood in Late 14th-Century England,'' *Studies in Medieval History Presented to F. M. Powicke* (Oxford, 1948).

tion should make it possible to specify the nature of the social custom. Those studies which hitherto have considered the habits of the times with regard to the educations of youths, including works of Langlois, Sainte-Palaye, Evans, and Schultz,[41] primarily have used romances as evidence of social custom and then discussed romances as mirrors of their age. This circularity of judgments perhaps may be broken by a more specific inquiry into several possible literary sources for the theme of the hero's education.

Three groups of sources credited with fostering other features of romance will be examined: Irish saga, classical literature, and medieval non-romantic literature. Two aspects of the education theme may be sought in these works. Although often interrelated, it is possible to distinguish between the specific elements of the education—its curriculum, periods, and tutors—and the more general concept of the knight as educated, or learned. Another distinction may be drawn in addition to that between narrative detail and philosophical concept of education within each text. A differentiation may be made between those works of primarily "fictional" nature and those which are essentially "theoretical." As exemplification of these categories, the education of Achilles in the *Iliad*, intrinsic as it is to the narrative, may be considered a fictional treatment of the education theme, as opposed to the didactic and philosophical statement of the education of the ruler in Plato's *Republic*. This distinction between fictional and theoretical treatments of the education theme is a convenient analytical device which will help impose order amidst disparate source materials. The texts to be quoted are only a few among the many which might exemplify the points made.[42] The rationale of this selection is to

41. Ch.-V. Langlois, *La vie en France d'après des romans mondains du temps* (Paris, 1924); J. B. Sainte-Palaye, *Mémoires sur l'ancienne chevalerie; considerée comme un établissement politique et militarie* (3 vols.; Paris, 1759-1781) (or that edited by J. C. E. Nodier [2 vols.; Paris, 1826]); Evans, *op. cit.*; A. Schultz, *Das höfische Leben* (Leipzig, 1889), I. Cf. A. Fourrier, *Le courant réaliste dans le roman courtois en France au moyen-âge* (Paris, 1960); and Friedrich Heer, *The Medieval World*, trans. Janet Sondheimer (Cleveland, 1962), pp. 123-57.

42. I have used Manitius as guide through the dark circles of the *PL*, and have depended upon L. K. Born's studies of the *specula principum* for corroboration of readings and courage to continue on. M. Manitius, *Geschichte der lateinischen Literatur des Mittelalters* (Munich, 1911-1931). Born's ''The

facilitate this consideration of possible origins of the education theme in the medieval Arthurian romances and to formulate the conclusion that such a review suggests.

Representing Celtic fictional literature, the Old Irish saga accounts of the *macnimrada* of Finn and Cuchulainn will be examined, as will be the Old Irish theoretical instruction books for princes and the collections of sententious sayings, the *tecosca*. Of the early classical fictional literature, the *Iliad, Odyssey*, and *Aeneid* have been chosen for consideration and will be followed by later classical fictional works of Ovid and Statius; then theoretical treatises of Plato, Seneca, and Plutarch will be examined. The coalescence between fictional and theoretical in classical panegyric poetry and classical prose romance also will be touched upon. Finally, as comparison to the fictional medieval romances, selected examples of non-romantic medieval literature will be considered for their expression of the theme of the hero's education. The testimony of *miroirs de princes* will be offered here. John of Salisbury's *Policraticus*, William Perrault's *De Eruditione Principum*, and Aegidius Romanus' *De Regimine Principum* are the main examples. The reflection upon the times afforded by Philippe de Beaumanoir's *Coutumes de Beauvaisis* will also be mentioned.

Celtic literature, which has been credited with the origin of so much else in Arthurian romance, including accounts of heroes' births, love affairs, and deaths, offers suggestive material for study of the *enfance* and education of the hero. Cuchulainn, Finn, and Lug are the Old Irish saga heroes for whom *enfances* exist and whom advocates of the Celtic hypotheses of Arthurian origins have most often called to witness.[43] Similarities between these Celtic

Perfect Prince: A Study in 13th- and 14th-Century Ideals,'' *Speculum*, III (1928), 470-504; ''The *Specula Principum* of the Carolingian Renaissance,'' *Revue belge de philologie et d'histoire*, XII (1933), 583-612; and the superb Introduction to his translation of Erasmus, *The Education of a Christian Prince* (''Columbia University Records of Civilization,'' No. 27 [New York, 1936]), hereafter referred to as *Erasmus*.

43. Works of Professor Roger Sherman Loomis are the major authority upon which material in this section on Celtic sources depends. Supplemented by reference to his predecessors and successors, enumerated in chap. ii, note 2, and chap. iii, notes 9, 10, and 22, the Celtic hypotheses for Arthurian *enfances* are best expounded in *Arthurian Tradition and Chrétien de Troyes* (New York, 1949); on Perceval, pp. 335-63; on Lancelot, pp. 239-40. On Ulrich's

heroes' youthful adventures and those of the three major Arthurian
heroes were given passing notice in the three previous chapters and
now will receive more detailed consideration.

None of the Old Irish heroes' childhood adventures has been
shown to have affected the learned ideal or details of the education
of Tristan. With circumspection, Miss Schoepperle, after comparing the feats of prowess and specific skills of Irish with Arthurian
heroes, concludes that Celtic sources for the *enfances* in Tristan
narratives are not possible to establish.[44] Her judgment is con-
firmed by Professor Newstead's correlation between Tristan's
enfance and English tradition.[45]

Cuchulainn's and Finn's youthful exploits, however, bear certain striking resemblances to Perceval's and to those heroes' whose
enfances are comparable to Perceval's. Taken together, the *macnimrada* of Finn and Cuchulainn offer an outline which may account for certain aspects of the Perceval *enfance* framework. Like
Perceval's, Finn's father is wounded in battle and later dies; his
son is raised in a forest by women. The youth's weapon is a casting
spear. Finn, his name meaning "fair one," is called by the epithets
"biauz fils" and "biauz sire"; he demands knighthood from a king
and does not reveal his heritage to this king when asked. Finn
later visits two uncles,[46] one a "fisher king's" father and a second,
to whom he recounts his history, a hermit dwelling in a "desert."[47]

Lanzelet, see Professor Loomis' Introduction and Notes to his and K. G. T.
Webster's translation of *Ulrich von Zatzikhoven, Lanzelet* (New York, 1951).

44. Gertrude Schoepperle, *Tristan and Isolt: A Study of the Sources of the
Romance* (2nd ed.; 2 vols.; New York, 1960), 281, 288. Rachel Bromwich
would place Tristan's *enfance* in the tradition of the Celtic formula of "exile
and return" ("Some Remarks on the Celtic Sources of 'Tristan,'" *Transactions of the Honorable Society of Cymmrodorion* [1953], pp. 32, 45). This
attribution, however, obscures more than it illuminates.

45. "The 'Enfances' of Tristan and English Tradition," *Studies . . .
Baugh*, ed. MacEdward Leach (Philadelphia, 1961), pp. 169-85.

46. Professor Loomis considers these eme-visits part of the *enfance*
(*Arthurian Tradition*, pp. 335 f.).

47. The texts, in translation, may be found in: T. P. Cross and C. H. Slover,
Ancient Irish Tales (New York, 1936), pp. 360-69; R. Thurneysen, *Die irische
Helden- und Königsage bis zum siebzehnten Jahrhundert* (Halle, 1921), pp.
268-73, 396-403. Valuable supplementary material may be found in Eleanor
Hull's *The Cuchullin Saga in Irish Literature* (London, 1898), as well as in A.
and B. Rees, *Celtic Heritage: Ancient Tradition in Ireland and Wales* (New
York, 1961), especially pp. 244 f.

Cuchulainn's *enfance* has certain resemblances to this version
of Finn's—which could account for their hypothetical intermin-
gling[48]—and even greater similarities to Perceval's *enfance*. Like
Perceval, Cuchulainn is brought up by his mother. He hears about
a royal court and announces his desire to seek his fortune there.
His mother consents only reluctantly. Armed with a javelin, he
arrives at the fortress of King Conchobar. From this maternal
uncle Cuchulainn receives training and arms.[49]

These paired *macnimrada* of Finn and Cuchulainn outline a
convincing parallel to Perceval's *enfance*. However, several objections may be recognized. Professor Loomis' inclusion of the
visits to the Grail Castle, (*Perceval*, 69-1698) and to the Hermit
Uncle (6238-6438) in the comparison between Finn's and Perceval's *enfances*—thus ranging virtually from the first through the
last lines of Chrétien's poem—makes the *enfance* somewhat extensive. Then, Cuchulainn's visit to King Conchobar's court bears as
many resemblances to Perceval's visit to King Arthur's court as it
does to Perceval's stay at Gornemant's, for which it is considered
the origin. Also, the most noteworthy correspondences between
Celtic and Arthurian heroes are found not in the early medieval
romance texts but rather in the late fourteenth-century, corrupt,
and uniformly unreliable Welsh *Peredur*.[50] But the chronology of
the Old Irish texts poses the greatest obstacle to certitude. The
"Youthful Exploits of Finn" were composed not before the twelfth
century and survive in manuscripts of much later date.[51] The
enfance of Cuchulainn, preserved as part of the *Cattle Raid of
Cooley*, which Thurneysen traces back to eighth-century composition,[52] is by no means of the same antiquity as the remainder of
the *Cattle Raid* story. Thurneysen says of Cuchulainn's education
with Scathach:

Mit den verschiedenen Bearbeitungen, die die Sage von CüChu-
lainns Aufenthalt bei der Scätach bis ins 12. Jahrhundert erfahren

48. Loomis, *op. cit.*, pp. 335 f.

49. Cross and Slover, *op. cit.*, pp. 137-50; Hull, *op. cit.*; Thurneysen, *op. cit.*

50. "Thanks to the cognate (though corrupt) version supplied by *Peredur*
we can feel assured of the descent of Perceval's "enfances" from the boyhood
deeds of Cuchulainn" (Loomis, *op. cit.*, p. 336).

51. Loomis, *op. cit.*, p. 338; Rees, *op. cit.*, pp. 244-58.

52. Cf. Loomis, *op. cit.*, p. 337.

hatte, fand sie noch keine Ruhe. Wohl der Moderisator etwa des 15. Jahrhunderts hat die Fassung III seinen Zeitgenossen mundgerecht gemacht; in dieser Gestalt ist sie dann in die modernen Volkserzählungen übergegangen. Die zahlreichen Abschriften, die d'Arbois, Essai d'un catalogue S.140 aufzählt, gehen nicht über das 18. Jahrhundert hinauf. Die älteste Handschrift scheint Edinburg, Advocates' Library XXXVIII S.81 zu sein, die Mackinnon dem Ende des 16. oder Anfang des 17. Jahrhunderts zuschreibt. . . .[53]

Assurance for the precedence of the Old Irish texts and proof of their subsequent influence upon the Arthurian romances are difficult when their chronology is so refractory. These several objections notwithstanding, the Old Irish *macnimrada* of Finn and Cuchulainn are analogous in pattern to Perceval's *enfance*.

Even if the Perceval *enfance* framework is dependent upon Celtic origins, the possibility remains remote that the Arthurian education details and ideals are simply reworkings of Celtic themes. Finn's *enfance*, while more clearly allied to Perceval's than to Tristan's or Lancelot's, does have some slight hints of a learned ideal, though without the narrative elements that could be called a youthful education. A remarkably precocious youth, Finn's "thumb of knowledge,"[54] the sign and instrument of his wisdom and divination, makes intelligence and display of gifts the signal qualities of his youthful exploits. Cuchulainn's *enfance*, on the other hand, possesses some narrative elements of youthful education but nothing of an educated ideal for the hero.[55] Cuchulainn's strength lies not in his thumb or his intellect; his attraction to knowledge and facility in attaining it is no more subtle than is his attraction to his beloved Emer, for whom no qualities of mind bestir Cuchulainn, but rather, her extraordinary chest. While the Arthurian material could have developed from these qualities of Finn and Cuchulainn, other possibilities offer less strained parallels.

53. *Op. cit.*, pp. 396 f.

54. A fascinating study on the origin and development of this "thumb" motif (as well as on the "salmon of knowledge," and the "highest wisdom" in the knowledge of animals' language) is by R. D. Scott, *The "Thumb of Knowledge" in Legends of Finn, Sigurd, and Taliesin* ("Columbia University Studies in Celtic and French Literature," [New York, 1930]).

55. Professor Loomis suggests that Cuchulainn's naïveté is the origin of Perceval's *Dümmling* qualities (*op. cit.*, p. 339).

The Irish sun-god Lug's relationship to Lancelot presents a Celtic and Arthurian correlation based upon both late and hypothetical texts. Lug's complete history compares to Lancelot's in eight features, three of which pertain to the *enfance*: the heroes' names are withheld; they are raised by foster mothers, who are queens, until ready to bear arms; they are trained in physical accomplishments by mermen.[56] For the education periods of Ulrich's Lanzelet, the theory promulgated is more detailed. In the first educational period in the fairy lake, the resemblances noted between Lug and Lanzelet are based upon Ulrich's statement that mermen instruct Lanzelet. Qualities of the sea god Manannan have been interpreted as those of a "merwunder"—hence, a merman— and the role of an educator has been attributed to him based upon material first recorded at the end of the nineteenth century.[57] As for Lanzelet's second period with Johfrit and its correspondence to Lug's, the involved supposition has been made that:

The name Johfrit may, like Jofreit fis Idol in Wolfram's *Parzival* and Jaufré, son of Dovon, hero of a Provençal romance, represent the French Giflet fis Do, which in turn goes back to the Welsh Gilfaethwy son of Don. Though the role of Ulrich's Johfrit corresponds to nothing related of either of these personages, it is an odd fact that Gilfaethwy's brother Gwydion reared Lleu or Llew, a prototype of Lanzelet, "until he could ride every horse," and that Prof. Gruffydd has argued that Gilfaethwy superseded Gwydion as father of Lleu. There may have been a Welsh tradition, therefore, that Gilfaethwy instructed Lleu in horsemanship, as Johfrit trained Lanzelet.[58]

While some general framework of Lancelot *enfances* might owe its beginning to Celtic tradition, scepticism seems justifiable upon this origin for the education of Lancelot.

Lug, Cuchulainn, and Finn, then, are the three saga heroes whose childhood adventures have been considered prototypes of Lancelot's and Perceval's. However, certain questions of chronology which are difficult to overcome, and the necessity for multiple hypotheses concerning texts and their relationships make for some-

56. *Lanzelet*, pp. 15-18, and notes 5-29, pp. 158-68.
57. *Ibid.*, pp. 163-64, and Introduction, pp. 16-17.
58. *Ibid.*, pp. 168-69.

thing less than certitude in the attribution of Celtic fictional sources for the educations of Arthurian romance heroes.

The theoretical Celtic literary type pertinent to this study—the *tecosca*[59]—has rarely been considered a possible influence upon medieval romance but deserves notice because of the general similarities in its content to the Arthurian romance educations. *Audacht Moriand, Tecosca Cormaic,* and *Senbrianthra Fithail*[60] are three major repositories of instructions and advice from fathers to sons and from tutors to students which exemplify the *speculum principum* in Early Irish literature.[61] Although no educational program is outlined in these texts of heroes' educations, most of which antedate the fifth century, advice given princes upon the uses of counsel, the administration of justice, and the efficacious handling of women is not dissimilar to sentiments set forth in romance educations.[62] Though the *tecosca* possibly affected aspects of the educations of Old Irish saga heroes, they probably had no direct influence upon the romance heroes whatsoever, but they bear intriguing and unexplored correspondences as *miroirs de princes*.

Celtic literature thus offers suggestive material for the study of Arthurian *enfances* but fails to offer conclusive relationships: conceivably Celtic fictional literature could have offered romancers both an ideal of a learned hero, derived from the *macnimrada*

59. Used by modern commentators upon the genre, *tecosc* is the singular form, *tecosca* the plural, of the Old Irish approximation of Latin *speculum*, with reference to "teaching" or "instuction" texts.

60. Editions and commentaries may be found in Morand, "Tecosc," ed. R. Thurneysen, "Morands Fürstenspiegel," in *Zeitschrift für Celtische Philologie*, XI (1917), 56-106; and XIII (1921), 297-305; as well as his other notices in *ZCP*, XII (1918); XVI (1927); and his *Irisches Recht* (Berlin, 1931). Other editions are cited in the notes to R. M. Smith's paper, indicated below.

61. "The *Speculum Principum* in Early Irish Literature" is the title of R. M. Smith's article, *Speculum*, II (1927), 411-45, upon which this brief discussion depends. Bezzola, (*op. cit.*, II, i, 148 f.) also discusses this Old Irish genre. On the historicity of the figures for whom *tecosca* were written, see Kuno Meyer, "The Wooing of Emer," *Archeological Review*, I (1888), 68 f.

62. *Tecosca Cormaic*, of the third century, is particularly interesting in these regards. See Smith, *op. cit.*, pp. 439, 441-43. Upon the literary relationship between these subjects of *tecosca* and earlier and later satire, a fascinating discussion is F. N. Robinson's "Satirists and Enchanters in Early Irish Literature," *Studies in the History of Religions, presented to C. H. Toy* (New York, 1912), pp. 95-130.

Finn, and details of a hero's education, based upon the *macnimrada* Cuchulainn; possibly the framework of the educations of Cuchulainn and Finn, particularly with regard to Perceval, might have been adapted from their coarse detail and supernatural interest to the sophisticated concern of medieval romance educations with curricula and courtliness. Celtic literature could have been the source for the *enfance* itself.[63] But earlier and later classical literature and contemporary medieval literary expressions offer parallels and detailed correspondences to the medieval romances which are less tenuous.

The form of the early classical epic, with its great action beginning *in mediis rebus*, negates the possibility of an *enfance*. Achilles', Odysseus', and Aeneas' childhood backgrounds are revealed only incidentally, and later in the poems. They are brought to the foreground[64] in scenes calculated to retard the action of the epics.[65] Aeneas' goddess mother reveals his early history in a retrospective recapitulation (Book VIII). Odysseus' scar excuses Homer's excursion into his hero's childhood adventures concerning his nurse, his grandfather, and his hunting prowess (Book XIX). As in the *Aeneid*, there is no hint of educational periods, tutors, or curricula; however, the dramatic parallel to Odysseus' scar is another Homeric "retardation" which does include an educational theme: Achilles' wrathful refusal of aged Phoenix's plea to return to battle (Book IX). Phoenix's plea introduces Homer's digression into Peleus' charge to Phoenix to teach the stripling Achilles to be "both a speaker of words and a doer of deeds." Homer details this upbringing, but this remembrance is the only extant scene in early epic comparable to the educations of Arthurian heroes.

Homer's Achilles, the son of the sea goddess Thetis, receives his first education from his mother (Book XVIII). Later sent by his father Peleus to Agamemnon, Achilles, as yet "unskilled in equal

63. Bezzola, *op. cit.*, II, i, 147.

64. "Background" and "foreground" are here used according to the definition of Erich Auerbach in his discussion of literary representation of reality, *Mimesis*, trans. W. Trask (New York, 1957), pp. 2-20.

65. Adapting ideas of Goethe and Schiller, Auerbach expounds the "retarding" element as a literary device in classical epic (*ibid.*, pp. 3 f.).

war and in debate wherein men wax preeminent,'' is instructed in
this second educational period by Phoenix. Recounted by this
tutor, the ''education text'' reads:

Yea, I reared thee to this greatness, thou godlike Achilles, with my
heart's love; for with none other wouldest thou go unto the feast,
neither take meat in the hall, till that I had set thee upon my knees
and stayed thee with the savoury morsel cut first for thee, and put
the wine-cup to thy lips. Oft hast thou stained the doublet on my
breast with sputtering of wine in thy sorry helplessness. Thus I
suffered much with thee and much I toiled, being mindful that the
gods in nowise created any issue of my body; but I made thee my
son, thou god-like Achilles, that thou mayest yet save me from
grievous destruction.[66]

Once in the Troad, Achilles' third period of education—for
''wisdom''—is overseen by aged Nestor (XI). Finally, at some un-
specified time during his youth, Achilles is taught medicine by the
centaur Chiron.[67]

Like Lancelot, Achilles is the son of a sea fairy, and like both
Lancelot and Perceval, Achilles' earliest upbringing is among
women. Like Arthurian heroes, the second educational period
is directed by a tutor who remains friend and mentor throughout
the hero's life of adventure. Like Lancelot and Eilhart's Tristrant,
Achilles has a period of instruction ''at court'' in which he is
guided by example of an established courtier. However, Homer
provides no program of instruction for ''speaking words'' and
''doing deeds'' beyond Phoenix's attempt to teach Achilles how to
eat.[68] There is no specification of Achilles' acquisition of that
''wisdom'' Nestor is charged to inculcate. This total education of
Achilles—separable into periods, presided over by tutors, and

66. Gilbert Highet (trans.), *The Iliad by Homer* (New York, 1950), p. 160.
67. This is revealed in Book XI when Eurypylos begs Achilles' friend
Patroclus to demonstrate the medical skill which Achilles, after having ac-
quired it from Chiron, had then in turn taught Patroclus.
68. While this wielding of bread and wine may be symbolic of some more
spiritual condition of learning, no other literal detail of youthful (virtually,
infantile) education appears in the *Iliad*. One wonders what Christian al-
legorists such as Fulgentius—who translated Virgil's ''arma virumque'' as
''courage and wisdom'' (cited by E. Curtius, *European Literature in the
Latin Middle Ages*, trans. W. Trask [New York, 1953], p. 175)—might have
done with this passage. Like Virgil, Homer might have been considered a
necromancer because of this prevision of communion!

containing some small detail of things taught—probably had no effect upon medieval romance *enfances*. The *Ilias latina*, the version of Homer known to the Middle Ages, does not contain an education for the hero. However, when viewing the education of the Arthurian hero within the context of the history of an "idea" (in the A. O. Lovejoy and Marjorie Nicolson definition), *Iliad IX* is the point of provenance.

For all his battle-lore and his ability in playing the cross-barred lyre, Homer's Achilles is not a learned hero, nor is Homer's Odysseus or Virgil's Aeneas. Their powers, their destinies, and their wraths are not effected by education. While, in the opposition of several characters, it is possible to establish the polarity of *sapientia–fortitudo* in early classical epic, as Curtius does,[69] there is no unity of wisdom and strength in a single major epic hero, except, perhaps, in Odysseus. Only in him do "heroism, proficiency in war, and wisdom appear to be in equilibrium."[70] But Odysseus' *sapientia* and his *fortitudo* are not synthesized into the learned arms or "armed letters" of a twelfth- or thirteenth-century Alexander, Tristan, or Lancelot. In classical epic, the *topos sapientia–fortitudo*, because it is exemplified by separate characters, is a concept valid only for the total narratives and not for the individual characters within them; in medieval courtly epic, however, this *topos* informs specific characters. Education and learning, the achievements of medieval romance heroes, play little part in the early classical heroic ideal.

Yet, later antiquity possesses fictional educations which, while containing little that could be construed as a learned ideal, nevertheless may have offered a framework to the Middle Ages for the educations of medieval knights. These texts challenge Celtic fictional literature as the probable origin of the outline of the Arthurian romance *enfances*. Achilles' education in Homer, the fullest of the early classical educations of heroes and the probable provenance of this *enfance* idea is an appropriate heroic education to trace through later classical versions.[71]

69. *Ibid.*, pp. 167-74.
70. *Ibid.*, p. 175.
71. Less pertinent but equally fascinating is study of earlier and later versions of other classical *enfances*, such as the education of Paris as a herdsman,

Homer's Thetis, Phoenix, and Nestor are not the only educators classical art and literature attribute to Achilles. The specific relationship between the hero and the centaur Chiron, which so often is represented in classical sculpture and fresco,[72] is not portrayed in the *Iliad*, nor is the even more frequently depicted sequestration and education of the hero among Lycomedes' virgin daughters on the isle of Scyros. Homer merely refers by indirection to Chiron's teaching (Book XI) and simply names Scyros as one of twelve cities captured on the way to Troy (Book IX, 667). However, these two episodes of Achilles' education—with Chiron at Thessaly and with Thetis and Deidamia at Scyros—are preserved by Ovid and Statius and undoubtedly were known in some form to medieval writers.[73]

Although Ovid did not write an Achillean epic, elements of the early exploits of the hero are recounted by reference and allusion in the *Fasti, Ars Amatoria,* and *Metamorphoses.*[74] In describing Chiron's death, accidentally caused by Achilles' poisoned arrows,[75]

Perseus as a fisherman, or Jason as Chiron's student. Pindar associates Jason with Chiron in Pythian Ode IV, v.100-120; Pindar, *Odes,* ed. Sir J. E. Sandys (''Loeb Library'' [Cambridge, Mass., 1957]). O. A. W. Dilke uses this reference wrongly to attribute to Pindar the first association of *Achilles* with Chiron; Statius, *Achilleid,* ed. O. A. W. Dilke (Cambridge, 1954), p. 10; cf. Karl Fehr, *Die mythen bei Pindar* (Zurich, 1936). All of these heroes, along with Achilles, and like heroes of myth and folklore of other cultures, are first exiled from their lands and deprived of their destined roles; second, disguised as well as protected in the guise of an ''underling'' or ''inferior'' being; third, given an opportunity to reveal their inherited nobility; fourth, given a specific trial by which they prove their worthiness; and fifth, ultimately returned and reinstated in their destined positions of rule.

72. Important for this subject is K. Weitzmann, *Greek Mythology in Byzantine Art* (Princeton, 1951), especially pp. 19-21, 85-87, 165-68, 192-93, and figs. 12-16, 205-11. Also, T. S. Duncan, *The Influence of Art on Description in the Poetry of P. P. Statius* (Baltimore, 1914); and Elizabeth C. Evans, ''Portraiture in Ancient Epic,'' *Harvard Studies in Classical Philology,* LVIII-LIX (1948), especially pp. 189 f., 214 f.

73. References appear in Curtius, *op. cit.,* pp. 48-54, and notes to these pages.

74. *Fasti,* ed. and trans. Sir J. G. Frazer (''Loeb Library'' [Cambridge, Mass., 1951]); *Ars Amatoria,* ed. and trans. J. H. Mozley (''Loeb Library'' [Cambridge, Mass., 1957]); and *Metamorphoses,* ed. and trans. F. J. Miller (''Loeb Library'' [Cambridge, Mass., 1958]).

75. J. G. Frazer notes the several interesting variations of Chiron's death, as related by Apollodorus, Diodorus Siculus, Servius, Tzetzes, Eratosthenes, Hyginus, and the scholiast on Caesar Germanicus (*The Fasti of Ovid: Commentary* [London, 1929], IV, 31-32).

Ovid refers to the hero's earlier learning of the art of lyre-playing from Chiron, as well as to this music master's methods of punishing his student's unsatisfactory performance (*Fasti*, V, 390; *Ars Amatoria*, I, 11-16). In Ovid's retelling of Deidamia's tragic tale, Achilles' education in womanly arts—of sewing, weaving, and gentle demeanor—among the ladies of Scyros is twice alluded to (*Metamorphoses*, XIII, 162-70; 179; *Ars Amatoria*, I, 681-704). Drawn from several works, these two educational periods form but a composite *enfance*. In direct contrast to the medieval *enfance*, this education of Achilles has no chronological nor artistic structure. Nonetheless, the Ovidian education of Achilles in music and in feminine crafts represents a variation from the components of the Homeric *enfance* of Achilles and reveals the narrative rudiments upon which Statius (or his source)[76] built an epic.

What Ovid reveals by indirection, Statius fully documents in his *Achilleid*.[77] The education of the hero, which is composed of two periods, directed by tutors, and embellished with curricular detail, constitutes Books I and II, the major extant portion of this first-century epic. A general description of Achilles' *enfance* in Book I provides detail only for the second educational period; the specific description of the first period of education is delayed until the second book. In Book I, Thetis—although a goddess she is also a fearful mother—seeks out Chiron's cave where her son had been educated by the aged centaur.[78] After hearing Chiron's report about Achilles' independent and irascible behavior, and after greeting Achilles' companion Patroclus, her son's equal in "ways of youth" but his subordinate in strength, Thetis joins Achilles.

76. Weitzmann maintains that the great frequency and wide distribution of representations of Achilles' childhood—including aspects which do not occur in Statius—demonstrate that although "the original Greek text for the stories of Achilles' youth is no longer extant . . . there must have existed an *Achilleis* of the Hellenistic period which Statius used for his *Achilleis*" (*op. cit.*, p. 166).

77. Ed. and trans. J. H. Mozley ("Loeb Library" [Cambridge, Mass., 1957]). Compare the edition of Dilke (*op. cit.*) for other readings. On Statius' use of Vergil and Ovid, a useful guide is Mozley's "Statius as an Imitator of Vergil and Ovid," *Classical Weekly*, XXVII (1933), 33 f.

78. Chiron, "far different from his wicked brethren," makes his only toil "to learn the herbs that bring health to creatures doubting of their lives, or to describe to his pupil upon his lyre the heroes of old time" (*Achilleid*, ed. J. H. Mozley, I, 217).

Mindful of the gods' dire predictions, she spirits him away to
Lycomedes' isle of Scyros, disguises Achilles as a maiden, counsels
him in feminine gait and demeanor, and, leaving him in this protec-
tive disguise, as well as offering last, whispered counsels, she finally
plunges back into the main. Achilles is further educated in female
graces by Lycomedes' daughter Deidamia, with whom he falls in
love. She instructs him to move with more modest grace, to spin
unwrought wool, and to weave expertly (551 f.). In return,
Achilles teaches Deidamia to play the lyre, to harp, and to sing
(572 f.).

Achilles' recapitulation in Book II of the program of his first
period of education under the guidance of Chiron is an answer to
the urging of Oenides to recount the "ways his spirit was first
trained," how "his valor grew," and "by what arts his limbs were
made strong and his courage fired" (589). Beginning modestly,[79]
Achilles describes the food he ate during "crawling infancy": the
entrails of lions and the bowels of she-wolves.[80] He then relates his
past practice for fearlessness and for physical prowess; both the
food and the exercise make him, by the age of twelve, capable to
"outpace swift hinds and Lapith steeds and running overtake the
flung dart" (591). Achilles next describes Chiron's teaching of
hunting (only for war-like, not for timid beasts), warfare (the
various fighting methods of neighboring countries), sports and
physical feats (leaping, climbing, "catching stones," wrestling,
flinging the quoit, boxing, "passing through burning houses"),
music (playing the lyre and singing of "the fame of ancient
heroes"), medicine (the juices and grasses which staunch blood,
succor disease, and close wounds), surgery (what ills can be
checked with the knife), and law ("precepts of divine justice").
Achilles fondly recalls Chiron's methods of instruction which

79. Statius specifically says: "Quem pigeat sua facti loqui? tamen ille
modeste/incohat, ambiguus paulum propiorque coacto" (II, 94-95). Dilke,
in his edition of *Achilleid*, describes this scene as a "boastful account" by
Achilles of his childhood in Thessaly (*op. cit.*, p. 8).
80. Discussions of the meaning of these culinary habits, and their probable
relationship to sympathetic magic, are Frazer's *The Fasti . . . : Commentary*,
IV, 30 f.; and D. S. Robertson, "The Food of Achilles," *Classical Review*,
LIX (1940), 177 f.

included encouragement by praise and challenge by ridicule.[81] With Achilles' abrupt "So much do I remember of the training of my earliest years," the extant portion of Statius' epic ends.

Just as for many other aspects of epic form and epic content, this education of the hero in Statius stands midway between classical epic and courtly epic.[82] Whereas Homer's *Iliad* preserves a retrospective *enfance* and education which serve as structural "retardation," and whereas medieval romances present the *enfance* in the narrative present, as the beginning of chronological "biographies," Statius offers elements of both of these epic structures. Mirroring Homer, Statius has a retrospective program of specific education for Achilles (Book II); but, prefiguring medieval romances, Statius delineates a general *enfance* in the narrative present (Book I). Whereas the content of the education program in Homer is vague, spare, and not calculated to forecast the later qualities and talents of the hero, and whereas the educations of medieval romance heroes are specific, detailed, and prefigure the knights' later exploits, Statius represents a mean between these qualities of epic content.[83] The separation of the education into two definable periods, the depiction of the tutor Chiron, and the detail devoted to subjects learned far exceed the meager statements of these education elements in Homer. However, although the three recurring features of medieval romance educations—periods,

81. References to Chiron and his pedagogical methods include p. 521 (his report to Thetis), p. 523 (Achilles' affection for him), p. 529 (Achilles' respect for him), p. 589 (his instruction by praise), p. 593 (his teaching by taunt and threat).

82. Curtius many times refers to Statius' intermediate literary position between antiquity and the Middle Ages (*op. cit.*, Index *sub* Statius).

83. The fragmentary nature of the *Achilleid* makes consideration of Statius' later development of *enfances* themes a speculative endeavor. But evidence of plastic arts as well as contemporary classical literature suggests that Statius' earlier themes would have been related to later themes. For example, Statius describes Patroclus as "replacing" Achilles in Thessaly and using the very implements of sport made for him, just as later, according to most other versions, Patroclus "replaces" Achilles in battle while using his accoutrements of war. In an elegiac soliloquy, Achilles, hidden at Scyros, laments: "Now Patroclus, now you aim my darts, bend my bow, mount the team nourished for me" (ed. J. H. Mozley, p. 557); in almost every version of Achilles' exploits, Patroclus later fights and dies wearing the armor specifically forged for Achilles. Statius might have included this *enfance* lament as prefiguration of this later incident with Patroclus which was traditional to the legend of Achilles.

tutors, and curricula—appear in Statius, his emphases and details
are different. In the depiction of Achilles' tutors and the subjects
of learning, the supernatural and the divine are omnipresent.
Chiron, for example, while an affectionate, stern, and loyal instructor, is the offspring and fosterer of immortals and possesses the
equine whinney and strong hoof of a marvelous man-half-horse.
While Achilles learns many skills from him, most are physical.
The hero's matchless speed, endurance, and might are cultivated by
his instruction in: spanning huge dikes by leaping, climbing, and
grasping the airy mountain peaks, catching flung stones on his arm,
passing through burning houses, catching the flying four-horse
team on foot, flinging the quoit to the sky, and standing against the
flooding river and hurling back its billows (593). Unlike the
Arthurian romancers, Statius' concern is not with a master's
transmission of "culture" to a noble charge, nor with books,
languages, seven arts, or courtly and chivalric refinements. Statius'
education of Achilles consists of supernatural physical training
for supernatural physical exploits of a supernatural hero.

Nevertheless, several features beyond general form and general
content are comparable between Statius' epic and medieval
romance *enfances*. The hero's disguise enforced by his (fairy)
mother who fears for his safety and the instruction and advice she
gives her son before they part also are aspects of the Perceval
stories. The tutor's pedagogical methods of encouragement and
challenge are emphasized both in the *Prose Lancelot* and in Gottfried's *Tristan.* The general details of a complaint by the tutor
against his charge, as well as the education of the hero with a
companion, appear in the *Prose Lancelot.* Finally, the young
Achilles' transmission of his knowledge and musical skill to his
beloved lady, Deidamia, is a theme comparable to the *translatio* of
knowledge in the Tristan versions.

While such details in Statius are similar to aspects of several
Arthurian educations, the education of Achilles does not seem to
have affected the *enfance* of any single Arthurian hero. However,
since Statius was known to the Middle Ages, this *enfance* could
have offered to romancers a framework for educations of their
knights.

Although the framework of the medieval Arthurian *enfance* seems more likely to be of classical fictional origin than of Celtic origin, the ideal of the hero's learnedness which pervades the medieval knight's education and the details which distinguish it have other origins. Classical theoretical literature offers suggestive material for the derivation of both this ideal and this detail. Both ideal and detail are specifically expressed in classical treatises of political theory, the *miroirs de princes*.[84] Many of these treatises, the "authorities" cited, and the passages quoted in the major *florilegia* of the Middle Ages, were known in full or in part to the clerically educated. Such classical theorists as Plato, Seneca, and Plutarch were among the "curriculum authors"[85] expounding the learned ideal and the program for cultivation of that ideal not for the classical fictional hero but, rather, for the theoretical ruler.

Primary education for a prospective guardian of Plato's Republic is composed of two branches, the first one for cultivation of the mind, the second, of the body. Two periods constitute this primary learning, the first in intellectual and physical studies, followed by a second, in military training. The second period in martial subjects generally corresponds to the martial aspects of the medieval knight's education, but the first period affords more congruent features. The Platonic curriculum consists of reading and writing ("Grammatic"); harp playing and singing of lyric poetry; those arts presided over by the Muses ("Music"), including music, art, letters, "culture," and philosophy; and finally, many sorts of athletic exercise ("Gymnastic"), (II, 376–III, 412).[86]

84. Following the usual critical classification of *miroirs de princes*, I examined works which their authors specifically addressed as instruction books for rulers (such as Isocrates' *Ad Nicoclem*) as well as those which, while of broader implication and dedication (such as Plato's *Republic*), yet are major works of statecraft theory. (L. K. Born similarly defines *miroirs, Erasmus*, pp. 44 f.). I also make no distinction in this section between Greek and Latin works, for although differences are discernible the subject has been carefully studied and the differentiation affects no conclusions of this chapter. See M. Lechner's *Erziehung und Bildung in der greichisch-römischen Antike* (Munich, 1933); and E. Bauker, *The Political Thought of Plato and Aristotle* (New York, 1906).

85. Cf. Curtius, *op. cit.*, pp. 48 f., with M. L. W. Laistner, *Speculum*, XXIV (1949), 260 f.

86. Plato, *Platonis opera*, ed. J. Burnet (5 vols.; Oxford, 1900-1907); and

With the exceptions of poetry and philosophy, the educational programs of romance heroes are not dissimilar. Indeed, many details of this primary education expounded by Plato are echoed in the better romance *enfances*. While the artistic intentions of the philosopher and the romancers of course are different, aspects of their works are comparable. The total education in both intellectual and physical pursuits leading to a harmonious development of character (III, 403) particularly distinguishes versions of the educations of Tristan and Lancelot. The idea of teaching concepts and practices of warfare by example (VII, 536) appears in romances of all three major Arthurian heroes.

Specifically noteworthy in the *Prose Lancelot* are Platonic as well as other classical pedagogical enjoinders for instruction without compulsion (VII, 535-41), recognition by means of gentle guidance of what the student's natural capacities suit him for (VII, 538), and inculcation of that maturity of character which castigates wailing and lamentation (II, 387). Especially interesting in Gottfried's *Tristan* are Platonic emphases upon the powers of music and upon the equality of educated women. Music's study gives insight into the harmonious order, the "cosmos" of the world (III, 401); and music, if man surrenders to it, tempers his highly spirited nature (III, 411).[87] So too in Plato's *Protagoras* the concept appears that the child's training in music introduces rhythm and harmony to his soul; this *consonantia* can be later shared. And a man's equal in cultivation as well as in temper of spirit is a woman educated in her youth (IV, 445–V, 470)—such as Gottfried makes his Isold.

No revanescence of Platonism in the Middle Ages need be postulated to explain any of these similarities. While romance writers, clerics or laymen clerically trained in classical authors,

---

The Republic ed. and trans. Paul Shorey ("Loeb Library" [New York, 1930-1935]).

87. Plato's ultimate rejection of the reliability of music in the perfect state further emphasizes his recognition of music's power. Gottfried also rejects music's reliability while delineating its might. The musical nourishment of the lovers in the *Minnegrotte* cannot endure permanently; Tristan and Isold are made to return to other "foods" and life at Mark's court. Gottfried, like Plato, recognizes the glories, warns of the dangers, and ultimately rejects the enveloping sensuality of music.

could have based their educations of knights upon Plato's precepts, more probably they adapted his ideas as they were transformed by theorists of their own epoch. But it is noteworthy that in addition to the learned ideal, specific details of the ruler's education, its periods, and its curriculum appear in this classical theory.

This ideal and these details reappear throughout classical treatises of statecraft. Plato has little to say on the subject of tutors—the third in the recurring features of periods, curricula, and tutors in the romance education texts. However, Seneca, writing the first Latin *miroir de prince*,[88] and Plutarch, uniting his Greek culture with his Roman experience, specifically discuss tutors' functions in their several treatises. Like Plato's, these texts could have offered to the Middle Ages both the ideal and the details of the educated hero.

In Seneca's *Moral Epistles* and *De Ira*,[89] the learned ideal is presented as the necessary emulation, by modern princes, of the rulers of the Golden Age (*Epistles* 90, 5) and consists of a consciously cultivated rational faculty (124, 3). Tutors, who must possess worthy qualifications of character (52, 8), must teach by their own good example (52, 9). Youthful education is not only important but must be guided carefully since the young mind is easily trained, whereas the faults of the older are difficult to correct (*Epistles*, 108, 3; *De Ira*, 18, 2).

Similarly, but with even greater emphasis and detail, Plutarch devotes full essays of the *Moralia*[90] to the ideal of the educated ruler and the requisite training for its achievement. Throughout the *Discourse to an Unlearned Prince* and the *Discourse on the Training of Children*, ideas are expounded which, in dramatic form, also infuse the better Arthurian romances. The need for a noble youth's nature to be nurtured (a prince without education is like a golden statue filled with sand) (*Unlearned Prince*, 2); the necessity and efficacy of good training in developing native ability

88. L. K. Born discusses Seneca's *De Clementia*, written for Emperor Nero, in *Erasmus,* pp. 66-69, and Plutarch's *miroirs,* pp. 71-73.
89. *Moral Epistles,* ed. and trans. R. M. Gummere (''Loeb Library'' [3 vols.; New York, 1917-25]).
90. In W. W. Goodwin (ed.), *Plutarch's Miscellanies* (6th ed.; 5 vols.; Boston, 1898).

(*Training of Children*, 4); the impressionability of young minds and thus their need for careful guidance (*Training of Children*, 4); the necessity and value of a good tutor and the dangers of a poor one (*Training of Children*, 17); the tutor's requisite qualities of virtue, manner, and experience (*Training of Children*, 7)—such precepts are similar to those dramatically expressed by Gottfried and the *Prose* writer.

As with Plato, the direct influence of Seneca or Plutarch upon medieval romancers is an unnecessary and probably invalid postulate. Apposite quotations from Aristotle's *Politics* and *Nicomachean Ethics*[91] could be added to Plato's; and Cicero's *Republic* and *Offices* as well as St. Augustine's *City of God* could reinforce the references to Seneca and Plutarch. Significant in all of these are the emphases upon the ideal of the learned leader and the details of his learning. The education theme appears constantly and consistently in theoretical works of antiquity dedicated to the proposition of the learned ruler.

Both aspects of this education theme, particularly the learned ideal, appear strikingly in classical panegyric poetry. Praise of rulers represents a coalescence of the dichotomy between fictional and theoretical, for both fiction and theory are put to the service of praise. Uniting compliment with prescription and reflection with obsequy, poems of praise enshrine the synthesis of *sapientia–fortitudo*. Myriad examples in Pliny the Younger, Quintillian, Statius, Dion of Prusa, Aurelius Victor, Ausonius, Claudian:[92] these display the same concern of the classical political theorists with the learned ruler and the details of his instruction.

Just as in classical panegyric poetry, so the education theme is specific in classical panegyric prose biographies, in the "historiography" of Plutarch's *Lives*, or in Pseudo-Callisthenes' *Life of Alexander*. Because of Alexander's significance as historical king of antiquity transformed by the Middle Ages to medieval hero of

91. Aristotle becomes exceedingly important in the later medieval *miroirs*, those written after the "rediscovery" of Aristotle in the mid-thirteenth century. Many of the thirteenth- and fourteenth-century *miroirs* consist almost entirely of quotations and paraphrases of his thought; his influence is most marked in the work of Aegidius Romanus, which will be discussed later.

92. These cited by Curtius suffice; *op. cit.*, pp. 176-77.

head, heart, and hand, he is the appropriate example to which to
return. Plutarch's idea of "biography" in the literary form of
prose romance justifies the emphasis upon education and its detail
in both his and other contemporary "lives" of Alexander: "It is
not Histories that I am writing, but Lives; and in the most il-
lustrious deeds there is not always a manifestation of virtue or vice,
nay, a slight thing as a phrase or jest often makes a greater revelation of character than battles where thousands fall, or the greatest
armaments, or sieges of cities."[93] Thus, not only is Alexander
portrayed both in Plutarch and Pseudo-Callistenes as the embodiment of courageous wisdom and learned might, but the periods,
tutors, and subjects of the education which made him so are indicated. "When he became a lad, his pedagogue was Lekretetis, a
negro, his foster-father Leukonides, his teacher of literature
Polyneices of Pella, and of music the Lemnian Alkippos, of geometry the Peloponesian Menippos, of rhetoric the Athenian Aristo-
menes, of Philosophy, Aristotle of Melos, and of warfare Lamp-
sakes. . . . So as time passed he was educated in formal knowledge
and began to think of ruling. . . ."[94] In classical prose biography
as well as in classical panegyric poetry, the unity between fiction
and theory displays in the education of heroes the unity between
prowess and learning.

Direct relationship between any of these antique expressions
and medieval dramatizations of the learned ideal and the details of
its acquisition is not a necessary hypothesis. Clerics and laymen
schooled in the classics adapted these same ideals to their own new
prescriptions for rulers of medieval Christianity. Classical ideals
emended by medieval predecessors and contemporaries, rather than
by the individual romancers themselves, would appear the more
likely origin of the Arthurian education theme. Ideas of the time
expressed in medieval theoretical works concerning rulers appear
to be the "realities" which Arthurian romances reflect in their
educations of heroes.

Before considering these medieval theoretical adaptations of

93. *Plutarch's Lives, Alexander,* ed. and trans. B. Perrin ("Loeb Library"
[New York, 1919]), VII, 225.
94. Pseudo-Callisthenes, *The Life of Alexander of Macedon,* ed. and trans.
Elizabeth Haight (New York, 1955), p. 21.

classical ideals of kingship, we might remark upon the medieval
fictional genre of national epic for its lack of expression of the
education theme. In Germanic epic the learned hero has no place.[95]
Siegfried, in his brief *enfance* in the *Nibelungenlied*, early expresses his preference for chivalry over kingship, but no ideal is
intimated nor detailed for his preparation for knighthood. Of his
enfance, before the tourney celebrating his knighting, we are told
only that: "By Siegmund's and Sieglind's command he was
dressed in elegant clothes, and experienced men well-versed in
matters of honour had him in their charge, as a result of which he
was able to win all hearts. He had grown to be strong enough to
bear arms expertly, and he possessed in abundance all the needful
qualities.'"[96]

In French national epic, many heroes of *chansons de geste* have
their childhood exploits recorded in specific and separate songs
within the epic cycles, such as the *Enfances Guillaume, Enfances
Vivien*, and *Enfances Ogier*.[97] These *enfances* are not restricted to

95. For their discussions of Germanic "ideals," two fascinating studies
upon learning and the hero in Anglo-Saxon epic are, Levin Schücking, "Wann
entstand der Beowulf? Glossen Zweifel und Fragen," *Beiträge zur Geschichte
der deutsche Sprache und Literatur*, XLII (1917), 347-410; and R. E. Kaske,
"*Sapientia et Fortitudo* as the Controlling Theme of *Beowulf*," *SP*, LV
(1958), 423-56. Schücking suggests that Beowulf may have been composed
for a Scandinavian prince, reigning in the Danelaw territory, as a *miroir de
prince*. Kaske details the fusion in *Beowulf* of Christian with Germanic concepts.

Not only is the learned hero essentially absent from Germanic epic, but he
does not appear in the legendary British history either, unless such *sapientia-
fortitudo* is found in Robert of Gloucester in Geoffrey of Monmouth's *Historia*
(as Professor Robert W. Hanning, Columbia University, suggested to me).
The chronicles of Geoffrey, Wace, and Layamon, despite their exhortations to
good behavior in rulers, do not seem to have influenced the Arthurian *enfances*.
Demonstrations of the total influence of the chronicles upon romances are
J. S. P. Tatlock, *The Legendary History of Britain: Geoffrey of Monmouth's
Historia . . . and its Early Versions* (Berkeley, 1950); and Robert W. Hanning,
*The Romantic Histories of Britain: Studies in the Relationship Between
Individual and Society in Early Medieval Historiography* (New York, 1964).
Geoffrey of Monmouth, *History of the Kings of Britain*, trans. S. Evans,
revised C. W. Dunn (New York, 1958); *Arthurian Chronicles Represented by
Wace and Layamon* (New York, 1928).

96. Trans. A. T. Hatto (Baltimore, 1965).

97. *Les Enfances Guillaume*, ed. Patrice Henry (Paris, 1935); *Les Enfances Vivien*, ed. C. Wahlund and H. von Feilitzen (Upsala and Paris,
1895); *Les Enfances Ogier par Adenés di Rois*, ed. M. A. Scheler (Bruxelles,
1874). (An interesting comparison is the *enfance* in the thirteenth century

programs of education and displays of youthful learning as are the Arthurian childhood exploits. Rather, they are concatenations of typical adult adventures of French epic heroes which, however, are engaged in before the ceremony of knighting. *Enfances* of the *chansons de geste* are closer in quality of content to Celtic *enfances* and accounts of legendary heroes of other cultures than to *enfances* of Arthurian romance. Those displays of youthful cultivation which do appear are physical exploits, not intellectual. Of Vivien's youthful hunting skill, for example, detail is given of his passion for the sport, his consequent disobedience to his foster parents, and his purchases for himself of a hunting dog and hawk (1339-46); later, his successful killing of a deer is described (6388-98). For Vivien and the other heroes of *chansons de geste*, the *enfances* are imbued with much *fortitudo*, but there is no expression of *sapientia* or its acquisition in these early adventures.[98]

These French epic *enfances*, all very late additions to the cycles,[99] are contemporaries of Arthurian romances. Without the two aspects of the education theme—learned ideal and educational detail—these *enfances* of the *chansons de geste* surely cannot be considered the possible origin for Arthurian *enfances*.[100] On the other hand, French epic *enfances*, while different in spirit and content, yet add weight to the supposition that the pattern of the hero's youthful exploits was extraordinarily prevalent in medieval

Aiol, ed. J. Normand and G. Raynaud [Paris, 1877], a *chanson de geste* with so many affinities to romance it is often called a romance. [For example, Evans, *op. cit.*, p. 118.])

98. While not directly concerned with the *enfances* of heroes, studies on the general qualities of the knights of national epics and of their adventures, particularly in relation to ''historical fact,'' include G. B. Fundenberg, *Feudal France in French Epic* (Princeton, 1918); and T. A. McGuire, *The Conception of the Knight* (Michigan, 1939). Also, R. W. and A. J. Carlyle, *A History of Medieval Political Thought in the West* (London, 1928), especially, III, 22 f. on the ''realistic'' qualities of epic as opposed to romance.

99. *Les Enfances Guillaume*, pp. xxx-xxxv, xli; and Bezzola, *op. cit.*, II, ii, 520.

100. Rather, the three possibilities for the origins of French epic *enfances* would seem to be: emulation of Alexander romances, reflection of the same general forces which shaped Arthurian romances, and specific imitation of Arthurian romances. The first supposition is offered by Bezzola (*op. cit.*, II, ii, 520; and II, i, 147); the second possibility is proposed by Henry (*op. cit.*, p. xli); and the third is intimated by M. Jeanroy (*Romania*, XXVI, 13, n. 1). Cf. O. Riese, *Untersuchungen über der Enfances Vivien* (Halle, 1900).

fictional literature. The specification of childhood exploits as education—its acquisition and its display—is the distinction of
Arthurian romance, as well as those romances whose courtly
princes, like Alexander, are made Arthurian in everything but
name.

This dedication of childhood to education is a major interest of
the important theoretical treatises of the Middle Ages, the *miroirs
de princes.*[101] Politics and ethics are not distinguishable in these
treatises, and learning is the bond between both disciplines. Ex-
pressing concerns of their time, demonstrating their debts to ideals
of antiquity, and comparing remarkably with educations of
romance heroes, the medieval *miroirs* promulgate the ideal of a
learned ruler and detail the program of his education.

These ideals are expressed in almost every medieval *miroir.*[102]
But differences are discernible between earlier works, such as John
of Salisbury's *Policraticus* and Hugh of Fleury's *Tractate*, when
compared to those later, such as William Perrault's *De Eruditione
Principum* and Aegidius Romanus' *De Regimine Principum*. The
details of the prince's education, its periods, his tutors, and his
curriculum, can be examined in these same works, with additional
reference to Gilbert of Tournai's *Eruditio Regum et Principum*,
and to such a typical reflection of laws and manners as Philippe de
Beaumanoir's *Coutumes de Beauvaisis*. No direct interrelationships between theoretical *miroir* and fictional romance will be
proposed, but rather, the suggestion will be made of the specific
topicality of the Arthurian romance educations of heroes. The
testimony of the medieval *miroirs* indicates that the attributes of

---

101. Excluded from the material of this chapter are the numerous clerically conceived and clerically dedicated medieval ''theoretical'' treatises which
discuss education. St. Bruno of Cologne's works, for example—while sharing
with romances certain classical ideas upon learning which are transformed by
Christianity—are addressed specifically to the cloister or the classroom. So too
for others cited by Reginald Poole, *Illustrations of the History of Medieval
Thought and Learning* (London, 1960) and Jean Leclercq, *The Love of
Learning and the Desire for God*, trans. Catherine Misrahi (New York, 1960).
Excluded also is the Bible as source for education themes, even though its
general qualities and precepts must have affected, very indirectly and very
diffusely, the pedagogy in romance.

102. Convenient summaries may be found in Born's works upon the
specula principum: Speculum, III (1928), and *Erasmus*, pp. 44-130.

the educated knight were adapted from the qualities proposed for
the learned ruler.

The ideal of the learned prince expressed in the twelfth-
through fourteenth-century *miroirs* is not dissimilar from that in
the first *miroir* known to literature, Isocrates' *Ad Nicoclem*, 374
B.C.[103] This learned ideal, which well might be the signal "idea"
for tracing a tradition of admonition from Isocrates through the
Renaissance humanists and beyond, remains constant through the
centuries, but its specific qualities vary from epoch to epoch. Differences are apparent between classical and medieval works, and
between earlier and later medieval treatises.[104] Characterizing the
medieval *miroirs*, L. K. Born states:

There is little originality displayed; the main argument is nearly
always supported by wholesale quotations; the methods and topics
are nearly all the same. . . . Before the twelfth century little space
is given to economic matters or to education in its strictest sense.
This is not so in the succeeding centuries. . . . In the political
thought of the thirteenth and fourteenth centuries (as in the
earlier centuries), the central figure about which the whole revolves
is the prince. This emphasizes the personal view toward rulership
which is characteristic of the period. Furthermore, in accordance
with the medieval attitude, the writers of these centuries considered
the real in terms of the ideal and were interested in nothing less
than the pattern of the perfect prince. . . . [The] combination of
Greek thought and Roman vigor, joined with medieval theology,
resulted in a mixture of idealism and practicability. . . . Every
one of the writers lays great stress upon the personal moral virtues
of the prince . . . emphasis [is placed] upon counsel which is so
regularly enjoined upon the ruling prince.[105]

Emphases in the medieval works upon the necessity for education, not merely wisdom; upon the prince's personal moral virtues;
and upon his instructors and advisors appear in Plato and other
classical theorists; but the *Republic*, for example, proposes the

103. *Isocratis Opera*, ed. and trans. G. Norlin ("Loeb Library" [New
York, 1928]). Born begins his history of the *miroir* genre with Isocrates
(*Erasmus*, pp. 46-49).
104. To the comprehensive bibliographies in Born's studies, and to the
selected works cited in Chap. II, notes 60-61, above, a recent work may be
added which expertly considers education during the centuries for which evidence is fragmentary: Pierre Riché, *Éducation and culture dans l'Occident
barbare, VIe-VIIIe siècles* ("Patristica Sorbonensia," No. 4 [Paris, 1962]).
105. *Erasmus*, pp. 125-27.

refinement through learning of many individuals before selection of
the one to rule. The medieval theorists, on the other hand, address
the one who by birth or political accident must be refined to reflect
the image of the perfect prince. Plato, it would seem, fits the noble
man to the learned pattern whereas the medieval theorist fits that
pattern to the man.

The learned ideal develops in quality from its expression in the
mid-twelfth century—contemporaneous, then, with the earliest
Arthurian romances—to its definition in the thirteenth and early
fourteenth centuries—comparable in time to Gottfried, Wolfram,
and the *Prose Lancelot*'s writer. John of Salisbury's *Policraticus*,[106]
written in 1159, the earliest medieval *miroir* to be considered,[107]
proposes that the perfect ruler be "learned in letters" as well as
guided by the council of men of letters (IV, 6). John continues: "I
do not know how it chances, but since the merit of letters has lan-
guished among princes, the strength of their military arm has
become enfeebled and the princely power itself has been as it were
cut off at the root. But no wonder, since without wisdom no government can be strong enough to endure or even to exist."[108] In John's
exposition of the learned ideal for the ruler—whose responsibility is
the commonwealth (the *universitas* whom he represents [IV, 2; V,
2, 4]) but who is himself responsible to God (IV, 3; IV, 6)—noble
mind is not only united with noble might, but without *nobilitas
mentis* there is no *nobilitas corporis*. This emphasis upon the
learned "root" of power is greatly elaborated by John's successors.[109] Indeed, from the earlier medieval *miroirs* to the later,
there is a definite progression from concern with *nobilitas corporis*
to preoccupation with *nobilitas mentis*.[110]

Yet, John's chapter heading for statement of this ideal of the
learned ruler reads: "That he should have the law of God ever

106. Ed. C. C. J. Webb, *op. cit.*
107. John of Salisbury's is the earliest medieval *miroir* which was written
at the same time as were the (earliest) Arthurian romances. In beginning
with John's work, I follow the precedent of Born, *Speculum*, III (1928),
470-504; and W. Berges, *Die Fürstenspiegel des hohen und späteren Mittelalters* (*MGH*, Schriften II) (Stuttgart, 1938).
108. *The Statesman's Book of John of Salisbury*, trans. John Dickinson
(New York, 1927), p. 29.
109. Berges, *op. cit.*, pp. 26, 52-59, 67-70, 123-29, 289-356.
110. *Ibid.*, pp. 9-10, 26, 62-67.

before his mind and eyes and should be learned in letters. . . ."
The necessity for knowledge of letters is the ability to read the law
of God. Similarly, Hugh of Fleury prescribes letters and defends
learning for a king "ut acuatur cotidie ejus ingenium lectione
divinorum librorum."[111] The implications, in Hugh and more so in
John of Salisbury, that personal knowledge of God's law fosters
noble action toward God's design, strengthen these otherwise com-
paratively brief statements of the ideal for learned rulers.[112] However, later medieval *miroirs* state the *nobilitas mentis* ideal so fully
that Christian virtue becomes dependent upon Christian learning;
the education of the ruler is his means to necessary public virtues
and to personal salvation. William Perrualt's (d. *ca.* 1275) thesis,
originally attributed to Thomas Aquinas,[113] that the princely
"head" which rules the "body" politic must be assiduously
"filled,"[114] makes him devote more than half of his *De Eruditione
Principum* to the elucidation of that ideal.[115] Aegidius Romanus'
(d. 1316) demonstration that the prince's "highest good" is in
"works of wisdom" is the major constituent in his *De Regimine
Principum.*[116]

From John of Salisbury to Aegidius Romanus, from earlier to
later *miroir*, there is a development from desirability of the learned
ideal[117] to necessity for that ideal. These later treatises augment

111. *Tractatus de Regia Potestate et Sacerdotali Dignitate* (i, 6), *MGH*,
Libelli de Lite, Vol. II.
112. John of Salisbury also says, later, that the prince must be learned in
law and military science (vi, 2).
113. Therefore, the edition of William Perrault's *De Eruditione Principum*
is found in Thomas Aquinas' *Omnia Opera* (Parma 1852-1871), XVI,
Opusculum xxxvii, pp. 390-476. An excellent bibliography is given by Berges,
op. cit., pp. 308-13 (who calls William "PseudoThomas").
114. This "organic analogy," used by Aquinas as well, was first formulated
by John of Salisbury, *Policraticus*, V, 2. (See Born, *Speculum*, III [1928],
472).
115. Book III and especially Book V, which nearly equals in length all the
other books put together, discuss the prince's education.
116. Since Philippe le Bel, to whom this *miroir* was dedicated, immediately
had it translated into French from Latin, and since this French text is the
best and most accessible in modern edition, this is the one which will be
quoted; ed. S. P. Molenaer, *Les Livres du gouvernement de rois* (New York,
London, 1899). On the education, see especially Book II, and I, i, iii. (Many
libraries catalogue Aegidius' works under: "Egidio Colonna.")
117. John of Salisbury, for example, proposes that while the prince

statements of ideal with minute proposals for its acquisition.
Marked similarities obtain between these details of theoretical
medieval rulers' educations and the *enfances* of romance heroes.

Just as the general configurations of *enfances* of Tristan, Perceval, Lancelot, and other romance heroes are distinguished by
educational periods, tutors, and curricula, so are the recommenda-
tions for young princes. Romance heroes spend their first several
years under the care and instruction of women, and their second
educational period under the tutelage of a male tutor, chosen for
his own specific qualities and charged with a definite curriculum
for cultivation of both mind and body of the future knight. In
the best romances the Arthurian knight's curriculum is separable
into "liberal" and "chivalric" studies, with special introduction
to the responsibilities of knighthood. So too with the *miroirs*.

The separation of romance heroes' educations into separate
periods is not an artifact of analysis. In both romances and *miroirs*
there is a definite transition point, often at the age of seven,
between educational periods of learning with women and learning
with men. This dichotomy Sainte-Palaye traces back to a "law"
of the Roman Emperor Julian.[118] Deschamps dramatically records
it: Il y a jusques a VII ans/Et plus encore trop de péris/Mais il
n'en chant a nos maris. William Perrault, carefully detailing his
plan of periods, advises the first seven of the prince's years to be
spent in learning essentials of polite behavior (V, 12, 13), and the
next seven years under a tutor's direction practicing courtly,
intellectual, and physical endeavors (V, 14-20). Aegidius Romanus
describes these educational periods even more systematically, devot-
ing separate chapters to elementary learning "des enfanz de cen
que il sont né jusqu'a VII anz apres" (II, xv), and the second
period of specific subjects, "quele cure l'en doit avoir des enfanz de
VII anz jusqu'a XIV anz" (II, xvi). Gilbert of Tournai proposes
in like manner the planning of educational periods.[119]

Presiding over these separate periods are first, a nurse, and then,

---

himself ought to be learned in letters, if he himself cannot be literate, then,
at least, his counselors must be lettered men (IV, 6).

118. *Op. cit.*, I, 28.

119. Gilbert of Tournai, *Le Traité Eruditio Regum et Principum*, ed. A. de
Poorter ("Les Philosophes Belges," IX [Louvain, 1914]), Book I, 2, 5.

more importantly, a tutor, each of whose careful selection is a topic
of special interest, dramatically in the romances, theoretically in
the *miroirs*. Comparable to the long romance disquisitions upon the
perils of acquiring suitable nurses—in *Galeran, Sone,* the "Seven
Sages" versions, and the Alexander texts[120]—are similarly forth-
right considerations of nurses in William (V, i) and Aegidius
(II, xv).[121] Similar to the romance portraits of tutors—the suit-
ability for his task of Tristan's Kurneval, for example, as well as
the *Prose Lancelot's* master's defaults of duty—are William's enjoinders to proper choice of tutors. The prince's master must
possess those personal and professional qualities which, in the
translatio of learning, will redound to the prince's honor. Of stable
character, the tutor must conduct his own life honorably, possess
lofty ideals, eloquence, skill in his profession (V, 9), and excellent
manners (V, 11).[122] Aegidius too details the character and qualifications of the good master (II, ix). Learned, capable of trans-
mitting his knowledge, and understanding the special "conditions
des enfanz qu'il doit enseignier" (II, ix, 13-14), the tutor must
be "sachanz es sciences de clergié et estre sages es euvres humaines
en cen que l'en doit fere, et qu'il soient prodons et de bone vie"
(II, ix, 34-37).[123]

The similarities between romance and *miroir* in separation of
the education into periods and in definitions of tutors are made more
striking when the curricula of knights are compared with those of
princes. The elementary learning of the first periods are similar:
rudimentary education in behavior toward God, men, and women.
The "liberal" curricula of the second periods correspond in both:

120. A striking contrast is Wolfram's unusual representation of Herzeloide
personally nursing her son Parzival. Notice of this is given in chap. iii, n. 38.
121. Compare Philippe de Beaumanoir, *op. cit.,* lxix.
122. Comparable to this (and also to the *Prose Lancelot's* portrait of the
hero raised with noble companions) are William Perrault's sentiments upon
the choice of the prince's companions, their necessary reliability, congeniality,
and desirable habits (V, 40, 42-43).
123. *Op. cit.,* p. 205. For qualities and functions of tutors examined from
a legal point of view, an interesting comparison is Philippe de Beaumanoir's
Coutumes, xvii, in which are discussed: the tutor's task, which is not only
to educate, but to "defendre et garantir, et pour leur droit maintenir et
garder" (570); the necessity for the tutor's periodic reports to the seigneur
who employs him (571); the tutor's salary, allotment of funds for the child's
needs, and adjustment of salary according to the care given (577).

studies in the "seven arts," refinements of manner, physical exercise, and laws and customs of the land. More remarkable, however, are affinities between romance and *miroir* elucidations of chivalry. Comparison of two scenes of chivalric indoctrination—Lancelot's tutelage by the Lady of the Lake in the *Prose* and Gurnemanz' initiation of Parzival in Wolfram's poem—with selections from John of Salisbury, Aegidius Romanus and others indicates that, just as for the other aspects of their educations, the proposed functions of these fictional romance knights are also those of theoretical rulers.

In William Perrault, the prospective first educational period is devoted to articles of religion, to speech, manners, dress, and conduct with elders (V, 12-13). In Aegidius, from birth until seven, the royal child, given rudimentary instruction in Christianity (II, v) and slowly introduced to refinements of conduct, must develop dexterity of body and elementary proficiency in language and music (II, vi; II, xv). For the liberal curriculum of the second period William proposes studies which he considers the major occupation of youth (V, 4) and the determinants of character (V, 7) —in the "seven arts," other sciences, sports, hunting, courtly games, horsemanship, and law (V, 22). Aegidius devotes his second period to "l'escience de clergié" (II, vii), specifically the seven "sciences franches et liberaus," plus several others which pertain to both a cleric and a king including, "nature," "divinité," "les droiz et les lois," "musique," "bones moeurs," and "languages" (II, vii, viii). Until the time of his knighting, the young prince ought to learn sports and "a chevaucher et a liutier et as autres euvres fere qui sont requises a chevalerie" (II, xvii). In these subjects of liberal learning and physical exercise, as well as in the elementary period, the educations of Arthurian heroes concur.

In their indoctrinations of their young men into the art of chivalry, romance and *miroir* agree in quality but differ in attribution: qualities ascribed to romance knights are in the *miroirs* the attributes of ideal rulers. John of Salisbury and Aegidius Romanus discuss knights essentially as warriors. John defines knighthood's duties as defending the Church, attacking unbelief, protecting the poor from injury, keeping the peace in the state, and pouring out one's blood for one's brothers (VI, viii).[124] Aegidius also considers chivalry only for its martial aspect: "chevalerie est un espece et une maniere de sens et d'avisement par quoi l'en seurmonte les ennemis et ceus qui deffendent et empeschent le bien et le profit commun du people" (III, iii, i, p. 372), and proceeds to discuss the climates and nations which produce the best soldiers, the age at which military training should begin, and the education of the knight in skills of arms, military drills, and gymnastic developments (II, III, VI, VII).[125] Such martial prowess, however, is but one of several responsibilities of romance knights.

The *Prose Lancelot's* Lady of the Lake challenges her noble foster son to accept the burdens of a knighthood, the responsibilities of which far exceed those which are simply martial, and resemble, instead, those of a ruler. She explains the major functions of chivalry as maintaining justice and protecting the Holy Church. In discussing the respective roles of the knight, the Church, and the people, she explains the symbolic significance of the knight's armor. These functions of the knight, his social role with respect to other men and institutions, and the very origins of chivalry are represented in John of Salisbury and other theorists as attributes of rulers.

According to the Lady of the Lake, chivalry's obligation toward justice—"Drois iugieres sans amour & sans haine · & sans amor daidier au tort por le droit greuer · & sans haine de nuire au droit por traire le tort auant"—demands certain personal qualities of

124. Elsbeth Kennedy cites this reference as example for comparison between the Lady of the Lake's speech and John's theory upon "chivalry" ("Social and Political Ideas in the French Prose *Lancelot*," *Medium Aevum*, XXVI (1957), 90-106). However, while here John merely states that defense of justice and church are the knight's duty, elsewhere, in great detail, John allots these duties *primarily* to the king; the knight executes the order of the king whose responsibility this defense is. Kennedy ignores all of the more numerous and more detailed affinities between the Lady of the Lake's definition of chivalry and John's discussion of kingship.

125. Pp. 371-85. Aegidius' whole section on chivalry and its functions, as well as the similar discussion upon warfare in John of Salisbury, are based upon Vegetius' *De re militari*; both medieval theorists quote this treatise at length. Aegidius Romanus disagrees with Vegetius in one regard. While Vegetius maintains that townsmen ("vileins") make the best soldiers, Aegidius favors noblemen, for they are more apt to endanger their lives for the sake of "honor" and less likely to flee when the chips are down! (p. 380).

the knight. He must be merciful, kind-hearted, just (114, 116), and inexorable toward the wicked (116). So too in John of Salisbury, the king responsible for justice must temper it with mercy (IV, 8) and be unswerving in his punishment of all those who commit injury and crime (IV, 2). In the Lady of the Lake's explication, maintaining justice for "the people" places the knight in relation to humanity as a rider is to his horse. The people deserving the knight's aid and protection carry him upon them, care for his needs, and carry him forward (115). Employing a different analogy with yet the same qualities, John of Salisbury likens the people (peasants) to the feet of the body of which the prince is the head—for these raise the prince, sustain him, and move him forward (V, 2).

Not only must the Lady of the Lake's knight defend justice for all but he has specific responsibilities toward those ordinarily defenseless: to widows, to orphans, to the old and weak (115). John's king similarly has duties to the very wise and the very foolish, to little children, to widows, to the weak and aged (IV, 3). The knight of the *Prose Lancelot* and the king of the *Policraticus* are servants of the people (*Prose Lancelot*, 115; *Policraticus*, IV, 7).

Both are also servants of God. (*Prose Lancelot*, 115; *Policraticus*, IV, 7). For the knight's defense of the Church he wears armor which has symbolic meaning. The Lady of the Lake explains that the "weakness" of the Church: "Car ele ne se se doit deuanchier par armes · ne rendre mal encontre mal · Et por che est a che establis le cheualiers quil garandisse chelui que tent la senestre ioe quant ele a este ferue en la destre" requires that the shield which shields the knight defend the Church (114). Similarly, the shield of John of Salisbury's prince is for the protection of the weak and must ward off the darts of the wicked from the innocent (IV, 2). This symbolic exposition of armor, its heritage extending back in time to St. Paul ("Ephesians," VI), is a commonplace of twelfth- and thirteenth-century theoretical literature.[126] Comparable are the Monk of Moiliens' symbolic description of the sword's edges and points and Philippe de Beaumanoir's elucidation of the double

126. Kennedy (*op. cit.*, p. 100, n. 52) cites a list of these given by Paul Meyer, "Nouvelles Catalanes inédites," *Romania*, XX (1891), 579-80.

swords which govern the people.[127] Thus armed as servants of God, the Lady of the Lake's knight and John of Salisbury's king must ultimately answer to God for their discharge of His assigned duties.[128] The knight not executing his obligations loses God's favor and the privileges of Heaven (116). The king not discharging his responsibilities properly is judged in Heaven and loses God's grace (IV, 1, 7, 10, 12).

Another fascinating correlation between romance fiction and *miroir* theory derives from the Lady of the Lake's exposition of the origins of chivalry.

Et tant sachies vous bien que cheualiers ne fu mie fais a gas ne establis · & non pas por che quil fuissent au commenchement plus gentil homme ne plus haut de lignage li un de lautre. Car dun peire et dune meire deschendirent toute gent. Mais quant enuie & couoitise commencha a croistre el monde. Et forche commancha a vaintre droiture. A chele eure estoient encore pareil & vn et autre de lignage & de gentilleche. Et quant li foible ne porent plus souffrir ne endurer encontre les fors. si establirent desor aus garans & desfendeors por garandir les foibles & les paisibles. Et tenir selonc droiture. Et por les fors bouter ariere des tors quil faisoient & des outrages. A cheste garantie porter furent establi chil qui plus ualoient · a lesgart del commun des gens. Che furent li grant & li fort · & li bel & li legier · & li loial & li preu & li hardi. Chil qui des bontes del cuer & del cors estoient plain.   (113-14)

This explanation of the development of knighthood as the redress to the conquering of right by might is elsewhere the history of kingship. John of Salisbury discusses the originally good state of society which needed no checks and laws (VIII, 17) until unjust power triumphed over right; then a prince was needed and was created (VI, 21).[129] Even closer to the Lady of the Lake's explanation of chivalry's origins is Philippe de Beaumanoir's explication of kingship:

Comment que pluseur estat de gens soient maintenant, voirs est qu'an commencement tuit furent franc et d'une meisme franchise,

127. Monk of Moiliens, *Li Romans de Carité et Miserere du Renclus Moiliens*, ed. Van Hamel (Paris, 1885), pp. 22-24; and Philippe de Beaumanoir, *op. cit.*, XLVI, 1474, p. 246.

128. Berges discusses God's ordination of monarchy, *op. cit.*, pp. 24 f.

129. John makes the analogy between human society and the social organization of the bees, which comparison is familiar from Virgil's *Georgics*, IV, 153-218.

car chascuns set que nous descendismes tuit d'un pere et d'une mere. Mais quant li pueples commença a croistre et guerres et mautalent furent commencié par orgueil et par envie, qui plus regnoit lors et fet encore que mestiers ne fust, la communetés du pueple, cil qui avoient talent de vivre en pes, regarderent qu'il ne pourroient vivre en pes tant comme chascuns cuideroit estre aussi grans sires l'uns comme l'autres : si eslurent roi et le firent seigneur d'aus et li donnerent le pouoir d'aus justicier de leur mesfès, de fere commandemens et establissemens seur aus; et pour ce qu'il peust le pueple garantir contre les anemis et les mauvès justiciers, il regarderent entre ceus qui estoient plus bel, plus fort et plus sage, et leur donnerent seignourie seur aus en tel maniere qu'il aidassent a aus tenir en pes et qu'il aideroient au roi, et seroient si sougiet pour aus aidier a garantir. Et de ceus sont venu cil que l'en apele gentius hommes. . . .   (XLV, 1453)

In the *Prose Lancelot*, the delineation of the hierarchy of power is significant. The Lady of the Lake skips one step in the creation of the chivalric social order. She omits the king. While in John and Philippe the creation of the king is primary, and the "gentius hommes" or knights are created secondarily to aid him, in the Lady of the Lake's explanation chivalry is primal. It is the first and highest calling.

Lancelot's introduction, then, to the origin, social role, and functions of chivalry is comparable to contemporary medieval discussions of political ideas.[130] However, what appears in John of Salisbury and Philippe de Beaumanoir as the province of the ruler is in the *Prose Lancelot* the responsibility of the knight. The topicality of these ideas emphasizes the narrative skill of the *Prose* writer by whom they were so dramatically transformed into a chivalric education of an Arthurian romance ruler-knight.

Parzival's chivalric education in Wolfram's poem also is comparable to theoretical educations of princes. Gurnemanz' chivalric Advice to Parzival, as Chapter II, above, suggests, is a magnificent elaboration upon the four short precepts of Advice in Chrétien's poem.[131] The speech in Wolfram has a specific and rigid structure in which twelve separate precepts are contained in four categories —of spiritual and ethical injunctions, of admonitions concerning

130. The best general discussion of the social "estates" in medieval literature is R. Mohl, *The Three Estates in Medieval and Renaissance Literature* (New York, 1933).
131. See pp. 60-66, 70-73, 88-97.

polite daily behavior, of chivalric precepts, and of suggestions for behavior with women. These four categories are addressed to the four *personae* of Parzival as the Neophyte Knight: the ruler, the boy, the warrior-knight, and the husband. The comprehensiveness of this didactic program and its arithmetic structure do not negate the dramatic power of Gurnemanz' wise words to his "adopted son." On the other hand, the poignancy of the setting and the diction of the poetry do not obviate the fact that within a scant eighty-four lines is compressed a virtually complete thirteenth-century *miroir de prince*.

Aegidius Romanus' *De Regimine Principum* may be compared to Gurnemanz' speech. Aegidius the theorist (1247-1316) and Wolfram the romancer (fl. 1200-1212) express the ideals of their epochs, specifically concerning Christian kingship. A similar scheme of correspondences might be executed for William Perrault's *miroir* and Wolfram's poem, or between Gilbert of Tournai's or Robert of Blois'[132] and Wolfram. But the enormous popularity of Aegidius' treatise[133] makes it a worthwhile comparison to Wolfram's introduction of Parzival to chivalry.

Gurnemanz' first category of spiritual and ethical injunctions (addressed to the ruler) corresponds to Aegidius' Book I, Part II. Not only are the sentiments parallel—the necessary virtues of the knight and of the prince must include *humilitas, misericordia,* and *mesura*—but they are emphasized similarly. Wolfram, for emphasis, begins with humility: Never lose your sense of shame, for the shameless man always sheds his honor (170:16-20). Also for emphasis, Aegidius concludes his list with humility and, like Wolfram, pairs it with honor (xxiv, xxv, xxvi): "Et por cen humilitez est meëne entre orgueil et avillance, quer humilité et

132. Gilbert of Tournai's edition is cited above, n. 119; Robert of Blois, *L'Enseignement des Princes*, ed. J. H. Fox (Paris, 1948). Cf. the education of the prince in Pierre du Bois, *De Recuperatione Terrae Sanctae*, ed. E. Langlois ("Collections de Textes pour Servir à l'Étude et à l'Enseignement de l'Histoire," IX [Paris, 1891]).

133. Testimony to the popularity of this work is Berges' enumeration of the translations and versions of Aegidius in Latin, French, Italian, Castilian, Catalan, Portuguese, Middle High German, Middle Dutch, Middle English, Old Swedish, and Hebrew (*op. cit.*, pp. 320-28). See also the critical catalogue of Aegidius' total works, by Gerardo Bruni, *Li Opere di Egidio Romano* (Firenze, 1936).

principaument a oster l'orgueil, par quoi li hons se retret mie des
hennours selon cen que il doit, et atempre l'avillance et la chaitiveté,
par quoi li hons se retret plus des hennours que il ne doit" (xxvi).
Next in Gurnemanz' speech is the need for compassion, generosity,
and kindness for the youth of high birth who is striving even
higher (21-24); comparable are Aegidius' injunctions about
liberality and magnanimity in princes (xx-xxiii). And similar to
Gurnemanz' appeal to Parzival for "maze," to be poor and rich appropriately, not profligate, not niggardly, are Aegidius' precepts
upon continence as opposed to incontinence (xv, xvi), liberality
but not prodigality (xvii, xviii), and magnificence within a mean
(xix).

The second category of Wolfram's enjoinders concerning polite
behavior (addressed to the boy) is paralleled by Aegidius' Book II,
Part II. The romance group of four counsels—shun bad behavior,
"unfuoge"; do not ask too many questions; do not disdain answers;
and let your seeing, hearing, tasting, and smelling bring you to
wisdom—with all their ramifications as a narrative device, and
despite their similarities to folklore proscriptions,[134] are yet within
the prince's training in elementary behavior. Addressing himself
to the prince upon shunning bad behavior, Aegidius writes: "quer
quant li hons s'encline a aucun mal, il se doit moult acostumer au
bien qui est contreire a celi mal . . . . [vi, 21-23] les enfanz espetiau-
ment doivent mult eschiver mauvese compaignie" (xiv, 28-30).
As for asking and answering questions, Aegidius forbids the use of
words which are "desatemprees" and "desapensees." While not
identical to Wolfram's, Aegidius' warnings are surprisingly
similar: "Quer les gennes genz, por cen que il sevent pou et ont pou
esprové, il parolent volentiers tost et desapenseëment, por quoi l'en
les doit amonestier que il ne respoignent mie tantost sanz penser a
cen que l'en lor demande, et les doit l'en acostumer a penser, por
cen que il ne dient paroles qui facent a reprendre et a blasmer"
(x, 33-40). Comparable to the last of the four romance counsels
concerning the senses, Aegidius recommends what and how children must speak, see, and hear (x), and apropos of taste and smell,
what and how children must eat (xi).

134. See pp. 59-60, notes 11-12; p. 78; p. 92.

Gurnemanz' third and shortest category (addressed to the warrior) upon temperance of justice with mercy, and the washing of rust from the face after bearing arms, has no exact parallel in Aegidius, although justice and mercy are discussed (I, Part II, x-xiii) as well as are practical chivalric precautions (III, Part III, i-vii).

In Wolfram, the final category of instruction concerns behavior with women (addressed to the husband). Its exposition of equality between man and woman who are husband and wife marks a major departure from Chrétien's courtly love interest. However, it finds a correspondence in Aegidius' Book II, Part I. Similar to Wolfram's emphasis upon unwavering devotion and lack of deception in the marriage relationship are Aegidius' chapters upon proper marital government (xvi), the husband's necessary continence (xvii), and his need to avoid jealousy (xix). Corresponding to Wolfram's statement of marital equality, "man and wîp diu sint al ein" (173:1), Aegidius' commands equality: "entre l'omme et la femme doit avoir egauté" (xii) and recommends implementing this equivalence in life (i-xii, xx-xi).

The ideas of Aegidius' *De Regimine Principum* appear to be epitomized in Wolfram's governance of a prince which Gurnemanz expresses. Wolfram's dramatic form, lacking systematic justifications for each precept and quotations from authority, nevertheless presents most of the basic content of Aegidius' *miroir*. While Aegidius addresses the prince, Wolfram's Gurnemanz, introducing identical considerations, advises Parzival on the conduct of a knight. Aegidius' work, to be sure, is a compendium of quotations from Aristotle—few pages can be turned without "le philosophe dit" appearing—and of commonplaces of other medieval moralists who are as much indebted as he is to classical writers. He, just like William Perrault or Gilbert of Tournai or Robert of Blois, expounds thirteenth-century ideas which undoubtedly were meant for a wider audience than one prince.[135] Indeed, a familiar phrase in *De Regimine* is that a particular quality ought to be possessed by

135. Some of these *miroirs*, though dedicated to a ruler, had a wider application and were really intended for the use of the children of all nobility. (Born, *Speculum*, III [1928], 471.)

"les gentiz hommes" but "meësmement les rois et les princes."
However, what is merely desirable for the nobleman is obligatory
for the prince. This special obligation of the prince: to God, to the
people, and to himself—this obligation to conform to the image of
princely perfection—is never left unsaid in Aegidius' work. In
Wolfram's poem this same obligation informs the knight's chivalric
learning.

These striking similarities between details of Lancelot's and
Parzival's chivalric educations with John of Salisbury's and
Aegidius Romanus' proposals for rulers add emphasis to the other
comparable features in both romance and *miroir*: the interest in
the liberal curricula, the concern with tutors, and the separation of
educations into periods. These many congruent details are but-
tressed by similar expressions of the ideal of an educated hero in
these fictional and theoretical works. Parallels between medieval
theoretical princes and medieval romance knights are too frequent
to be fortuitous. They must have been influenced by common ideas.
It seems likely that the romancer's concern with heroes' educations
and their conception of the knight as educated or learned reflect
those similar concerns and conceptions of the epoch that pertain to
kingship. Late twelfth- through fourteenth-century educations of
princes, proposed by and probably reflected by *miroirs de princes*,
offer the closest congruence of ideals and details with the prevalent
romance theme of the education of the Arthurian hero.

Thus the narrative pattern of the Arthurian hero's education
which was so excellently adapted to special artistic functions by
Gottfried, Chrétien, Wolfram, and the *Prose Lancelot* writer was
prevalent in romance of the Middle Ages. The fluorescence of
enfances and educations of heroes in romances of the late twelfth
through early fourteenth centuries, both those of superb quality
and those of indifferent artistic worth, was not confined to romances
of Tristan, Perceval, and Lancelot. Lesser romance heroes too, such
as Galeran, Wigalois, Wigamur, and Sone de Nausai, possess educations comparable in content to those of major Arthurian heroes.
Non-Arthurian romances of the same positions in time as the major
and minor Arthurian romances and partaking of many of their
qualities—those of the "Seven Sages" and Alexander—also dis-

play *enfances* and educations of their heroes. These non-Arthurian youthful exploits preserved in several versions display the same progressions from simpler to more complex education texts in earlier to later versions that characterize the major Arthurian heroes' versions. While it is possible to postulate interrelationships between these major and minor Arthurian romances, and between Arthurian and non-Arthurian romances, with regard to the hero's education, the similarities among them all suggest their independent though similar development of a common theme.

The provenance of this frequent narrative interest in the medieval hero's education has been sought in fictional and theoretical works of Celtic, classical, and medieval literature. Irish saga, early classical epic, but more importantly, late classical epic, classical political theory, and medieval theory in the classical tradition offer the closest ideals and details to the medieval romance education theme. Old Irish saga accounts of Cuchulainn's and Finn's *macnimrada* outline an *enfance* which may relate to that of medieval heroes, particularly Perceval's. Homer's *Iliad* (IX) preserves the first literary example of the education of a hero and is probably the ultimate origin of the *enfance* idea which captivated succeeding poets' minds. While this "idea" of an education may originate in Achilles' retrospective *enfance*, the actual classical influence upon medieval romance more probably derives from such a late epic as Statius' *Achilleid*, and from educational theory recorded in classical *miroirs de princes*. The classical ideas in *miroirs*, reassessed and revised, are basic to medieval discussions of kingship. Of all the possibilities, medieval theory in the *miroirs de princes* offers the closest parallels to the education theme and its content in medieval romance.

A review of the possible provenances of the *enfance* idea suggests a tripartite conclusion. The basic framework of the *enfance* and education of the Arthurian hero may be of Celtic origin but more probably is of late classical provenance in such an epic as Statius' *Achilleid*. However, the ideas and sentiments which determine the details and inform the concepts within this education "outline" are ideals of the epoch regarding kingship; these ideas, derived from antiquity and transformed by Christianity, are expressed, theoretically, in contemporary medieval *miroirs de princes*. Finally, from this medieval pattern of the learned ruler the romancers formed the educations of their heroes and the conceptions of their knights as learned. The best Arthurian romance authors present these details and this concept in their own artistic configurations of chivalry, of Christianity, and of love. For each of these subjects the education both predicts and depicts standards which the hero either must achieve or must transcend. Consideration of the prevalence and provenance of the romance education theme suggests that delineation of a hero's education is a necessary factor in his characterization and hence necessary to the complete romances. Just as the Arthurian hero as a knight must love, so as a prince must he learn.

⟨ Conclusion

The education of the Arthurian hero as it is delineated in the *enfances* of Arthurian romances is both sufficiently delimited and significant to invite thorough investigation. Circumscribed by the narrative limits of birth and knighting yet essentially unbound by traditional proscription, the *enfances* and educations discussed have revealed general attributes of the romance art as well as individual qualities of each romancer's craft. Close examination of these prodigious childhoods has highlighted the artistic methods and the philosophical attitudes of each of the romancers. Some literary interrelationships between romances have been proposed on the basis of this analysis. The study has made possible the identification of some pervasive qualities, developmental characteristics, and literary progressions of this relatively unstudied pattern of romance art: the education within the *enfance* of the Arthurian hero.

This *enfance* has been seen to consist primarily of the hero's education. Preceded by parental history, which reveals the inherited qualities with which the hero is endowed, and succeeded by adventures which display the qualities of his learning, the essential core of the *enfance* is a program of education. Three recurring features have been noted in the education texts. First, the education is distinctly partitioned. The earliest period is overseen by women, the next is directed by a male tutor, and the last, if present, is guided by a courtier of the king. Second, the male tutor's qualities of character and his pedagogical methods are delineated with noteworthy emphasis. This tutor is often seen to be a significant figure later in the romance, and his teaching exerts an extensive influence upon the hero's adult adventures. Third, the young hero's curriculum, with few exceptions, consists of subjects whose nature can be divided into "liberal" and "chivalric" content. These include, first, "liberal arts," reading, instrumental and vocal music, law, hunting, and exercise in sport; second, there is tutelage in chivalry's practical and philosophical precepts. These educational periods, these fully characterized tutors, and these divisions of curricula appear as the constant components of an *enfance* pattern to which still other embellishments were added by individual Arthurian romancers.

The *enfances* and educations of Tristan, Perceval, and Lancelot, the three major Arthurian figures whose adventures are preserved in multiple versions, were subjected to close analysis. Study of the several extant versions of these *enfances* revealed certain qualities specific to each hero and indicated developments in the education theme from the simpler to the more sophisticated texts. Tristan's *enfance* is a portrait of precocity exemplifying the artistic reconciliation of the battle between *miles* and *clericus*. In the young Tristan learning and artistry supersede mere martial prowess. Tristan's antithesis is Perceval who in his youth is purposefully uneducated and intentionally deprived of chivalry and courtliness. Perceval's belated education, however, is a carefully controlled progress from rustic *Dümmlingheit* to potential wisdom. Lancelot's *enfances* portray him in one instance, like Perceval, a *Dümmling* hero, and in the other, like Tristan, a precociously learned youth. This inconsistency in portraiture was shown to contribute to an understanding of significant literary relationships and divergent literary origins.

Three major texts were considered in the detailed study of Tristan's education and *enfance*. The tripartite education in Eilhart von Oberg was seen to offer a curriculum of *hovelichen dingen* which, however, was but an enumeration of subjects without subsequent importance for the romance. Though educated, Eilhart's hero is not learned. Thomas of Britain's Tristan, on the other hand, is an intellectual hero and a musician. In this text, concern with education and its effects was striking. While not so fully catalogued as in Eilhart, Thomas' hero's learning was displayed in action, and his passions for music, languages, hunting, and artful ceremony, as well as certain configurations of his youthful training, were stressed later in the romance. Close examination of this character and event revealed marked similarities to details ascribed by Jean de Marmoutier, in his *Historia Gaufredi Ducis Normannorum et Comitis Andegavorum*, to the historical figure Count Geoffrey the Handsome of Anjou. The congruences suggest the possibility that Thomas' characterization of Tristan may have been inspired by this learned Angevin count. From Thomas' learned knight, Gottfried von Strassburg derived a Tristan as perfect artist. Augmenting the usual tripartite educational framework, Gottfried detailed the nature of the education, the character of the educator, and the uses and effects of learning. Among Gottfried's innovations are his emphases upon the quality of Tristan's music and musicianship, the apprehension through education of the pain in learning, of the necessity for restraint, of the uses of guile, and of the concept of preparation before action. In the study of this remarkably embellished *enfance*, many incidents wrought with humor, irony, and parody were also cited in suggesting qualities of the romance which make it poetry with which, as Gottfried himself said, noble hearts can laugh. Three minor and less perfected Tristan versions—*Sir Tristrem*, the *Prose Tristan*, and Malory's "Book of Sir Tristram of Lyones"—were also considered. In these, the education is neglected, absent, or unelaborated; the significance of these *enfance* texts consists simply in their preservation of the education theme in rudimentary form.

In the consideration of Perceval's education and *enfance*, five minor and artistically cruder romance versions—*Sir Perceval*,

Peredur, Carduino, "Bliocadran's Prologue," and the *lai* of *Tyolet*—and two major works—Chrétien de Troyes' *Perceval* and Wolfram von Eschenbach's *Parzival*—were studied. Like the less refined Tristan stories, the minor texts contain only the barest outlines of the education theme. Study of Chrétien's poem, however, reveals specific structural functions for the education both within the *enfance* and later in the poem. Perceval's first two periods of learning, with his mother and with Gornemant de Gohort, are combined with a structurally parallel third period, with his Hermit Uncle, to form an educational progress. Recognition of this progress permits an understanding of the architectonic design of the *Conte del Graal* and allows an alignment of otherwise anachronistic incidents within this narrative of preparations and culminations. Appreciation of this framework is necessary to understanding Chrétien's excellent humor in applying his romance art. In Wolfram von Eschenbach's poem, the moral and spiritual implications of the *Dümmling's* education are explicated and amplified. The tripartite education shows that Parzival's two periods of education, with his mother Herzeloide and with Gurnemanz de Graharz, plus a later third period with Trevrizent, are structurally not unlike those in Chrétien's poem. But in Wolfram they also mark a spiritual and chivalric progress from destructive chivalry to chivalric nobility. In depicting Parzival's parental heritages of diverse qualities and their conflict within him, and in the realistic portrayal of the hero as a child, Wolfram entirely transforms Chrétien's rustic *Dümmling* and neophyte knight. New details are lavished on the tutor Gurnemanz, who is Chrétien's apparently original character Gornemant. Wolfram grants him an attendant daughter, a quality of sorrow, and a more defined influence upon Parzival's chivalry, religion, and love. Gurnemanz' initiation of Parzival into chivalry is a scene remarkable not only for its ethical purpose and its arithmetic design but also for a definition of the chivalric temper that is unmatched in romance.

Lancelot's educations in Ulrich von Zatzikhoven's *Lanzelet* and the *Prose Lancelot* have not shown the same significances for the total romances as have the *enfances* of Tristan and Perceval. A study of the educational periods, tutors, and curricula of these two educations of Lancelot, however, suggests their independence from one another and offers some indication of their possible origins. The *enfance* of Ulrich's Lanzelet reveals such affinity with the youthful exploits of Wolfram's Parzival that *Parzival's* influence upon *Lanzelet* seems undeniable. Lanzelet's *Dümmling* character and the actions attributed to him parallel those of Parzival. Lanzelet's tutor Johfrit, his family, as well as his method of teaching, correspond to the like details ascribed to Parzival's Gurnemanz. The mode of Lanzelet's transition from chivalric awkwardness to knightly excellence replicates the outline of Parzival's progress. Philological evidence adduced by other scholars indicating a relationship between Wolfram and Ulrich seems corroborated by this detailed examination of characterization and event within the *enfances*. In the *Prose Lancelot*, the hero's education shows no correspondence to the *Dümmling* qualities and ingenuous marvels of Ulrich's poem. Concern with Christian humanism, in general, and educational theory, in particular, emerges from an analysis of the hero's first educational period with the Lady of the Lake and his second period at the court. Delineation of the antagonism between precocious prince and inadequate master and dramatization of the philosophical dichotomy between Nature and Nurture compose the *Prose* writer's portrait of Lancelot's precocity.

Remarkably prevalent in other Arthurian romances as well as in non-Arthurian romance, the education of the hero seems to have been a necessary element in his characterization and, consequently, a necessary component of romance narrative. Minor Arthurian knights such as Galeran, Wigalois, Wigamur, and Sone de Nausai, as well as non-Arthurian figures such as Alexander and the "Seven Sages" heroes, have educations prefixed to their adult adventures and *enfances* which, both in quality and in development, correspond to those of the major Arthurian knights. The presence of educations within the medieval *enfances* transcends barriers of language, century, and artistic merit.

In an attempt to determine the provenance of this prevalent romance theme, Celtic, classical, and non-romantic medieval literature were investigated. A distinction was made between "fictional" and "theoretical" works. Style was used as the basis for this separation, with dramatic narratives such as Homer's *Iliad* being termed fictional, and didactic philosophical texts such as Plato's *Republic* being termed theoretical. Within this material two aspects of the education theme were sought—the constellation of educational detail and the statement of the philosophical concept of the learned hero. Analyzed in this way, Celtic theoretical works, the *tecosca*, appear to have no relationship to the development of Arthurian *enfances*. Early classical fictional epics, though having no direct effect, yet were seen to preserve the earliest extant education of the hero in the retrospective *enfance* of Achilles in the ninth book of the *Iliad*. Celtic fictional saga such as in the *macnimrada* of Cuchulainn and Finn possibly might have offered a basic framework to the medieval romancers' *enfances*. It seems far more probable, however, that late classical fictional epics, particularly the *Achilleid* of Statius, determined the medieval *enfance* outline. The sentiments and ideas which inform the concept of the educated hero and determine its specific details appear to be medieval theoretical adaptations of classical theoretical expositions of kingship. While marked correspondences obtain between qualities of romance educations and those proposed in classical *miroirs de princes*, such as Plato's and Plutarch's, the most remarkable congruence between fiction and theory is to be noted between medieval romances and medieval *miroirs* written in the classical tradition—such as John of Salisbury's *Policraticus* and Aegidius Romanus' *De Regimine Principum*. Thus derived from antiquity and transformed by Christianity, these ideals and details ascribed to the theoretical ruler depicted in the medieval *miroirs* are found to be presented as the attributes of the fictional knight in medieval romance. The investigation of the education within the *enfance* pattern, the identification of its varying artistic usages, and the inquiry into its origins illuminates the methods and achievements of the major Arthurian romancers, for whom the portrait of the pursuit of learning, like the pursuits of damsels and dragons, jousts and justice, and honor and love, seems to have been an essential of the Arthurian adventure.

ℴ Bibliography

To facilitate further investigation in the *enfances*, this bibliography is separated into four sections which correspond to the four chapters of the study. Occasionally, a work is pertinent to more than one chapter and therefore is cited more than once. Each section is subdivided into lists of texts and of secondary works. However, an edited text used solely for its critical apparatus is listed as a secondary work. Books cited in the notes to the Introduction appear in Section IV.

I. TRISTAN

TEXTS

Bédier, J. (ed.). *Le Roman de Tristan par Thomas.* 2 vols. Paris, 1902.

Benedetto, Luigi di (ed.). *La Leggenda di Tristano.* ("Scrittori D'Italia," Vol. 189.) Bari, 1942.

Golther, Wolfgang (ed.). *Tristan und Isolde von Gottfried von Strassburg.* Berlin, Stuttgart, 1888.

Halphen, Louis, and Poupardin, Réné (eds.). Jean de Marmoutier, *Historia Gaufredi Ducis Normannorum et Comitis Andega-vorum*, in *Chroniques des comtes d'Anjou et des seigneurs d'Amboise*. Paris, 1913.
Howlett, R. (ed.). *Chronicles of the Reigns of Stephen, Henry II, and Richard I.* London, 1886.
Kölbing, Eugene (ed.). *Sir Tristrem.* Vol. II of *Die nordische und die englische version der Tristan-sage.* Heilbronn, 1882.
———. (ed.). *Tristams Saga ok Isondar.* Vol. I of *Die nordische und die englische version der Tristan-sage.* Heilbronn, 1878.
Lichtenstein, Franz (ed.). *Eilhart von Oberge.* [Tristrant.] ("Quellen und Forschungen zur Sprach und Culturgeschichte de Germanischen Volker," Vol. XIX.) Strassburg, London, 1877.
Löseth, E. (ed.). *Le roman en prose de Tristan, le roman de Pala-mède, et la compilation de Rusticien de Pise. Analyse critique d'après les manuscrits de Paris.* Paris, 1891.
Malory, Sir Thomas. *Le Morte D'Arthur*, ed. William Caxton. 2 vols. London, New York, 1956.
Marchegay, Paul, and Salmon, André (eds.). *Chroniques des comtes d'Anjou receuilliés et publiées pour la Société de l'his-toire de France.* Paris, 1856-1871.
Northup, C. T. (ed.). *El Cuento de Tristan de Leonis.* Chicago, 1928.
Ranke, Friedrich (ed.). *Gottfried von Strassburg, Tristan und Isold.* Berlin, 1963.
Thomas of Britain. *Tristram and Ysolt*, trans. R. S. Loomis. New York, 1951.
Vinaver, Eugène (ed.). *The Works of Sir Thomas Malory.* 3 vols. Oxford, 1947. [Winchester MS edition.]
Wind, Bartina H. (ed.). *Les Fragments du Tristan de Thomas.* Leiden, 1950.

SECONDARY WORKS

Bechstein, A. *Tristan und Isolt.* 5th ed. Leipzig, 1930.
Bergemann, Bernhard. *Das höfische Leben nach Gottfried von Strassburg.* Halle, 1876.
Bezzola, Reto Roberto. *Les Origines et la formation de la littéra-ture courtoise en occident, 500-1200.* Paris, 1944-1960.
Boethius. *Anicii Manlii Torquati Severini Boetii, De institutione musica*, ed. G. Friedlein. Leipzig, 1867.
Brinkmann, Hennig. *Entstehungsgeschichte des Minnesangs.* Halle, 1926.

Bromwich, Rachel. "Some Remarks on the Celtic Sources of 'Tristan,' " *Transactions of the Honorable Society of Cymmrodorion* (1953), pp. 32-60.
de Bruyne, E. *L'esthétique du moyen-âge.* Bruges, 1947.
Cary, George. *The Medieval Alexander.* Cambridge, 1956.
Carney, James. *Studies in Irish Literature and History.* Dublin, 1955.
Carpenter, Nan Cooke. *Music in the Medieval and Renaissance Universities.* Norman, Okla., 1952.
Chroniques des églises d'Anjou, ed. L. Halphen. Paris, 1903.
Curtius, Ernst. *European Literature in the Latin Middle Ages.* Trans. W. Trask. New York, 1953.
Deutschbein, M. *Studien zur Sagengeschichte Englands.* Cöthen, 1906.
Fétis, F. *Histoire générale de la musique.* Paris, 1869-1876.
Gerbert de Montreuil. *La Continuation de Perceval,* ed. M. Williams. Paris, 1922-1925.
Gérould, T. *La musique au moyen-âge.* Paris, 1932.
Golther, W. *Die Sage von Tristan und Isolde.* Munich, 1887.
Gombert, Johannes. *Eilhard von Oberg und Gottfried von Strassburg.* ("Beiträge zur Tristanforschung.") Rotterdam, 1927.
Gower, J. *Confessio Amantis,* ed. G. C. Macauley. Oxford, 1899-1902.
von Hahn, J. G. *Sagwissenschaftliche Studien.* Jena, 1876.
Halphen, Louis. *Le comté d'Anjou au XIe siècle.* Paris, 1906.
Härtsen, Jkvr. M. J. *Der Zweispalt in Gottfrieds "Tristan" und die Einheit der Ritterlich-Höfischen Kultur.* Amsterdam, 1938.
Haskins, Charles H. *Studies in Medieval Culture.* 2nd ed. New York, 1958.
Hatto, A. T. (trans.). *Gottfried von Strassburg's Tristan.* Baltimore, 1960.
Heer, Friedrich. *The Medieval World,* trans. Janet Sondheimer. Cleveland, 1962.
Henri d'Andeli. *La bataille des septs arts,* trans. L. J. Paetow. *The Battle of the Seven Arts.* Berkeley, 1914.
Hentsch, A. A. *De la littérature didactique du moyen-âge s'adressant spécialement aux femmes.* Paris, 1903.
Hibbard, Laura. *Medieval Romance in England.* New York, 1924.
Historia Apolonii regis Tyri, ed. A. Riese. Leipzig, 1893.
Hübner, A. *Die mittelhochdeutsche Ironie.* Leipzig, 1930.
Hughes, Muriel. *Women Healers in Medieval Life and Literature.* New York, 1943.
Jackson, W. T. H. "Gottfried von Strassburg," *ALMA,* pp. 145-56.

——. "The Role of Brangaene in Gottfried's *Tristan*," *GR*, XXVIII (1953), 290-96.

——. "Tristan the Artist in Gottfried's Poem," *PMLA*, LXXVII (1962), 364-72.

Jacobius, H. "Die Erziehung des Edelfräuleins in alten Frankreich nach Dichtungen des XII, XIII, und XIV Jahrhunderts," *ZRPh*, XVI (Halle, 1908).

Jonin, Pierre. *Les personnages féminins dans les romans français de Tristan au XII⁰ siècle. Étude des influences contemporaines.* ("Publications des Annales de la Faculté des Lettres d'Aix-en-Provence," N. S. No. 22.) Gap, 1958.

Kelly, Amy. *Eleanor of Aquitaine and the Four Kings.* Cambridge, Mass., 1952.

Ker, W. P. *The Dark Ages.* Edinburgh, 1904.

Klebs, Elimar. *Die Erzählung von Apollonius aus Tyrus.* Berlin, 1899.

Kolb, H. *Der Begriff der Minne und das Entstehen der höfischen Lyrik.* Tübingen, 1958.

Kuhn, Hugo. *Dichtung und Welt im Mittelalter.* Stuttgart, 1959.

Kühn, Oscar. "Medizinisches aus der altfanzösischen Dichtung," *Abhandlungen zur Geschichte der Medizin.* Breslau, 1904.

Kühne, U. *Das Herrscherideal des Mittelalters und Kaiser Friederich I.* ("Leipziger Studien auf dem Gebiet der Geschichte," V.) Leipzig, 1898.

Küpper, H. *Bibliographie zur Tristansage.* Jena, 1941.

Lachmann, K. (ed.). *Des Minnesangs Frühling.* New ed. Stuttgart, 1959.

Laurie, Simon Sommerville. *The Rise and Early Constitution of Universities, with a Survey of Medieval Education.* New York, 1903.

Le Gentil, P. "La légende de Tristan vue par Béroul et Thomas. Essai d'interprétation," *RP*, VII (1953), 117 f.

Lehmann, P. *Die Parodie im Mittelalter.* Leipzig, 1922.

Lejeune, Rita. "Rôle littéraire d'Aliénor d'Aquitaine et de sa famille," *Cultura Neolatina*, XIV (1954), 5-57.

Loomis, R. S. *Burlington Magazine*, XLI (1922), 54-64.

——. *Illustrations of Romance on Tiles from Chertsey Abbey.* ("University of Illinois Studies in Language and Literature," Vol. II, No. 2.) Urbana, 1916.

——. "Tristram and the House of Anjou," *MLR*, XVII (1922), 24-30.

——, and Loomis, Laura Hibbard. *Arthurian Legends in Medieval Art.* New York, 1938.

Loomis, R. S. (ed.). *Arthurian Literature in the Middle Ages.* Oxford, 1959.

Lot, Ferdinand. "Geoffroi Grisegonelle dans l'épopée," *Romania,* XIX (1890), 377-93.

Lot-Borodine, M. "Tristan et Lancelot," *Medieval Studies in Honor of Gertrude Schoepperle Loomis,* ed. R. S. Loomis. Paris, New York, 1927. Pp. 21 f.

Lumiansky, R. M. *Malory's Originality: A Critical Study of Le Morte Darthur.* Baltimore, 1964.

Märkisch, R. *Die altenglische Bearbeitung der Erzählung von Apollonius von Tyrus.* Berlin, 1899.

Mergell, B. *Tristan und Isolde.* Mainz, 1949.

Meyer, Paul. *Alexandre le Grand dans la littérature française du moyen-âge.* 2 vols. Paris, 1886.

Mitchell, Philip. "Scandanavian Literature," *ALMA,* pp. 462-71.

Mohr, Wolfgang. "*Tristan und Isold* als Künstlerroman," *Euphorion,* LIII (1959), 153-74.

Moret, A. "Qu'est-ce que la Minne? Contribution à l'étude de la terminologie et de la moralité courtoise," *Études Germanique,* IV (1949).

Muret, E. "Eilhart d'Oberg et sa source française," *Romania,* XVI (1887).

Newstead, Helaine. "The 'Enfances' of Tristan and English Tradition," *Studies in Medieval Literature in Honor of Albert Croll Baugh,* ed. MacEdward Leach. Philadelphia, 1961.

———. "King Mark of Cornwall," *RP,* XI (1958), 240-53.

———. "The Origin and Growth of the Tristan Legend," *ALMA,* pp. 122-33.

Nickel, E. *Studien zum Liebesproblem bei Gottfried von Strassburg,* in *Königsberger deutsche Forschungen,* I. Gräfe, 1927.

Norgate, Kate. *England Under the Angevin Kings.* 2 vols. London, New York, 1887.

Obermeyer, J. *The French Element in the Tristan of Gottfried of Strassburg.* Venlo, Holland, 1928.

Paetow, L. J. *The Arts Course at Medieval Universities, with Special Reference to Grammar and Rhetoric.* Urbana, 1910.

Pelan, Margaret. *L'Influence du Brut de Wace sur les romanciers français de son temps.* Paris, 1931.

Piquet, F. *L'originalité de Gottfried de Strasbourg.* ("Travaux et Mémoires des Facultés de l'Université de Lille," N.S. No. 5.) Lille, 1905.

———. "Le problème Eilhart-Gottfried," *Revue Germanique,* XX (1929), 109-54.

Ranke, R. *Die Allegorie der Minnegrotte in Gottfrieds Tristan.*

("Schriften der Königsberger Gelehrten Gesellschaft, geisteswissenschaftliche klasse," Vol. II, No. 2.) Königsberg, 1925.
———. *Tristan und Isold*. Berlin, 1925.
Rashdall, Hastings. *The Universities of Europe in the Middle Ages*. 3 vols. Oxford, 1895.
Reese, Gustave. *Music in the Middle Ages*. New York, 1940.
Remigereau, François. "Tristan 'Maître de Vénerie' dans la tradition anglaise et le roman de Tristan," *Romania*, LVIII (1932), 218-37.
Richey, Margaret. *Essays on the Medieval German Love Lyric*. Oxford, 1943.
Richter, M. T. "The Allegory of Love's Hunt." Unpublished Ph.D. dissertation, Columbia University, 1962.
Rühlmann, J. *Die Geschichte der Bogeninstrumente*. Braunschw., 1882.
Rumble, Thomas C. "The Tristan Legend and its Place in Malory's Morte Darthur." Unpublished Ph.D. dissertation, Tulane University, 1955.
Ruodlieb, ed. E. Zeydel. Chapel Hill, 1959.
Savage, H. L. "Sir Gawain 'Fer Ouer þe French Flod,'" *JEGP*, XLVII (1948), 44-52.
Schmid, P. "Die Entwicklung der Begriffe 'Minne' und 'Liebe' im deutschen Minnesang bis Walther," *ZDP*, LXVI (1941).
Schoepperle, Gertrude. *Tristan and Isolt: A Study of the Sources of the Romance*. 2nd ed. 2 vols. New York, 1960.
Schoolfield, George W. *The Figure of the Musician in German Literature*. Chapel Hill, 1956.
Schröder, W. J. "Vindaere wilder maere. Zum Literaturstreit zwischen Gottfried und Wolfram," *Beiträge*, LXXX (1958), 269 f.
Schultz, A. *Das höfische Leben zur zeit der Minnesinger*. 2 vols. Leipzig, 1889.
Schwietering, J. *Die deutsche Dichtung des Mittelalters*. Potsdam, 1941.
———. *Die Tristan Gottfrieds von Strassburg und die Bernhardische Mystik*. Berlin, 1943.
Singer, S. *Apollonius von Tyrus, Untersuchungen über das Fortleben des antiken Romans in spätern Zeiten*. Halle, 1895.
Smyth, A. B. *Shakespeare's Pericles and Apollonius of Tyre*. Philadelphia, 1898.
Sneyders de Vogel, K. "L'Éducation d'Alexandre le Grand," *Neophilologus*, XXVIII (1942-1943), 161-71.
Sommer, H. Oscar (ed.). *Le Morte Darthur: The Original Edition of William Caxton*. . . . 3 vols. London, 1889-1891.

Stolte, H. *Eilhard und Gottfried, Studien über Motivreim und Aufbaustil.* Halle, 1941.

Tax, Petrus W. *Wort, Sinnbild, Zahl in Tristanroman.* Berlin, 1961.

Thrupp, Sylvia. *The Merchant Class of Medieval London.* Ann Arbor, 1962.

Vinaver, Eugène. *Études sur le Tristan en prose: Les sources, les manuscrits, bibliographie critique.* Paris, 1925.

―――. *Le roman de Tristan et Iseut dans l'oeuvre de Thomas Malory.* Paris, 1925.

Vincent of Beauvais. *De Eruditione Filiorum Nobilium,* ed. Arpad Steiner. Cambridge, Mass., 1938.

Voretzsch, C. *Epische Studien.* Halle, 1900. I, 144-46.

Weber, G. *Gottfrieds von Strassburg Tristan und die Krise des hochmittelalterlichen Weltbildes um 1200.* Stuttgart, 1953.

Whitehead, Frederick. "The Early Tristan Poems," *ALMA,* pp. 134-44.

Winfrey, L. E. (Review of E. Vinaver's *Le Roman*). *MP,* XXVI (1928-1929), 231-33.

Wolf, Ferdinand. *Über die Lais, Sequenzen und Leiche.* Berlin, 1841.

II. PERCEVAL

TEXTS

Campion, J., and Holthausen, F. (eds.). *Sir Perceval of Gales.* Heidelberg, 1913.

Hilka, Alfons (ed.). "Bliocadran's Prologue," in *Der Percevalroman.* . . . Halle, 1932. Pp. 430-54, 489-90.

Hilka, Alfons (ed.). *Der Percevalroman von Christian von Troyes.* Halle, 1932.

Jones, G., and Jones, T. (trans.). *Peredur,* in *The Mabinogion.* London, New York, 1957.

Lachmann, K. (ed.). *Parzival,* in *Wolfram von Eschenbach.* 6th ed. Berlin, 1926.

Paris, G. (ed.). *Tyolet,* in *Romania,* VIII (1879), 40-50.

Rajna, Pio (ed.). *Carduino,* in *Poemetti Cavallereschi.* Bologne, 1873.

Williams, Mary (ed.). *Gerbert de Montreuil. La Continuation de Perceval.* Paris, 1922-1925.

SECONDARY WORKS

Aarne, A. *The Types of the Folktale*, trans. Stith Thompson. ("Folklore Fellows Communications," No. 74.) 2nd ed. Helsinki, 1961.

Adolf, Helen. "The Theological and Feudal Background of Wolfram's 'Zwîvel,'" *JEGP*, XLIX (1950), 285-303.

————. *Visio Pacis: Holy City and Holy Grail: An Attempt at an Inner History of the Grail Legend*. State College, Pa., 1960.

Ariès, Philippe. *Centuries of Childhood: A Social History of Family Life*. New York, 1963.

Arnold, F. C. *Das Kind in der deutschen Literatur des XI-XV Jahrhunderts*. Griefswald, 1905.

Bernheimer, R. *Wild Men in the Middle Ages*. Cambridge, Mass., 1952.

Boeheim, W. *Handbuch der Waffenkunde*. Leipzig, 1890.

Boestfleisch, K. *Studien zum Minnegedanken bei Wolfram von Eschenbach*. Königsberg, 1930.

Bolte, J., and Polivka, G. *Anmerkungen zu den Kinder- und Hausmärchen der Brüder Grimm*. Leipzig, 1913.

Brown, A. C. L. "The Grail and the English Sir Perceval," *MP*, XVII (1919), 361 f.; XVIII (1920), 211-21.

Brugger, E. "Ein Beitrag zur Arthurischen Namenforschung. Alain de Gomeret," *Aus romanischen Sprachen und Literaturen, Festgabe für H. Morf*. Halle, 1905.

————. "Bliocadran, the Father of Perceval," *Medieval Studies in Honor of Gertrude Schoepperle Loomis*, ed. R. S. Loomis. Paris, New York, 1927. Pp. 147 f.

————. "Der schöne Feigling in der arthurischen Literatur," *ZRPh*, LXI (1941); LXIII (1943); LXV (1949); LXVII (1951).

Cabrol, F. (ed.). *Dictionnaire d'archéologie chrétienne et de liturgie*. Paris, 1907-1932.

Campbell, Joseph. *The Hero with a Thousand Faces*. New York, 1956.

Chamberlain, A. F. *The Child and Childhood in Folk-Thought*. New York, London, 1896.

Chydenius, J. *The Theory of Medieval Symbolism*. Helsingfors, 1960.

Cross, T. P. *Motif-Index of Early Irish Literature*. ("Indiana University Publications, Folklore Series," No. 7.) Bloomington, 1952.

Curtius, Ernst. *European Literature in the Latin Middle Ages*. Trans. W. Trask. New York, 1953.

Dickson, A. *Valentin and Orson: A Study in Late Medieval Romance.* New York, 1929.

Droulers, E. *Dictionnaire des attributs, allégories, emblèmes, et symboles.* Turnhout, 1948.

Eberwein, E. *Zur Deutung mittelalterlicher Existenz.* Bonn, Cologne, 1933.

Eggers, H. "Literarische Beziehungen des Parzival zum Tristrant Eilharts von Oberg," *Beiträge,* LXXII (1950), 39-51.

―――. "Strukturprobleme mittelalterlicher Epik dargestellt am *Parzival* Wolframs von Eschenbach," *Euphorion,* XLVII (1953), 260-70.

Ehrismann, G. *Geschichte der deutschen Literatur.* München, 1918-1935.

―――. "Die Grundlagen des ritterlichen Tugendsystems," *ZDA,* LVI (1919), 137-216.

―――. "Märchen in höfischen Epos," *PBB,* XXX (1905), 14 f.

―――. *ZDA,* XLIX (1909), 442-49.

Ellis, T. P. "Urien Rheged and his Son Owain," *Welsh Outlook,* XVIII (1931), 121-85.

Everett, Dorothy. "A Characterization of the English Medieval Romances," in *Essays on Medieval English Literature,* ed. Patricia Kean. Oxford, 1955.

Fellinger, F. *Das Kind in der altfranzösischen Literatur.* Göttingen, 1908.

Ferguson, G. *Signs and Symbols in Christian Art.* New York, 1960.

Fourquet, J. *Wolfram d'Eschenbach et le Conte del Graal.* Paris, 1938.

Fowler, David C. *Prowess and Charity in the Perceval of Chrétien de Troyes.* Seattle, 1959.

Frappier, J. *Chrétien de Troyes, l'homme et l'oeuvre.* Paris, 1957.

Friedmann, H. *The Symbolic Goldfinch, its History and Significance in European Devotional Art.* Washington, 1946.

Golther, W. *Chrestiens conte del graal in seinem verhältniss zum walschen Peredur un zum englischen Perceval.* Munich, 1890.

―――. *Die Gralssage bei Wolfram von Eschenbach.* Rostock, 1910.

―――. *Parzival und der Gral.* Munich, 1908.

Griffith, R. H. *Sir Perceval of Galles: A Study of the Sources of the Legend.* Chicago, 1911.

Hatto, A. T. "Archery and Chivalry: A Noble Prejudice," *MLR,* XXXV (1940), 40-54.

―――. "The Lime-Tree and Early German, Goliard, and English Lyric Poetry," *MLR,* XLIX (1954), 205 f.

―――. "Parzival 183, 9," *MLR,* XL (1945), 48-49.

Heckel, Hermann. *Das ethische Wortfeld in Wolframs Parzival.* Würzburg, 1939.

Heer, Frederick. *The Medieval World.* Trans. Janet Sondheimer. Cleveland, 1962.

Henninger, E. *Sitten und Gebräuche bei der Taufe und Namengebung in der altfranzösischen Dichtung.* Halle, 1891.

Hertz, W. *Parzival von Wolfram von Eschenbach.* 7th ed. Berlin, 1927.

Hilka, A. "Die Jugendgeschichte Percevals im *Prosa-Lancelot* und im *Prosa-Tristan,*" *ZRPh,* LII (1932), 513 f.

Holmes, U. T. *A New Interpretation of Chrétien's Conte del Graal.* ("University of North Carolina Studies in Romance Languages and Literature," VIII.) Chapel Hill, 1948.

———, and Klenke, A. *Chrétien, Troyes and the Grail.* Chapel Hill, 1959.

Jackson, W. T. H. *The Literature of the Middle Ages.* New York, 1960.

———. "The Progress of Parzival and the Trees of Virtue and Vice," *GR,* XXXIII (1958), 118-24.

———. "Tristan the Artist in Gottfried's Poem," *PMLA,* LXXVII (1962), 364-72.

Jodogne, Omer. "Le Sens chrétien du jeune Perceval dans la *Conte du Graal,*" *Lettres Romanes de Louvain,* XIV (1960), 111-21.

Jung, C. *Das göttliche Kind.* Amsterdam, 1941.

———. *Das göttliche Mädchen.* Amsterdam, 1941.

Jusserand, J. J. *Les Sports et les jeux d'exercice dans l'ancienne France.* Paris, 1901.

Keferstein, G. *Parzivals ethischer Weg, Ritterlicher Lebenstil im deutschen Hochmittelalter.* Weimar, 1937.

Kellerman, W. *Aufbaustil und Weltbild Chrestiens von Troyes im Percevalroman.* Beihefte zur *ZRPh,* LXXXVIII (1936).

Klenke, Sister A. *Liturgy and Allegory in Chrétien's Perceval.* Chapel Hill, 1951.

Königer, H. *Die Darstellung der Personen bei Crestien von Troyes.* München, 1936.

Kuhn, Hugo. *Dichtung und Welt im Mittelalter.* Stuttgart, 1959.

Kühne, U. *Das Herrscherideal des Mittelalters und Kaiser Friedrich I.* ("Leipziger Studien auf dem Gebiet der Geschichte," V.) Leipzig, 1898.

Laking, G. F. *A Record of European Arms and Armour.* London, 1920.

Langlois, Ernest. *Les Origines et Sources du Roman de la Rose.*

("Bibliothèque des Écoles Françaises d'Athènes et de Rome," LVIII) Paris, 1891.

Lichtenstein, F. "Zur Parzivalfrage," *Beiträge*, XXII (1897), 1-93.

Loomis, R. S. *Arthurian Tradition and Chrétien de Troyes*. New York, 1949.

Los, F. C. J. *Das Keltentum in Wolframs Parzival*. Amsterdam, 1927.

Mathew, G. "Ideals of Knighthood in Late Fourteenth-Century England," *Studies in Medieval History Presented to F. M. Powicke*. Oxford, 1948.

Mennung, A. *Der Bel Inconnu des Renaut de Beaujeu in seinem Verhältnis zum Lybeaus Desconus, Carduino und Wigalois*. Halle, 1890.

Mergell, B. *ADA*, LVIII (1939), 121-25.

————. *Der gral in Wolframs Parzival*. Halle, 1952.

————. *Wolfram von Eschenbach und seine französischen quellen*. Münster, 1936.

Meyer, H. *Der Typus des Sonderlings in der deutschen Literatur*. Amsterdam, 1943.

Mielke, W. *Die Charakterentwicklung Parzivals*. Gartz, 1904.

Misch, A. *DVLG*, V (1926).

Mockenhaupt, B. *Die Frömmigkeit im Parzival Wolframs von Eschenbach*. Bonn, 1942.

Mohr, W. "Parzivals ritterliche Schuld," *Wirkendes Wort*, II (Feb.-March, 1952), 151 f.

Morgan, B. "On Wolfram's Use of Numbers," *Monatshefte für deutsche Unterricht*, XXXI (1938), 170-76.

Morillot, M. "De la condition des enfants nés hors mariage dans l'antiquité et au moyen-âge," *Revue historique du droit français et étranger*, XII (Paris, 1866).

Mühlhausen, W. *ZRPh*, XLIV (1924), 465-543.

Mustard, Helen M., and Passage, Charles E. (trans.). *Wolfram von Eschenbach, Parzival*. New York, 1961.

Naumann, E. "Der Streit um das ritterliche Tugendsystem," *Erbe der Vergangenheit: Festschrift für K. Helm*. Tübingen, 1951.

Newell, W. W. *The Legend of the Holy Grail and the Perceval of Chrestien of Troyes*. Cambridge, Mass., 1902.

Newstead, H. "Perceval's Father and Welsh Tradition," *RR*, XXXVI (1945), 3-31.

Nitze, W. A. *Perceval and the Holy Grail*. Berkeley, 1949.

————. "The Sister's Son and the Conte del Graal," *MP*, IX (1912), 291 f.

Nutt, A. T. "The Aryan Expulsion-and-Return Formula," *Folk-Lore Record*, IV (1881), 1-44.
———. *Studies on the Legend of the Holy Grail.* London, 1888.
Ogle, M. B. "The Discovery of the Wonder Child," *American Philosophical Association, Proceedings and Transactions*, LIX (1928), 179-204.
Oschinsky, H. *Der Ritter Unterwegs und die Pflege der Gastfreundshaft im alten Frankreich.* Halle, 1900.
Pace, R. B. " 'Sir Perceval' and the 'Boyish Exploits' of Finn," *PMLA*, XXXII (1917), 598-604.
Painter, S. *French Chivalry.* Ithaca, 1957.
Panzer, F. *Gahmuret: Quellenstudien zur Wolframs Parzival.* Heidelberg, 1940.
Paris, G. "Études sur les romans de la table ronde: Lancelot du Lac," *Romania*, X (1881), 473 f.
Philipot, E. (Review of W. H. Schofield's *Studies*), *Romania*, XXVI (1897), 296-300.
Ploss, H. *Das Kind in Sitte und Brauch der Völker.* Leipzig, 1884.
Preissl, F. *Hroswitha von Gandersheim und die Entstehung des mittelalterlichen Heldenbildes.* ("Erlanger Arbeiten zur deutschen Literatur," XII.) Erlangen, 1939.
Rachbauer, M. A. *Wolfram von Eschenbach, A Study of the Relation of the Content of Books III, VI, and IX of the Parzival.* Washington, 1934.
Ramondt, M. "Zur Jugendgeschichte des Parzival," *Neophilologus*, IX (1923), 15-22.
Raglan, Lord. *The Hero, A Study in Tradition, Myth, and Drama.* London, 1949.
Rank, O. *Das Inzestmotiv in Dichtung und Sage.* Leipzig, Wien, 1926.
———. *Der Mythus von der Geburt des Helden.* Leipzig, Wien, 1922.
Reinhard, J. R. *The Survival of 'Geis' in Medieval Romance.* Halle, 1933.
Richey, M. F. *Gahmuret Anschevin.* Oxford, 1923.
———. *MLR*, XLVII (1952), 350-61.
———. *Studies of Wolfram von Eschenbach.* London, 1957.
Robertson, D. W., Jr. "Chrétien, Cligès, and the Ovidian Spirit," *Comparative Literature*, VII (1955), 32-42.
———. *Preface to Chaucer.* Princeton, 1962.
Roques, Mario. *Le Graal de Chrétien et la demoiselle au Graal.* Paris, 1955.
———. Review of O. Jodogne's "Le sens chrétien . . . ," *Romania*, LXXXI (1960), 271-73.

Ruodlieb, ed. F. Seiler, Berlin, 1882.

Ruodlieb, ed. E. Zeydel. Chapel Hill, 1959.

Saintyves, P. [pseud.]. *Les vierges mères et les naissances miraculeuses*. Paris, 1908. [This title is catalogued *sub* E. Nourry.]

Scherb, H. *Das Motiv von starken Knaben in den Märchen der Weltliteratur*. Tübingen, Stuttgart, 1930.

Schirling, V. *Die Verteidigungswaffen im altfranzösischen Epos*. Marburg, 1887.

Schneider, Hermann. *Parzival-Studien*. ("Sitzungsberichte der Bayerische Akademie der Wissenschaften, Philos.-Hist. Klasse, 1944-6," IV.) München, 1947.

Schofield, W. H. *Studies on the Libeaus Desconus*. Boston, 1895.

Schröder, W. J. "Der Dichterische Plan des Parzivalromans," *Beiträge*, LXXIV (1952), 160-92, 409-53.

————. *Der Ritter zwischen Gott und Welt: Idee und Problem des Parzivalroman Wolframs von Eschenbach*. Weimar, 1952.

————. "Vindaere wilder maere, Zum Literaturstreit zwischen Gottfried und Wolfram," *Beiträge*, LXXX (1958), 269 f.

Schultz, A. *Das höfische Leben zur zeit der Minnesinger*. 2 vols. Leipzig, 1889.

Schwietering, J. *Parzivals Schuld. Zur Religiosität Wolframs in ihrer Beziehung zur Mystik*. Frankfurt am Main, 1946.

Snyder, Susan B. "The Paradox of Despair: Studies in the Despair Theme in Medieval and Renaissance Literature." Unpublished Ph.D. dissertation, Columbia University, 1963.

Sparnaay, H. *Verschmelzung legendarischer und weltlicher Motive in der Poesie des Mittelalters*. Gröningen, 1922.

Springer, Otto. "Wolfram von Eschenbach's *Parzival*," *ALMA*, pp. 218-50.

Stapel, W. "Die kleine Obilot," *Deutsches Volkstum.*, XVIII (1936), 108-14.

Strucks, C. *Der junge Parzival im Wolframs von Eschenbach Parzival, Crestiens von Troyes Conte del Gral, englischen Syr Percyvelle und italienischen Carduino*. Borna, Leipzig, 1910.

Thompson, S. *Motif-Index of Folk Literature*. 6 vols. Bloomington, 1958.

de Vries, J. *Betrachtungen zum Märchen*. Helsinki, 1954.

Wapnewski, P. *Wolframs 'Parzival': Studien zur Religiosität und Form*. Heidelberg, 1955.

Weber, G. *Der Gottesbegriff des Parzival*. Frankfurt, 1935.

————. *Parzival, Ringen und Vollendung*. Oberursel, 1948.

Weigand, Hermann J. "Die epischen Zeitverhältnisse in den

Graldichtungen Chrestiens und Wolframs," *PMLA*, LIII (1938), 917-50.

Wentzlaff-Eggebert, F. W. "Ritterliche Lebenslehre und Antike Ethik," *DVLG*, XXIII (1949), 47 f.

Wessels, P. B. *Der höfische Ritter, ein Wanderer zwischen zwei Welten.* Nijmegen, 1952.

Weston, J. L. *The Legend of Sir Perceval.* London, 1906.

Williams, Blanche Colton. *Gnomic Poetry in Anglo-Saxon.* New York, 1914.

Williams, Mary R. *Essai sur la composition du roman gallois de Peredur.* Paris, 1909.

III. LANCELOT

TEXTS

Bräuner, G., Becker, H., and Bübinger, H. (eds.). [The *Prose Lancelot*], *Marburger Beiträge zur romanischen Philologie*, II (1911); VI (1912); VIII (1912).

Hahn, K. A. (ed.). *Ulrich von Zatzikhoven. Lanzelet.* Frankfurt, 1845.

Sommer, H. O. (ed.). *The Vulgate Version of Arthurian Romance.* Washington, 1913. Vol. III, [The *Prose Lancelot*].

Webster, K. G. T. (trans). *Ulrich von Zatzikhoven. Lanzelet*, rev. R. S. Loomis. ("Columbia University Records of Civilization Sources and Studies.") New York, 1951.

SECONDARY WORKS

Ackerman, R. "Arthur's Wild Man Knight," *RP*, IX (1955), 115-19.

Adler, A. "The Education of Lancelot: 'Grammar'-'Gramarye,' " *BBSIA*, IX (1957), 101-7.

App, A. J. *Lancelot in English Literature.* Washington, 1929.

Bächtold, J. *Der Lanzelet des Ulrich von Zatzikhoven.* Frauenfeld, 1870.

Brown, A. C. L. "The Grail and the English 'Sir Perceval.' " *MP*, XVI (1919), 553 f.; XVII (1919), 361 f.; XVIII (1920), 201 f.; 661 f.

Bruce, J. D. "The Composition of the Old French Prose *Lancelot*," *RR*, IX (1918); X (1919).

———. *The Evolution of Arthurian Romance from the Beginning Down to the Year 1300.* Göttingen, Baltimore, 1928.

Brugger, E. "Ein Beitrag zur Arthurischen Namenforschung...,"
Festgabe für H. Morf. Halle, 1905.

Campion, R. (Review of S. Singer, *Aufsätze* ... [1912]), *MLN,*
XXXII (1917), 416-21.

Carter, C. H. "Ipomedon, an Illustration of Romance Origins,"
Haverford Essays in Honor of Gummere. Haverford, 1909. Pp.
248-55.

Castets, F. (ed.). *Maugis d'Aigremont.* Montpellier, 1893.

Chrétien de Troyes. *Erec et Enide,* ed. M. Roques. Paris, 1955.

Cross, T. P., and Slover, C. H. *Ancient Irish Tales.* New York, 1936.

————, and Nitze, W. A. *Lancelot and Guinevere: A Study in the
Origins of Courtly Love.* Chicago, 1930.

Dufourt, N. *La jeunesse de Lancelot du Lac, d'après les romans de
la Table Ronde.* Villeurbanne, 1946.

Federn, P. *Die Vaterlose Gesellschaft. Zur Psychologie der Revolution.* Leipzig, Wien, 1919.

Fellinger, F. *Das Kind in der altfranzösischen Literatur.* Göttingen, 1908.

Foerster, W. (ed.). *Christian von Troyes ... IV, Der Karrenritter
und das Wilhelmsleben.* Halle, 1899.

Frappier, J. " 'L'Institution' de Lancelot dans le *Lancelot en
prose*," *Mélanges de philologie romane et de littérature médiévale offerts à Ernst Hoepffner.* ("Strassburg Université Faculté
des Lettres, Publications," No. 113.) Paris, 1949.

————. "The Vulgate Cycle," *ALMA,* pp. 295-318.

Gruffydd, W. J. *Math vab Mathonwy.* Cardiff, 1928.

Von der Hagen and Büsching (eds.). *Wigamur,* in *Deutsche
Gedichte des Mittelalters.* Berlin, 1808.

Harward, Vernon J., Jr. *The Dwarfs of Arthurian Romance and
Celtic Tradition.* Leiden, 1958.

Hertz, W. (ed.). *Parzival von Wolfram von Eschenbach.* 7th ed.
Berlin, 1927.

Hilka, A. *Der Percevalroman von Christian von Troyes.* Halle,
1932.

Jonckbloet, W. J. A. (ed.). *Roman van Lancelot.* Gravenhage,
1846-1849.

Kaluza, M. (ed.). *Libeaus Desconus.* ("Altenglische Bibliotek,"
V.) Leipzig, 1890.

Kluge, R. (ed.). *Lancelot. Deutsche Texte des Mittelalters,* XLII.
Berlin, 1948.

Langlois, E. (ed.). *Roman de la Rose.* Paris, 1914-1924.

————. *Les Origines et les Sources du Roman de la Rose.* (Bibliothèque des Écoles Françaises d'Athènes et de Rome," LVIII.)
Paris, 1891.

van der Lee, A. *Zum literarischen Motif der Vatersuche.* ("Verhandelingen der Koninklijke Nederlands Akademie van Wetenschappen, Afd. Letterkunde, Nieuwe Reeks," Deel LXIII, No. 3.) Amsterdam, 1957.

Leitzmann, A. "Zu Ulrichs *Lanzelet*," *Beiträge,* LV (1931), 293-305.

Loomis, R. S. *Arthurian Tradition and Chrétien de Troyes.* New York, 1949.

————. "Objections to the Celtic Origins of the 'Matière de Bretagne,' " *Romania,* LXXIX (1958), 57-62.

Lot, F. "Celtica," *Romania,* XXIV (1895), 322 f.

————. *Étude sur le Lancelot en prose.* Paris, 1918; new ed., 1954.

Lütjens, A. *Der Zwerg in der deutschen Heldendichtung des Mittelalters.* Breslau, 1911.

Märtens, P. "Zur Lanzelotsage," *Romanische Studien,* V (1880), 557 f.

Mennung, A. *Der Bel Inconnu des Renaut de Beaujeu in seinem Verhältnis zum Lybeaus Disconus, Carduino, und Wigalois.* Halle, 1890.

Meyer, Hermann. *Der Typus des Sonderlings in der deutschen Literatur.* Amsterdam, 1943.

Micha, A. "Symmetry in the *Prose Lancelot*," *ZRPh,* LXVI, 369-71.

Nitze, W. A. "Some Remarks on the Grail-Lancelot Cycle," *RP,* I (1947), 137-41.

Newstead, Helaine. *Bran the Blessed in Arthurian Romance.* New York, 1939.

————. "Perceval's Father," *RR,* XXXVI (1945), 3-31.

Paris, G. "Études sur les romans de la Table Ronde: Lancelot du Lac," *Romania,* X (1881), 471-96; XII (1883), 459 f.; XV (1886), 1-24.

Paton, L. A. *Studies in the Faery Mythology of Arthurian Romance,* rev. R. S. Loomis. 2nd ed. New York, 1960.

Pauphilet, A. *Études sur la Queste del Saint Graal.* Paris, 1921.

Philipot, E. (Review of W. H. Schofield's *Studies*), *Romania,* XXVI (1897), 296-300.

Potter, Murray A. *Sohrab and Rustem: The Epic Theme of a Combat between Father and Son: A Study of its Genesis, Use in Literature, and Popular Tradition.* London, 1902.

Radermacher, L. "Söhne zweier Väter," *Forschungen und Forschritt,* VII (1931), 172 f.

Renaut de Beaujeu. *Le Bel Inconnu,* ed. G. P. Williams. Paris, 1929.

Richey, M. *The Story of Parzival.* Oxford, 1935.

Richter, W. *Der Lanzelet des Ulrich von Zatzikhoven. Deutsche Forschungen,* XXVII. Frankfurt, 1934.

———. "Der literarische Raum des Lanzelet," *ZDA,* LXXV (1938), 33-39.

Rosenfeld, H. "Das Hildebrandslied. Die indogermanischen Vater-Sohn-Kampf Dichtungen und das Problem ihrer Verwandtschaft," *DVLG,* XXVI (1952), 431 f.

Sayers, Dorothy (trans.). *Song of Roland.* Middlesex, 1957.

Schoepperle, Gertrude. *Tristan and Isolt: A Study of the Sources of the Romance.* 2nd ed. 2 vols. New York, 1960.

Schofield, W. *Studies on the Libeaus Desconus.* Boston, 1895.

Schütze, P. *Das volkstümliche Element im Stil Ulrichs von Zatzikhoven.* Griefswald, 1883.

Schultz, A. *Das höfische Leben.* 2 vols. Leipzig, 1889.

Singer, Samuel. *Aufsätze und Vorträge.* Tübingen, 1912.

Slover, C. H. "Sir Degarre: A Medieval Hack Writer's Methods," *University of Texas Studies in English,* XI (1931), 5-23.

Sparnaay, H. "Hartmann von Aue and His Successors," *ALMA,* pp. 436-39.

Thurneysen, R. *Die irische Helden- und Königsage bis zum siebzehnten Jahrhundert.* Halle, 1921.

Wais, K. K. T. *Das Vater-Sohn-Motif in der Dichtung bis 1880.* Berlin, Leipzig, 1931.

Wallner, W. *Anzeiger für deutsches Altertum,* LIV (1935), 171 f.

Webster, K. G. T. *Guinevere: A Study of Her Abductions.* Milton, Mass., 1951.

———. "Ulrich von Zatzikhoven's 'Welsches Buoch,'" *Harvard Studies and Notes in Philology and Literature,* XVI (1934), 203-28.

———. "Walter Map's French Things," *Speculum,* XV (1940), 272 f.

Weston, J. L. *The Legend of Sir Lancelot du Lac.* London, 1901.

———. *The Romance of Morien.* New York, 1901.

———. *The Three Days' Tournament, a Study in Romance and Folklore.* London, 1902.

Williams, Harry F. (ed.). *Floriant and Florete.* Ann Arbor, 1947.

Wirnt von Gravenberg. *Wigalois.* ed. F. Pfeiffer. Leipzig, 1947.

Witthoff, J. *Das Motif des Zweikampfes zwischen Vater und Sohn in der französischen Literatur.* Nürnberg, 1921.

IV. PREVALENCE AND PROVENANCE

TEXTS

Aegidius Romanus. *De Regimine Principum*, ed. S. P. Molenaer. *Les livres du gouvernement de rois.* New York, London, 1899.

Aiol, ed. J. Normand and G. Raynaud. Paris, 1877.

Alanus de Insulis. *Anticlaudianus*, ed. Migne. *PL*, CCX.

St. Bernard. *De laude novae militiae. PL*, CLI, 576.

Brunet, C., and Montaiglon, A. de (eds.). *Li romans de Dolopathos.* Paris, 1856.

Campbell, Killis (ed.). *Seven Sages of Rome.* New York, 1907.

Castets, F. (ed.). *Maugis d'Aigremont.* Montpellier, 1893.

Chronique Artésienne, ed. F. Funck-Brentano. Paris, 1899.

Deux Redactions des Sept Sages, ed. G. Paris. Paris, 1876.

"Les Enfances Gauvain: fragments d'un poème perdu," ed. P. Meyer, *Romania*, XXXIX (1910), 1-32.

Les Enfances Guillaume, ed. Patrice Henry. Paris, 1935.

Les Enfances Ogier par Adenés di Rois, ed. M. A. Scheler. Bruxelles, 1874.

Les Enfances Vivien, ed. C. Wahlund and H. von Feilitzen. Upsala, Paris, 1895.

Étienne de Fougères. *Le Livre des Manières*, ed. J. Kremer. Marburg, 1887.

Frazer, R. M. (trans.). *The Trojan War.* Bloomington, 1965.

Geoffrey of Monmouth. *History of the Kings of Britain*, trans. S. Evans, rev. C. W. Dunn. New York, 1958.

Gilbert of Tournai. *Eruditio Regum et Principum*, ed. A. de Poorter. ("Les Philosophes Belges," IX.) Louvain, 1914.

Goldschmidt, M. (ed.). *Sone von Nausai.* Tübingen, 1899.

Gordon, R. K. (ed.). *The Story of Troilus.* New York, 1964.

Highet, Gilbert (trans.). *The Iliad by Homer.* New York, 1950.

Hincmar of Rheims. *De Regis Persona et Regio Ministerio. PL*, CXXV.

Hubert, J., and Porter, M. (eds. and trans.). *The Romance of Flamenca.* Princeton, 1962.

Hugh of Fleury. *Tractatus de Regia Potestate et Sacerdotali Dignitate. MGH*, Libelli de Lite, Vol. II.

Isidore of Seville. *De Principis Honestate. PL*, LXXXII-LXXXIV.

Isocrates. *Isocrates Opera*, ed. and trans. G. Norlin. ("Loeb Library.") New York, 1928.

Johannis de Alta Silva. *Dolopathos*, ed. A. Hilka. Heidelberg, 1913.

John of Salisbury. *Policraticus*, ed. C. C. J. Webb. Oxford, 1909 and London, 1932.

——. *The Statesman's Book of John of Salisbury*, trans. John Dickinson. New York, 1927.

Jonas of Orléans. *De institutione rego*, ed. J. Reviron. *Les idées politico-religieuses d'un évêque du IXe siècle*. Paris, 1930.

Julius Valerius. *Juli Valeri Alexandri Polemi res gestae Alexandri Macedonis translatae ex Aesopo graeco*, ed. B. Keubler. Leipzig, 1888.

LaDu, Milan S. (ed.). *The Medieval French Roman d'Alexandre*. ("Elliott Monographs," Vols. 36-41.) Princeton, 1937 and on.

Lamprecht, P. *Das Alexanderlied*, ed. F. Maurer. Leipzig, 1940; reprint, 1964.

Meyer, Paul (ed.). *Alexandre le Grand dans la littérature française du moyen-âge*. 2 vols. Paris, 1886.

——. (ed.). *Le roman de Flamenca*. Paris, 1933.

Misrahi, J. (ed.). *Le roman des Sept Sages*. Paris, 1933.

Monk of Moiliens. *Li Romans de Carité et Miserere du Renclus Moiliens*, ed. Van Hamel. Paris, 1885.

Morand. "Tecosc," ed. R. Thurneysen. "Morands Fürstenspiegel," *ZCP*, XI (1917), 56-106; XIII (1921), 297-305.

Muller, H. E. (ed.). *Die Werke des Pfaffen Lamprecht*. Munich, 1923.

Nibelungenlied, trans. A. T. Hatto. Baltimore, 1965.

"De Ortu Walwanii," ed. J. D. Bruce. *Hesperia*. Göttingen, Baltimore, 1913.

Ovid. *Ars Amatoria*, ed. J. H. Mozley. ("Loeb Library.") Cambridge, Mass., 1957.

——. *Fasti*, ed. Sir J. G. Frazer. ("Loeb Library.") Cambridge, Mass., 1957.

——. *Metamorphoses*, ed. F. J. Miller. ("Loeb Library.") Cambridge, Mass., 1958.

Perlesvaus, ed. W. A. Nitze. Chicago, 1932-1937.

Perrault, William. *De Eruditione Principum*, in Thomas Aquinas, *Omnia Opera*. Parma, 1852-1871. Vol. XVI, Opusculum xxxvii, pp. 390-476.

Philippe de Beaumanoir. [Philippe de Rémi, sire de Beaumanoir.] *Les Coutumes de Beauvaisis*, ed. A. Salmon. Paris, 1899-1900.

Philippe de Novare. *Les Quatres Âges de l'Homme*, ed. M. de Fréville. Paris, 1888.

Pierre du Bois. *De Recuperatione Terrae Sanctae*, ed. E. Langlois. ("Collections de Textes pour Servir à l'Étude et à l'Enseignement de l'Histoire," X.) Paris, 1891.

Pindar. *Odes*, ed. Sir J. E. Sandys. ("Loeb Library.") Cambridge, Mass., 1957.

Plato. *Platonis opera*, ed. J. Burnet. 5 vols. Oxford, 1900-1907.

――. *The Republic*, ed. Paul Shorey. ("Loeb Library.") New York, 1930-1935.

Plutarch. *Moralia*, in W. W. Goodwin (ed.), *Plutarch's Miscellanies*. 6th ed. 5 vols. Boston, 1898.

――. *Plutarch's Lives, Alexander*, trans. B. Perrin. ("Loeb Library.") New York, 1919. Vol. VII.

Pseudo-Callisthenes. *The Life of Alexander of Macedon*, ed. and trans. Elizabeth Haight. New York, 1955.

Renart, Jean. *L'Escoufle*, ed. [H. Michelant and] P. Meyer. Paris, 1894.

――. *Galeran de Bretagne*, ed. L. Foulet. Paris, 1925.

Robert of Blois. *L'Enseignement des Princes*, ed. J. H. Fox. Paris, 1948.

Ruodlieb, ed. E. H. Zeydel. Chapel Hill, 1959.

Seneca. *Moral Epistles*, ed. R. M. Gummere. ("Loeb Library.") 3 vols. New York, 1917-1925.

Statius. *Achilleid*, ed. O. A. W. Dilke. Cambridge, 1954.

――. *Achilliad*, ed. and trans. H. Mozley. Cambridge, Mass., 1957.

Von der Hagen and Büsching (eds.). *Wigamur*, in *Deutsche Gedichte des Mittelalters*. Berlin, 1808. Vol. I.

Wace. *Brut*, ed. I. Arnold. Paris, 1938-1940.

Wace. *Arthurian Chronicles Represented by Wace and Layamon*. New York, 1928.

Williams, Harry F. (ed.). *Floriant and Florete*. Ann Arbor, 1947.

Wirnt von Gravenberg. *Wigalois*, ed. J. M. N. Kapteyn. ("Reinische Beiträge und Hülfsbucher zur Germanischen Philologie und Volkskunde.") Bonn, 1926.

――. *Wigalois*, ed. F. Pfeiffer. Leipzig, 1847.

SECONDARY WORKS

Auerbach, E. *Mimesis*, trans. W. Trask. New York, 1957.

Bartsch, K. "Das Fürstenideal des Mittelalters im Spiegel deutscher Dichtung," *Gesammelte Vorträge und Aufsätze*. Freiburg, 1883.

Bauker, E. *The Political Thought of Plato and Aristotle*. New York, 1906.

Berges, W. *Die Fürstenspiegel des hohen und späteren Mittelalters*. (*MGH*, Schriften II.) Stuttgart, 1938.

Bezzola, R. R. *Les Origines et la formation de la littérature court-oise en occident, 500-1200.* Paris, 1944-1960.

de Boer, C. (ed.). *Ovide moralisé.* Amsterdam, 1915-1938.

Booz, E. *Die Fürstenspiegeln des Mittelalters bis zur Scholastik.* Freiburg, 1913.

Born, L. K. (ed.). *Erasmus. The Education of a Christian Prince.* ("Columbia University Records of Civilization," No. 27.) New York, 1936.

———. "The Perfect Prince: A Study in 13th- and 14th-Century Ideals," *Speculum,* III (1928), 470-504.

———. "The *Specula Principum* of the Carolingian Renaissance," *Revue belge de philologie et d'histoire,* XII (1933), 583-612.

Bromwich, Rachel. "Some Remarks on the Celtic Sources of 'Tristan,'" *Transactions of the Honorable Society of Cymmrodorion* (1953).

Bruni, Gerardo. *Le Opere di Egidio Romano.* Firenze, 1936.

Buisson, F. *Dictionnaire pedagogique et d'instruction primaire.* Paris, 1882-1887.

Burnet, J. *Aristotle on Education.* Cambridge, 1928.

Carlyle, R. W., and Carlyle, A. J. *A History of Medieval Political Thought in the West.* London, 1928.

Cary, George. *The Medieval Alexander.* Cambridge, 1956.

Cross, T. P. and Slover, C. H. *Ancient Irish Tales.* New York, 1936.

Curtius, E. *European Literature in the Latin Middle Ages,* trans. W. Trask. New York, 1953.

Dennis, L. "The Boy Called Ambrosius," *MLN,* XLVI (1931), 23-24.

Duncan, T. S. *The Influence of Art on Description in the Poetry of P. P. Statius.* Baltimore, 1914.

Ehrismann, G. *Geschichte der deutschen Literatur.* München, 1918-1935.

Evans, Elizabeth C. "Portraiture in Ancient Epic," *Harvard Studies in Classical Philology,* LVIII-LIX (1948).

Evans, Joan. *Life in Medieval France.* Oxford, 1925; 2nd ed. London, 1957.

Faral, E. *Recherches sur les sources latines des contes et romans courtois en moyen-âge.* Paris, 1913.

Fehr, Karl. *Die mythen bei Pindar.* Zurich, 1936.

Fourrier, A. *Le courant réaliste dans le roman courtois en France au moyen-âge.* Paris, 1960.

Frazer, J. G. *The Fasti of Ovid: Commentary.* London, 1929.

Fundenberg, G. B. *Feudal France in French Epic.* Princeton, 1918.

Gruffydd, W. J. *Math vab Mathonwy.* Cardiff, 1928.

Hanning, Robert W. *The Romantic Histories of Britain: Studies in the Relationship Between Individual and Society in Early Medieval Historiography.* New York, 1964.

Hartland, E. S. *The Legend of Perseus.* London, 1896.

Heer, Friedrich. *The Medieval World,* trans. Janet Sondheimer. Cleveland, 1962.

Hull, Eleanor. *The Cuchullin Saga in Irish Literature.* London, 1898.

Hummel, F. *Die Kulturhistorischen Element in Sone de Nausay.* Rostock, 1929.

————. *Zu Sprache und Verstechnik des Sone de Nausay.* Berlin, 1913.

Jackson, W. T. H. "Tristan the Artist in Gottfried's Poem," *PMLA,* LXXVII (1962), 364-72.

Kaske, R. E. "*Sapientia et Fortitudo* as the Controlling Theme of *Beowulf,*" *SP,* LV (1958), 423-56.

Kennedy, E. "Social and Political Ideas in the French Prose *Lancelot,*" *Medium Aevum,* XXVI (1957), 90-106.

Ker, W. P. *Epic and Romance.* London, 1897; New York, 1957.

Kittredge, G. L. *Arthur and Corlagon.* Boston, 1903.

Klebs, Elimar. *Die Erzählung von Apollonius aus Tyrus.* Berlin, 1899.

Laistner, M. L. W. (Review of Pierre Courcelle, *Histoire Littéraire des grandes invasions germaniques* [Paris, 1948]), *Speculum,* XXIV (1949), 260 f.

Langlois, Ch.-V. *La vie en France au moyen-âge d'après des romans mondains du temps.* Paris, 1924.

————. *La vie en France au moyen-âge d'après quelques moralistes du temps.* Paris, 1925.

————. (ed.). *Le Roman de la Rose.* Paris, 1914-1918.

Lechner, M. *Erziehung und Bildung in der griechisch-römischen Antike.* Munich, 1933.

Leclercq, Jean. *The Love of Learning and the Desire for God,* trans. Catherine Misrahi. New York, 1960.

Lewis, C. B. *Classical Mythology and Arthurian Romance.* London, 1932.

Loomis, R. S. *Arthurian Tradition and Chrétien de Troyes.* New York, 1949.

Loth, J. "L'origine de la légende d'Arthur fils d'Uter Pendragon," *Revue Celtique,* XLIX (1932), 132-49.

Luzarche, L. (ed.). *La Vie du Pape Gregoire le Grand.* Tours, 1857.

McGuire, T. A. *The Conception of the Knight.* Michigan, 1939.

Magoun, F. P. *The Gestes of King Alexander of Macedon.* Cambridge, Mass., 1929.

Manitius, M. *Geschichte der lateinischen Literatur des Mittelalters.* Munich, 1911-1931.

Mathew, G. "Ideals of Knighthood in Late 14th-Century England," *Studies in Medieval History Presented to F. M. Powicke.* Oxford, 1948.

Mausser, O. E. *Reimstudien zu Wigamur.* Munich, 1906.

Meller, W. C. *A Knight's Life in the Days of Chivalry.* London, 1924.

Meyer, F. *Jugenderziehung im Mittelalter dargestellt nach den altfranzösischen Artus- und Abenteuerromanen.* Solingen, 1896.

Meyer, Kuno. "The Wooing of Emer," *Archaeological Review,* I (1888), 68 f.

Meyer, Paul. "Nouvelles Catalanes inédites," *Romania,* XX (1891), 579-80.

Mohl, R. *The Three Estates in Medieval and Renaissance Literature.* New York, 1933.

Mozley, J. H. "Statius as an Imitator of Vergil and Ovid," *Classical Weekly,* XXVII (1933), 33 f.

Newstead, Helaine. "The 'Enfances' of Tristan and English Tradition," *Studies in Medieval Literature in Honor of Albert Croll Baugh,* ed. MacEdward Leach. Philadelphia, 1961.

Norwood, G. *Pindar.* Berkeley, 1956.

Ownbey, E. S. *Merlin and Arthur: A Study of Merlin's Character and Function in the Romances Dealing with the Early Life of Arthur.* Nashville, 1933.

Poole, Reginald. *Illustrations of the History of Medieval Thought and Learning.* London, 1960.

Rees, A., and Rees, B. *Celtic Heritage: Ancient Tradition in Ireland and Wales.* New York, 1961.

Rein, W. *Encyclopädisches Handbuch der Pädagogik.* Langensalza, 1898. Vol. V.

Richardson, H. G., and Sayles, G. O. *The Governance of Medieval England from the Conquest to Magna Carta.* Edinburgh, 1963.

Riché, Pierre. *Éducation et culture dans l'Occident barbare, VIe-VIIIe siècles.* ("Patristica Sorbonensia," No. 4.) Paris, 1962.

Richter, G. *Studien zur Geschichte der älteren arabischen Fürstenspiegel.* Leipzig, 1932.

Riese, O. *Untersuchungen über des Enfances Vivien.* Halle, 1900.

Robertson, D. S. "The Food of Achilles," *Classical Review,* LIX (1940), 177 f.

Robinson, F. N. "Satirists and Enchanters in Early Irish Literature," *Studies in the History of Religions, presented to C. H. Toy.* New York, 1912.

Röder, J. *Das Fürstenbild in den mittelalterlichen Fürstenspiegeln.* Münster, 1933.

Rust, E. *Die Erziehung des Ritters in der altfranzösischen Epos.* Berlin, 1888.

Sainte-Palaye, J. B. *Mémoires sur l'ancienne chevalerie; consideřée comme un etablissement politique et militaire.* 3 vols. Paris, 1759-1781.

————. *Mémoires sur l'ancienne chevalerie; considerée comme un etablissement politique et militaire,* ed. J. C. E. Nodier. 2 vols. Paris, 1826.

Sanches Reyes, E. *Les sept enfants de Lara.* Santander, 1941.

Sarrazin, G. *Wigamur, Eine Literarhistorische Untersuchung.* Strassburg, 1879.

Schoepperle, G. *Tristan and Isolt: A Study of the Sources of the Romance.* 2nd ed. 2 vols. New York, 1960.

Schönherr, F. *Die Lehre von Reichfürstenstande des Mittelalters.* Leipzig, 1914.

Schücking, Levin. "Wann entstand der Beowulf? Glossen Zweifel und Fragen," *Beiträge zur Geschichte der deutsche Sprache und Literatur,* XLII (1917), 347-410.

Schultz, A. *Das höfische Leben zur Zeit der Minnesinger.* 2 vols. Leipzig, 1889.

Scott, R. D. *"The Thumb of Knowledge" in Legends of Finn, Sigurd and Taliesin.* ("Columbia University Studies in Celtic and French Literature.") New York, 1930.

Smith, R. M. The *Speculum Principum* in Early Irish Literature," *Speculum,* II (1927), 411-45.

Sneyders de Vogel, K. "L'Éducation d'Alexandre le Grand," *Neophilologus,* XXVIII (1942-1943), 161-71.

Sparnaay, H. "Hartmann von Aue and His Successors," *ALMA,* pp. 430-42.

Steele, R. (ed.). *Opera hactenus inedita Rogeri Baconi.* Oxford, 1920.

von Stromer-Reichenbach. *Der deutsche Fürstenspiegel.* Dresden, 1925.

Tatlock, J. S. P. *The Legendary History of Britain: Geoffrey of Monmouth's Historia . . . and its Early Versions.* Berkeley, 1950.

Thurneysen, R. *Die irische Helden- und Königsage bis zum siebzehnten Jahrhundert.* Halle, 1921.

————. *Irisches Recht.* Berlin, 1931.

Webster, K. G. T. "Walter Map's French Things," *Speculum*, XV (1941), 272 f.

Weitzmann, K. *Greek Mythology in Byzantine Art*. Princeton, 1951.

Wentzlaff-Eggebert, F. W. "Ritterliche Lebenslehre und Antike Ethik," *DVLG*, XXIII (1949).

Werminghoff, A. "Die Fürstenspiegel der Karolingerzeit," *Historische Zeitschrift*, LXXXIX, 193-214.

———. "Drei Fürstenspiegeln der 14 und 15 Jahrhunderts," *Studien . . . A. Hauck*. Leipzig, 1916.

Wilmotte, M. "Rodlieb, notre premier roman courtois," *Romania*, XLIV (1916-1917), 373 f.

Zeller, P. "Die täglichen Lebensgewohnheiten im altfranzösischen Karlepos," *Ausgaben und Abhandlungen*, XLII (Marburg, 1885).

ᏋᏒ Index

This list is both a name index and a topic index. Names of authors, characters, and places are listed with appropriate modifications and some cross-references. Topics—under which are subsumed "themes" and recurring ideas in this book—have somewhat more extensive cross-references; they may suggest "thematic" investigations related to but not attempted in this volume. Thus "the educated heroine," "the hero as a child" "the arrival at court," "humor in romance," and "structural patterns in romance," are topics susceptible to thematic analysis similar to that used in *The Education of the Hero in Arthurian Romance.*

Numbers in italics indicate major discussions.

A NOTE ABOUT THIS BOOK

The text is set in Linotype DeVinne

The composition and printing by
SEEMAN PRINTERY, DURHAM, NORTH CAROLINA

The binding by
SEEMAN PRINTERY, DURHAM, NORTH CAROLINA

The paper is Publisher's Eggshell by
WARREN'S PAPER COMPANY

Designed and published by
THE UNIVERSITY OF NORTH CAROLINA PRESS
CHAPEL HILL, NORTH CAROLINA